AMERICAN HISTORY

Major Controversies Reviewed

Third Edition

Richard Kezirian
Monterey Peninsula College

KENDALL/HUNT PUBLISHING COMPANY
4050 Westmark Drive   Dubuque, Iowa 52002

TO THE MEMORY OF MY DEAR FATHER

Contents

List of Illustrations

DRAWINGS BY RUTH A. DEOUDES

Preface

This series of essays is intended to introduce college history students and other interested readers to "debates" among historians on various key issues in the American past. Many students are annoyed by the lack of consensus among historians as to the causes and effects of great events. I, too, have often wished that the answers were more self-evident and certain. However, the excitement of history is often found in the debate that it generates. With this idea in mind, I have set about discussing these important and perplexing questions, and the controversies involved.

Most college texts which examine historical controversies select only a few examples and then include very difficult selections from famous monographs as examples for each aspect of the debate. The editorial remarks included in such works are helpful, but the monographic selections are often too intricate and complicated for the beginning college student. On the other hand, one noted historian, Thomas A. Bailey, has published a two-volume work which introduces approximately 650 historical arguments and "myths" of the American past. However, since he deals with such a large number of issues, there is little opportunity for extensive development and elaboration.

My aim is to provide a book that will be like the porridge in "Goldilocks and the Three Bears"—just right. I focus on fifty important issues which have a special relevance to students in the 1990s. There are no monographic selections from the works of other authors; rather each essay is written by me. Admittedly, the choice of subject matter is arbitrary. There are other significant issues which could have been chosen with equal profit to the reader. Perhaps, then, the method is as important as the subject matter. For the most part, in each essay I have three objectives. First, I delineate the historiographic debate surrounding each issue. Second, I attempt to convey the insights that the newest documents and the latest scholarly literature have to offer. Last, I inject my own personal organization and approach to clarify the situation and to heighten the reader's interest. With this method I expect the student and the general reader to emerge from their study of history with an enhanced appreciation for the intriguing controversy that can be engendered by a study of the past. I also expect new insights to emerge as contrary aspects of vital questions are considered. Finally, I believe the reader will gain an enhanced understanding of how closely historical interpretations mirror the contemporary mood and concerns of the times in which they are written. Throughout my research, I have been influenced by A.J.P. Taylor's ingenious comment: "Events are well enough in their way; what historians write about them is much better."

In any undertaking requiring special dedication, there are those upon whom one must depend, no matter how individual the effort. Barbara Mitchell, William Pardue, Bruce Lannes

Smith, David and Katherine Yamada, Kathy Herbig, and Josef Gamper generously gave of their time and submitted ideas which I invariably used to improve these essays. All are valued friends, and in the case of Bruce, David, Josef, and Kathy, also outstanding colleagues in the teaching profession. Together they kept me from making errors of scholarship. Any errors that may remain are none of their doing.

Albert Cross, President and General Manager, and Susan Bernhardt, Sunday Editor, of the *Monterey Peninsula Herald*, initially found merit in my idea for a series of newspaper articles on American history, and then went on to present those articles to their readers. That proved to be the inspiration for this book, and I want to thank both Al and Susan for that initial support, and for permission from the *Monterey Peninsula Herald* and the *San Diego Union* to use and/or revise material from these articles for inclusion in this book.

I have been blessed these many years, from elementary school through college, with exceptional teachers. I would like to take this opportunity to recognize them: Les Holmberg, Greg Dunshee, Charles Tilghman, Lewis Carpenter, Michael Gordon, Joachim Remak, Elliot Brownlee, and especially, Donald Larson and Alfred Gollin.

I want to add special thanks to Ruth Deoudes, whose gifted artistry has added immensely to the attractiveness of this Third Edition. In our mutual endeavor, Ruth's talent was matched only by her enthusiasm and good humor.

My best friend, Renee, to whom I owe the greatest debt, gave me much-needed encouragement and love. Without her aid this volume could not have been completed. She served in a variety of roles: proofreader, critic and counselor. Most important, she has been a dedicated and loving wife.

My dear father, Edward, to whom I dedicate this book, served as a beacon and guide throughout my life. He had an indefatigable curiosity about our world—especially for the people and ideas that enlivened it—and an uncanny ability to convey wisdom to all who knew him. On a more private level, the strength of his character served as a standard of excellence to both family and friends.

R.P.K.

U.S. HISTORY TO 1877

> *The sun never shined on a cause of greater worth. 'Tis not the affair of a city, a country, a province, or a kingdom, but of a continent—of at least one eighth part of the habitable globe. 'Tis not the concern of a day, a year, or an age; posterity are virtually involved in the contest, and will be more or less affected, even to the end of time, by the proceedings now. Now is the seed time of continental union, faith and honor. The least fracture now will be like a name engraved with the point of a pin on the tender rind of a young oak; the wound will enlarge with the tree, and posterity read it in full grown characters.*
>
> Thomas Paine
> Common Sense

Jamestown gained eight years of peace with the Indians as a result of the marriage of Pocahontas to John Rolfe in 1614. That brief interlude of restraint probably sealed the fate of Virginia's Indians. Their eventual disillusionment is best revealed in Chief Logan's famous speech to Lord Dunmore, royal governor of Virginia, in 1774: "I appeal to any white man to say, if ever he entered Logan's cabin hungry, and he gave him not meat: if ever he came cold and naked, and he cloathed him not. During the course of the last long and bloody war Logan remained idle in his cabin, an advocate for peace. Such was my love for whites, that my countrymen pointed as they passed, and said, "Logan is the friend of white man." I had even thought to have lived with you, but for the injuries of one man. Colonel Cresap, the last spring, in cold blood, and unprovoked, murdered all the relations of Logan, not even sparing my women and children. There runs not a drop of my blood in the veins of any living creature. . . . Who is there to mourn for Logan?—Not one."

1

Could the Colonists Have Survived without the Indians?

Few aspects of America's past have received more attention, and yet have been more misunderstood, than that of Indian history. Though the subject continues to be fascinating, it is still more often confused than clarified. For instance, historians of Colonial America traditionally overlooked the importance of Indian aid, and attributed eventual English success to the Protestant virtues of hard work, religious dedication, good government, and the like. When Indians were mentioned it was most often as obstacles to be overcome, along with mountains, rivers, deserts, and wild animals. Much like the landscape they inhabited, Indians were portrayed as "passive objects," incapable of determining their own destiny, primarily taking cues from the more advanced European peoples. They were viewed as unbending in the face of time, unable and unwilling to meet the challenges of a new age. They were also characterized as a "hunting and gathering" people who were ineptly exploiting the potential which the rich American lands offered.

In sum, European accomplishments were emphasized and those of the Indians were not. Squanto's aid to the Pilgrims, the marriage of John Rolfe to Pocahontas, and some of the "trivial" contributions of the Indians such as canoes and snowshoes were mentioned and became folklore. But the real reasons for the success or failure of a European settlement were said to lie solely within European control. As the Virginia Company recorded in its colonial records, the newly improved charters which allowed for more individual initiative and profit were "the real and substantial food by which Virginia hath been nourished."

The first significant challenge to the traditional view of Indian history came in the 1960s. As with so many other areas of American society, culture, and scholarship, the 1960s witnessed a revolution in approaches to the Indian question. The first and most often used was the "contributions" approach. Aiming to capture the Indian past more truthfully, historians in the 1960s avidly searched for more significant contributions than the ones mentioned above. Not surprisingly, they found many that had influenced America politically, socially, and economically. For instance, it was calculated that well over half of America's modern agricultural products (e.g. corn, tobacco, tomatoes, beans and squash) were introduced by Indians.

Another historical innovation of the 1960s was the "heroes" approach. From this perspective, historians publicized the great men and women of the Indian past and made them familiar

3

figures in history textbooks. Soon young students were acquainted with details of the lives of such men as Pontiac, Tecumseh, and Chief Joseph.

There was also the "fraud-and-dispossession" approach. Here historians scoured documents which revealed white men's treaty betrayals, fraudulent practices, and broken promises. The aim of historians was not only to describe the wrongs done, but to offer detailed explanations of white greed and prejudice as motivations behind these wrongs. Thus, in the 1960s, the story of America's past was broadened to include the Indian minority, and white actions were often morally condemned.

Historians of the 1970s and 1980s expanded on the story even more. They recognized the good intentions of historians of the 1960s but argued that the latter approach was not completely fair to the Indians. For, implicitly, Indians were still being judged in terms of white values. For instance, the "contributions" approach recognized the Indian legacy only in terms of white standards. If an Indian invention proved useful to Europeans, and was understood and appreciated by later Americans, then the contribution was publicized. Historians now believe that this is unfair. This approach takes the Indian story out of its cultural context and underrates the valuable and rich diversity of the Indian experience. Similarly with the "fraud-and-dispossession" approach; it, too, is steeped in the language of white morals and cultural needs. It serves as an exercise in relieving white guilt, rather than truly recognizing the Indian as an active individual pursuing his own destiny. As for the "heroes" approach, it is merely a reversal of the chauvinism of whites. As such, though useful to some extent, it has severe limitations when the truth of the overall story is pursued.

Historians of the 1990s, as a result, plan to become more fluent in a truly Indian-centered history. The task is indeed difficult, for describing the diversity of the American experience is overwhelming. Nonetheless, historians of the 1990s believe that the task must be undertaken. Hence, these historians are preparing themselves in other disciplines; i.e., archaeology, linguistics, ethnography, anthropology, oral history, demography, and geography. By using a broader ethnohistorical approach, scholars are seeking the cultural essence of each Indian tribe and the ways in which each Indian tribe dealt with the changing circumstances of America's past.

With the perspective of the 1990s, then, we can explore the question posed at the beginning of this essay: Could the colonists have survived without the Indians? Englishmen when they first landed were outnumbered, unfamiliar with the terrain and with fighting in the forests, unschooled in the raising of crops in a new land; without Indian help, the colonists would have had to make a go of it within the confines of fortified walls.

Taking the Pilgrims first, one finds the aid of Chief Massasoit and his Wampanoags was the salvation of that struggling colony. The story of Squanto and the famous Thanksgiving dinner is familiar to all Americans. Not as well known is that the Wampanoags exchanged aid to the Pilgrims for an alliance against the Narragansetts. The Wampanoags gave their surplus corn to the Pilgrims, taught them how to farm in the new land, showed them the habits of the prey in the area, pointed out the locations of the best fishing places, and explained the peculiarities of the climate and weather.

Similar parallels occurred in Jamestown. Chief Powhatan, not fearing the permanency of white settlement, for he had witnessed innumerable failures earlier (e.g. English and Spanish), befriended John Smith and his fellow settlers in the early difficult days. It was the Virginia Indians who taught the Jamestown men how to raise tobacco—the crop which finally ensured the success of the colony. The strategic marriage of Pocahontas to John Rolfe was not the love affair that it is portrayed to be, but a political alliance whereby Powhatan exchanged Pocahontas as an insurance of peace with the English in return for aid against enemy Indian tribes in Virginia's piedmont region. As John Smith admitted: ". . . it pleased God (in our extremity) to move the Indians to bring us Corne, ere it was half ripe, to refresh us, when we rather expected . . . they would destroy us. . . . Had not the Indians fed us, we directly had starved." Population statistics bear out Smith's statements. In the first three years more than 900 settlers went to Virginia, yet by the winter of 1609–10, as a result of disease, malnutrition, and crop-failure, only 60 survived.

Still other insights might be gained into our original question by investigating Colonial ecological history. Students of Colonial America commonly assume that the first European settlers arrived in the New World to find an untamed wilderness. It was not a virgin or primeval forest which confronted the first colonists in the early seventeenth century. Rather the Indians had already placed their imprint on the New World environment. Even before the Europeans, the Indians had modified the American landscape in a significant way to suit their needs. (For purposes of clarification, I will focus on southern New England).

One universal perception of the New World is accurate, however, and that involved the incredible summer abundance of wildlife, in forests which were majestic and awe-inspiring. Accounts of scores of fish, birds, and mammals are legion, as are accounts of the beauty, openness, and parklike nature of the southern New England forests where trees towered and grasslands flourished.

What colonists failed to make was the connection between the Indian's lifestyle and the richness of the new land. Europeans did not recognize that the Indian practice of burning the undergrowth in large sections of forests once or twice a year was largely responsible for the nature of both the forests and the game which inhabited them.

The subtle effects of these annual burnings were numerous. First, the thick, woody underbrush was yearly cleared from the forests allowing the taller, larger species of trees to survive and thrive.

Second, in this open atmosphere, forest nutrients were more readily recycled, and grasses, shrubs, and nonwoody plants grew luxuriantly. It was no accident that on their arrival the colonists in the Spring were met with luscious wild strawberries, blackberries, and raspberries.

Third, with the more open forest canopy, and with the entry of more light, the soil of southern New England was warmer and drier. And finally, the annual burnings helped eliminate the pests and diseases which often were characteristic of damp, cold wilderness areas.

In addition, the Indians were creating what has been called the "edge effect," the boundary area between the forest and the grasslands which provided the ideal habitats for wildlife of all kinds. In a sense, by enhancing the edge habitats the Indians created their own abundance which they then "harvested" when they hunted and trapped.

Europeans on their arrival were generally oblivious to the significance of these Indian practices. From the European point of view, only the Indian women deserved respect, for only they worked hard at raising the crops and dispensing with important agricultural tasks. For Europeans, the Indian men were idling away their time with wanton burning, fishing, and hunting.

Indian farming practices in New England also had subtle ecological consequences. Maize was the chief crop grown, a crop which required careful tending and constant watchfulness. Five or six seeds would be planted in a large mound and as the plants grew, more earth would be built up around the roots for ensured stability. Because maize was a time-consuming and difficult crop to grow, to promote efficiency, Indian farm plots were used for more than just the maize. Beans were planted amidst the maize, the maize plants themselves serving as beanpoles. Squash, too, was added to the potpourri for its broad leaves and ground-hugging growth curbed the spread of weeds.

To Europeans, this approach to farming seemed a jumbled mess. But again the consequences were interesting. This type of farming brought high yields per acre, kept weeds under control, and better retained soil moisture. Because the ground was not deeply stirred or plowed, erosion was held to a minimum.

Though it is debatable whether the Indians themselves knew this, soil exhaustion was lessened, for the nitrogen-fixing beans planted with the corn helped counter the loss of soil nutrients. And from a nutritional standpoint, beans and corn together provided the right combination of amino acids for a balanced diet of vegetable protein.

After a time, when an area of land finally did become less productive, the Indians would simply move. It is a myth that the Indians used fish as a fertilizer. Though the story is famous that Squanto taught this practice to the Pilgrims, in reality, Squanto probably learned about fish use in agriculture while being held captive in Europe. Peasants living in the low-lying areas of Western Europe, such as eastern England, the Netherlands, and Jutland, had experimented with fish as a fertilizer since at least the early fifteenth century. For the Indians, the carrying and carting of fish to their fields was an unnecessary labor. When a piece of land lost its productivity, it was simply more convenient to move on to another plot of ground. This was readily done because of low population density and because land with available water and potting clay was easily found.

In sum, though overlooked and disregarded by the Europeans at the time, Indian burning and agricultural practices suited their purposes quite admirably, and laid the basis for the legendary accounts of abundance in Colonial New England.

The changes that the Europeans were to make in this ecological situation were devastating. First of all, the Europeans looked upon land as a private commodity rather than as a public commons. Hence, rarely were ecological considerations prominent in the decisionmaking. Labor was scarce and accumulated capital even scarcer. The result was an economy which looked to the land and all that it offered as the route to success and wealth. Land was soon divided into numbered parcels and sold on the open market. This approach gave to the new parcels an abstract quality independent of the environment, the climate, and their best use.

Second, there was a rush to deforest, subdivide, cultivate and occupy. The subsequent results are not hard to discern. There was an immediate reduction in the edge-dwelling species; i.e., elk, deer, beaver, hare, porcupine, turkey, quail, ruffed grouse, and so on. The composition of the plants in the forests themselves changed. With deforestation, the landscape became hotter in summer, and colder in winter. In fact, temperatures in general came to fluctuate more widely. In the winter, the ground froze more deeply, the water-holding capacity of the soil was reduced, and the runoff increased and became more erratic. Flooding became a problem, and in poorly-drained areas, flooding led to the appearance of swamps and marshes, with their accompanying diseases and fevers. The water tables in New England fell.

The European monocultural crop practices led to other disruptions. Deep plowing caused a faster loss of soil nutrients, while the disturbed soil was more susceptible to erosion. Since colonial farmers treated their land as a resource to be mined until it was exhausted, rather than as a precious commodity to be conserved, soil exhaustion was a problem. Nor were the colonists careful about their fertilization practices, and when soils began to lose their nutrients, as an expedient, Europeans turned to the use of fish, which in turn had the result of spoiling fields with their oiliness.

With the Europeans, too, came the introduction of livestock, and even more problems. Grazing animals were among the chief agents in transmitting to America one of the central characters of European agriculture, the weed. Because Indians kept no cattle, and because their mixed-crop, hoe agriculture provided a relatively dense ground cover, weeds had not been a problem in New England. It was not long before colonial agriculture was to be plagued by weeds, especially ones imported to New England from the Old World such as dandelions, chickweeds, bloodworts, mulleins, mallows, nightshades, and stinging nettles.

Finally, European farming practices unintentionally created habitats conducive to diseases and pests. There were increased problems with native pests, and of course, with the coming of the Europeans, new pests were brought to the New World. Some Old World pests first introduced to the New World by Europeans were the Hessian fly, the black fly, the cockroach, the gray rat, and the house mouse.

A particularly devastating disease for New England farming in the seventeenth century was the "blast," or black stem rust. It was the barberry bush which served as the host for one phase of the black stem rust's life cycle. In this case, a European weed had brought with it a European disease.

In sum, from an ecological point of view, deforestation, grazing, plowing, and erosion all contributed to problems that became endemic to colonial agriculture in New England: soil exhaustion and plant diseases.

The history of the settlement of Africa offers a final perspective to our discussion. There Europeans found, for the most part, hostile natives and an inhospitable terrain. As a result, and in contrast to America, European colonies in Africa remained only small enclaves amidst an unsettling environment. Not surprisingly, therefore, most of Africa today remains in the hands of its natives, and the majority of Europe's colonies have vanished.

To conclude, more than simple technological superiority was needed to achieve success in America. To conquer the land, and pacify other Indians, whites needed Indian allies. Luckily for English colonists first landing in America, the natives along the Atlantic coast did not consider the ownership of private property, along the English model, the ultimate purpose of life. What if the private ownership of land had been the most desired symbol of success among the Indians? If this had been the case, could the colonists have dispossessed them of their land so easily? It is more likely that the African experience would have been reenacted here in America.

SELECTED BIBLIOGRAPHY

1. Axtell, James T. *The European and the Indian: Essays in the Ethnohistory of Colonial North America.* New York: Oxford University Press. 1981.
2. Berkhofer, Jr., Robert F. *The White Man's Indian.* New York: Random House. 1979.
3. Cronon, William. *Changes in the Land.* New York: Hill and Wang. 1983.
4. Jacobs, Wilbur R. *Dispossessing the American Indian.* New York: Charles Schribner's Sons. 1972.
5. Jennings, Francis. *Invasion of America.* Chapel Hill: University of North Carolina Press. 1975.
6. Martin, Calvin. *Keepers of the Game.* Berkeley: University of California Press. 1978.

7. Nash, Gary B. *Red, White, and Black*. Englewood Cliffs, N.J.: Prentice-Hall, Inc. Second Edition. 1982.
8. Prucha, Francis Paul. *The Indians in American Society: From the Revolutionary War to the Present*. Berkeley: University of California Press. 1985.
9. Washburn, Wilcomb E. *The Indian in America*. New York: Harper and Row. 1975.
10. Wright, Jr., J. Leitch. *The Only Land They Knew*. New York: Free Press. 1981.

A Counterpoint to British Colonization in America: Father Serra and the Spanish Impact on Alta California: Salvation or Exploitation?

The 200th anniversary of any great historical event is meant to be a time for nostalgia and rejoicing. It is a time to release romantic inclinations, to bring forth sentimental words of commemoration and praise, to unabashedly indulge oneself in a grand celebration of the past. Such celebrations, after all, are invigorating and cathartic. They are a way both of revering the past and expressing hope for the future.

It was surprising, then, to find the emotive 200th anniversary of Father Serra's death (August 28, 1984) swirling with controversy. This controversy was especially perplexing when one considers the inherent drama of the Father Serra story. Father Serra, as the founder and first Father–President of the Alta California mission system bears comparison with the Puritans of New England. Like Serra, they were initiators of a new civilization. Like Serra, they were the torchbearers of a broader policy of state–controlled colonization by the mother country. The mission held center–stage in the colonization of Alta California by Spain, and the challenges and achievements were, on the surface, spectacular.

The Franciscan missionaries faced unparalleled problems from an isolated frontier, inhabited by countless natives. Surrounded by thousands of potential enemies, they had to endure lives filled with everpresent physical danger. To even begin to cope with this situation, a Franciscan padre had to be courageous and dedicated. He had to possess considerable administrative skill and political know-how, and have immense quantities of physical stamina. Any slight laziness on his part, or any flaw in his intellectual and spiritual armor, and his efforts would surely be doomed.

Seemingly, the Franciscan friars possessed these qualities. At the peak of the mission experience, no more than fifty friars held sway over 20,000 converted Indian Christians, and successfully managed hundreds of thousands of head of livestock and millions of acres of land. It is with trepidation, especially considering the inherent disadvantages facing Father Serra and his Franciscan brothers in the first place, that one dares to question such an achievement.

Nonetheless, nothing seems to escape the critical eye of modern-day anthropologists and historians and the legacy of Father Serra and the Spanish colonization of Alta California is no exception.

Modern critics lament that students of California history have too often focussed on the intentions of the Franciscan padres rather than on their results, that these students have emphasized the goals of the missionaries rather than the impact on the Indians. In reality, these critics argue, the Franciscan policies and the Spanish impact were quite disturbing.

Because the padres aimed to transform the Indian into a fully "civilized" and Christian citizen, they wrenched the California Indians from their native ecological niches, and brought them into the mission environment without regard for the consequences.

The California Indians along the coast were a hunting-and-gathering people. The richness of the California environment with its unfailing annual supply of acorns, pine nuts, berries, and fish and game made existence relatively easy for the Indians, and afforded them an easygoing and carefree lifestyle. In aboriginal times California had the densest Indian population north of Mexico.

The Spanish missionaries, with lessons for effective colonization dating back to Columbus, lured the Indians into the missions, and then forcibly kept them there. The Indians were taken from a comfortable, sparsely populated, homogeneous setting, and placed in the crowded, alienating, confusing mission environment. The results were catastrophic.

Death and disease become the everyday reality in the mission. The Indians, having no natural immunities to the white man's diseases, fell prey to one semi-epidemic after another: smallpox, measles, dysentery, pleurisy, pneumonia, and syphilis. It has been estimated, utilizing the padres' own records, that the total loss of the mission Indian population was 72 percent. By 1810, 50 percent of the Indian children born at the missions perished. By 1820, that figure had reached the staggering proportion of 86 percent. It is no wonder that the Indian women at the missions came to practice abortion and infanticide at an ever-increasing rate.

One of the great pioneers of California Indian studies, A.L. Kroeber, has written: "It must have caused many of the Fathers a severe pang to realize, as they could not but do daily, that they were saving souls only at the inevitable cost of lives. And yet such was the overwhelming fact. The brute upshot of missionization, in spite of its kindly flavor and humanitarian root, was only one thing, death."

In a letter written at that time, one Spanish government official commented: "The missions lack all medicines and there is no other physician than the Providence of God." Between 1776 and 1825 there was only one truly qualified physician in all of Alta California, and the missionaries themselves were not trained in medical matters.

Other aspects of the mission system have also come under spirited attack. Consider, for instance, the padres' restriction of Indian sexual relations. An uninhibited attitude on the part of the Indians was juxtaposed with one of the most narrow-minded and rigid interpretations of sexual relations of that time. Natural sexual expression on the part of the Indians was curbed as the padres built separate dormitories for young Indian men and women, and forcibly monitored their sexual activities.

The missionaries were mistaken, too, critics say, in attempting to change the Indians' diet. Because of their concern to eliminate all of the traditional Indian ways, the padres forced the natives to take up agriculture and animal husbandry. But since the Indians were unused to a settled agrarian way of life, before long, the old hunting-and-gathering skills were lost by the mission Indians, and a precarious food supply replaced a formerly abundant situation.

The forced labor practices of the missionaries come under attack, too. The Indians had been accustomed to a more seasonal approach to hard work in their struggle for existence, therefore, the Indians often had to be forced to take up daily work on agricultural estates through the use of severe punishments. The French nobleman, Jean F.G. de la Perouse, on a visit to California, commented on his impression of mission life:

> We declare with pain that the resemblance [to slave colonies in Santo Domingo] is so exact that we saw both the men and the women loaded with irons, while others had a log of wood on their legs; and even the noise of the lash might have assailed our ears as that mode of punishment is equally admitted, although it is employed with little severity. . . .

> Corporal punishments are inflicted on the Indians of both sexes who neglect their pious exercises, and many faults which in Europe are wholly left to divine justice are here punished with irons or the log.

Critics also question the extent of the missionaries' success in converting the Indians to Christianity. In the end, they say, the overwhelming impact of the padres' Christian teaching was nil. At best, the Indians retained the basics of their former beliefs, simply adding the Christian Trinity to their pantheon of deities. At worst, the Indians' natural social and intellectual expression was destroyed and replaced with one which led the Indians into an attitude of spiritual and psychological demoralization.

In sum, critics argue that the mission system, even before the notorious secularization under Mexican rule in 1834, was in an advanced state of material and spiritual degeneration. The padres never lived up to their original goal of preparing the Indians for civilization. Instead, by treating the natives as children, by failing to develop a respect for the native ways of life, the missionaries left the mission Indians as helpless dependents—spiritually, psychologically, and physically demoralized. In the end, the mission system as a method of colonization was a great tragedy for the Indians and also a political failure for Spain.

Father Serra himself has not escaped criticism. Malcolm Margolin offers the following thumbnail sketch in a recent book:

> Serra was a man driven by a passion for saving souls. . . . Serra was also driven by inner torments and a quest for personal martyrdom. In imitation of Saint Francis of Assisi, founder of the Franciscan order, he carried with him a chain with which he repeatedly beat himself before congregations of awestruck Indians. . . . When the chain was not sufficient to humiliate the flesh, Serra would stand upon the pulpit, clutch the image of the crucified Christ in one hand, and, seizing a heavy stone in the other, would strike himself again and again on the chest, pounding with such ferocity that the spectators feared he would fall dead before their very eyes. Yet there were times when even the stone was not enough. For such occasions Serra used a large burning candle with four wicks, which, after opening the bosom of his habit, he would hold against his naked chest. . . . Indeed, the chain, the stone, and the burning candle may well have been the attributes of a saint. But they were not, perhaps, the best attributes for a missionary to bring to the California Indians.[7]

On the other side of coin, the historians who hail the import of the Spanish legacy are equally persuasive in their point of view, and so highly laudatory of Father Serra himself that they believe that he truly deserves sainthood in the Catholic Church.

First of all, this school of historical thought argues that the perspective of history must be remembered in any valid judgment of the mission system. To judge the missions by twentieth-century standards is very distorting. Western Europeans believed themselves to be the heirs of the Americans. Imperialism was an unquestioned fact of life in those centuries after Columbus's discovery. In fact, there was a great ocean rivalry to see which European nation would reign supreme in the New World. It is in this context that the Spanish experience must be judged.

11

From this perspective, the Spanish come off very well. The key fact of the Spanish missions, after all, was that they were built *for* the Indian. The Spanish found the Indians worthy of conversion. To be sure, they expected the Indians to work and learn European ways, but they also permitted them to *live*.

This approach should be compared with the English efforts in colonization where conversion of the Indian was not a significant concern. It is said about the English that upon arrival in the New World, they first fell upon their knees, and then they fell upon the Indians.

As late as 1886 an American politician of note, namely Theodore Roosevelt, would say: "I don't go so far as to think that the only good Indians are the dead Indians, but I believe nine out of every ten are, and I shouldn't like to inquire too closely into the case of the tenth. The most vicious cowboy has more moral principle than the average Indian." Nor does the Spanish mission approach compare with the wanton genocide of the California Indians when the Anglo-Americans appeared on the scene after 1846.

The Spanish aimed to colonize with native inhabitants. Every Indian was to be eligible to become a Spanish citizen. Deaths did occur in the missions. But these were purely unintentional and due to factors beyond the understanding of anyone at that time. Indian deaths at the expense of the white man's diseases were prevalent throughout the conquest of the Americas.

A better perspective on the Franciscan missionaries in their own time would be a comparison with the later American Abolitionists, those mid-nineteenth-century advocates of an immediate end to slavery. (See Chapter 15). True, like the Franciscans, the Abolitionists exhibit many shortcomings in the eyes of modern historians. For instance, very few Abolitionists rejected the white supremacy doctrines of their own time. They were more anti–slavery in their thought than truly pro–black. They had a tendency to view black people as an abstraction and modern–day historians lament these facts. But perhaps more relevant, given the virulently racist environment of those days, the Abolitionists were still able to make a leap of faith and expect that some day, given an environment of freedom, the slavery-stunted black people would "catch-up" with whites. Abolitionists may deserve credit for opposing slavery despite their shortcomings and their inabilities to regard blacks as truly equal to whites.

The same might be said of the Franciscans in California. In their own time their dedication and efforts stand in a category by themselves, truly unequalled in the Americas.

Historians sympathetic with the padres also claim that the specific criticisms of life at the missions are exaggerated. These historians emphasize that the Indians entered their new way of life voluntarily, and that the natives had the option of leaving almost at will. Further, it is argued that the work required of the Indians was relatively easy, that the padres understood that the Indians, given their unique traditions, could not be expected to work at agricultural tasks as vigorously as the Western European peasant.

As a result, there was extensive leisure time, numerous recreations, and an abundant number of holidays. The Indians suffered little punishment at the hands of the padres. In fact, physical punishment was used only as a last resort, and most offenses were handled with a paternal scolding. Materially, the Indians were given clothing and food, and lived a very secure existence. In sum, it is argued that on the whole the Indians enjoyed their associations with the missionaries and in most cases profited considerably from these associations.

As for Father Serra, himself, extra-special praise is reserved. For in the beginning only he foresaw the potential of the mission system in Alta California. He is described as heroic in his courage and spirited in his defense of the mission system against the vicious exploitation of the Spanish soldiers. In personal relations with the Indians, he is described as meek, humble, self-facing, and totally dedicated to their well-being. In this regard, special note should be taken of his trip to Mexico City to present a list of thirty-two demands to Viceroy Bucareli, many of which aimed at improving the life and conditions of the Indians in the missions. This trip was made even though the great priest was sixty years old at the time, and permanently lame as a result of an injury suffered years before. This trip was made, too, against the wishes of Governor Fages, the key Alta California administrator antagonistic to Serra's reforms.

These are the two sides of the argument. Does one dare to try to resolve these conflicting points of view? Can there ever be a completely dispassionate point of view on an issue involving religion? Can there ever be a completely dispassionate point of view on an issue involving the clash of cultures?

Perhaps the following points might serve as a beginning, as partial resolution of the meaning of the Spanish impact on our own time.

First of all, Father Serra's greatness is unquestioned. His dedication and selflessness were exceptional. He stands in a special category as the heroic moral ideal revered throughout all history. More significantly, his impact on history warrants his greatness. The mission was the key in the Spanish colonization experiment and Father Serra's string of missions brought Western civilization to Alta California.

Second, the Spanish influence has been a part of our past, and to better understand ourselves we need to understand it. The Spanish episode has molded and shaped our world today. We have the Spanish place names, much of their vocabulary, many of their former celebrations, fiestas, and rodeos as an integral part of our lives.

There is a vast art and literature from and about the Spanish period in our history. And there are the missions themselves—beautiful treasures in the American landscape which have inspired our imaginations and our art and our architecture.

Indeed, Spanish culture, religion, law and language have come to play a preponderant role in our whole hemisphere. Millions still speak the language and worship the religion that the Spanish brought to this New World. If there were twenty-one missions in California, we need to remember that there were about the same number of missions in Texas, even more in Florida and perhaps twice as many in New Mexico.

When one realizes the extent of the distance covered by the line of missions from Saint Augustine in Florida to San Francisco in California, the Spanish frontier was about twice as long as the Rhine–Danube frontier held by the Roman Empire. All this was accomplished by a nation in the midst of almost constant religious wars on the European continent, and plagued incessantly by the French, English, and even the Russians, in the race for the New World—quite an accomplishment and quite an impact!

A third point involves the way in which Spanish control of much of the American West shaped the future of the United States. It is fortunate for the U.S. that Spain was the first Western nation along the shores of California and the first in many areas of the western U.S. For if an even stronger nation, say the English or the Russians, had settled here first, the chances for future American acquisition might have been greatly jeopardized or prohibited.

A final point has even more urgency for our own time. On the way toward making this point we need to understand that historical significance is a protean factor. It has a symbiotic relationship with the present. It depends on time and circumstance. As the shadows and perspectives of time lengthen, historical significances shift and settle.

For ourselves today, perhaps we need to ask more of the past than a calculation of the sum total of the influences that we have undergone. Perhaps we ought truly to re-scrutinize and reweigh the merit of the ideas and influences of our great historical figures in light of our atomic age. What has been considered exemplary in a non-nuclear world perhaps has to be revised for our more terrible times of potential mass destruction.

Conceivably, then, we should ask of Serra and the Franciscans a greater question. Serra is said to have loved the Indians. Indeed, because he was a Christian, his life and work with the Indians is said to illustrate this love. But, as Tzvetan Todorov asks in a recent book: "Can we really love someone if we know little or nothing about his identity; if we see, in place of that identity, a projection of ourselves or of our ideals? Is there not already a violence in the conviction that one possesses the truth oneself, whereas this is not the case for others, and that one must furthermore impose that truth on those others?"[9]

This is not to say that Father Serra could have acted any differently. But today are not the ideals of self-determination and non-interference more crucial? Does not the imposition of one's will upon others deny them a large part of their humanity? In our time, is not nonviolent communication a must, and is it not imperative that we distinguish very carefully between what is *imposed* and what is *proposed* to others?

By winning on the one side the Spanish lost on the other. By not recognizing the true dignity of the Indian they diminished their own humanity.

SELECTED BIBLIOGRAPHY

1. Bolton, Herbert E. *The Mission as a Frontier Institution in the Spanish-American Colonies.* El Paso, Texas: Western College Press. 1962.
2. Cook, Sherburne F. *The Population of the California Indians, 1769-1970.* Berkeley: University of California Press. 1976.
3. _____. "Historical Demography." In *California*, ed. Robert F. Heizer, Vol. 8 of *Handbook of North American Indians*, general editor, William C. Sturtevant, pp. 91-98. Washington: Smithsonian Insititution. 1978.
4. Englebert, Omar. *The Last of the Conquistadors: Junipero Serra.* New York: Harcourt. 1956.
5. Guest, Francis F. "An Examination of the Thesis of S.F. Cook on the Forced Conversion of the Indians in the California Missions." *Southern California Quarterly*. Vol. 61. pp. 1-77. 1979.
6. Heizer, Robert F. and Alan F. Almquist. *The Other Californians: Prejudice and Discrimination under Spain, Mexico and the United States to 1920.* Berkeley and Los Angeles: University of California Press. 1971.
7. Margolin, Malcolm. *The Ohlone Way: Indian Life in the San Francisco–Monterey Bay Area.* Berkeley: Heyday Books. 1978.
8. Phillips, George Harwood. *Chiefs and Challengers: Indian Resistance and Cooperation in Southern California.* Berkeley: University of California Press. 1975.
9. Todorov, Tzvetan. *The Conquest of America.* New York: Harper and Row. 1984.

3

How Puritanical Were the Puritans?

For most present-day Americans, mere mention of the Puritans conjures up a vivid and negative image. We imagine militant Protestants rigidly disciplined in their belief in predestination and unflinching in the idea that God's grace had placed them above and apart from the rest of humanity. We see them in the chilly confines of colonial New England, and picture them dressed in severe clothes of black. We associate them with extreme asceticism and abhorrence of the pleasures of the body, with neurotic sexual inhibitions, and with hostility to the enjoyment of art and music. We believe they were fanatically repressive in their political views. Indeed, the term "puritanical" has come to mean rigidly austere, narrow-minded, and self-righteous.

The great nineteenth century British historian, Thomas Macaulay, concurred with this image when he gibed: "The Puritan hated bear baiting, not because it gave pain to the bear, but because it gave pleasure to the spectators." Macaulay's American contemporary, Nathaniel Hawthorne, added credibility to the stereotype of the Puritans in his classic novel, *The Scarlet Letter*. Its heroine was condemned to wear the scarlet letter "A" (Adultress) upon her dress for the rest of her life, while the secret father of her child, a prominent young minister in colonial Boston, went through the agonies of guilt and remorse. The novel was replete with images of rigidity and repression, and it portrayed a somber people in an inhibiting environment. In the twentieth century, the caustic American critic, H. L. Mencken, continued the gloomy portrayal when he wrote: "Puritanism is the haunting fear that someone, somewhere, may be happy."

Historians in the early decades of the twentieth century went along with these popular images. During the years after World War I Americans were turning away somewhat from Europe, and subconsciously many of America's scholars were busy deriding the European influence in our national past, and with it the English Puritans who first came to settle here. Further, these were the years of Prohibition; and intellectuals saw in the self-righteous prohibitionist a twentieth-century Puritan. Indeed, not just an ordinary Puritan was visualized, but one with a blue-tipped nose, and perhaps a hatchet, who invaded the privacy of ordinary citizens in his search for immoral behavior and caches of liquor.

Lately, however, historians have been more sympathetic in their portrayal of the Puritans. Each of the stereotyped characteristics mentioned has been restudied and the harsher aspects of the above portrait have been softened. First of all, the image of the rigorous masochist rejecting all bodily pleasures has been clarified. For, as Protestants, Puritans never accepted the ascetic and monastic ideals of medieval Catholicism. Puritans typically saw themselves as workers in the world, and did not idealize the isolation and seclusion of monasticism. Further, Puritans did not totally reject pleasures of the body. Their attitude toward liquor is just one example. None other than the devoted Puritan leader and minister, Increase Mather, admitted that "wine is from God." A look at the immense quantities of alcohol and wine that colonial Puritans consumed can serve as verification that Puritans heartily relished God's munificence in this regard.

Similarly, Puritan attitudes towards sex are no longer associated with the inhibitions and hushed voices of the stereotype. Puritans were open and frank about the importance of sex in a happy and healthy marriage, and it is simply incorrect to talk of them as sexually inhibited or characterized by sexually repressive attitudes. One prominent Puritan minister, Samuel Willard, more than once expressed his disapproval of "that Popish conceit of the Excellency of Virginity."

Equally exaggerated is the image of Puritans somberly clad in black. True, the vegetable dyes of those days limited the range of colors available. Nonetheless, the Puritans did not restrict themselves to black. Their clothing inventories show that "russet," or various shades of orange-brown were among their favorites, along with many items in red, blue, green, yellow, purple, and so forth. Nor were the Puritans opposed to music and art per se. What they objected to was their display in the meetinghouse. Outside the church, however, art and music were often highly esteemed.

It is even more of a mistake to characterize Puritans as intellectually repressive. Though faith was, of course, the bedrock of their beliefs, Puritans also set great value on the idea that a person's intellect and reasoning had to be finely cultivated for a true understanding of God's Word. Their sermons, for instance, were noted for their high intellectual caliber, and their ministers were often among the best-educated people in the New World. More than 100 graduates of Oxford and Cambridge settled in New England before 1640, most of them ministers, while all of Virginia could not claim even five men with a similar background. The high value Puritans placed on education was exemplified by their founding of "The College" in 1636, later named Harvard University. Other religious sects soon followed suit. By the time of the American Revolution, there were nine colleges in the English colonies, only one which was not founded under the auspices of a church. It is interesting to note that England did not establish its third university until the nineteenth century.

One must not go too far in the reversal of the Puritan stereotype, however. While destroying one myth, I do not mean to create another. These people, after all, did not call themselves "Puritans" for nothing. I surely do not want to turn the Puritans into "rakes of the Renaissance" with one arm lustfully cuddling Priscilla and the other hoisting a tankard of ale. Though the traditional stereotype went too far, the Puritans were a serious lot. Puritan society was not one in which twentieth-century Americans would feel comfortable. Though Increase Mather might say that "wine is from God," he also remarked that "the Drunkard is from the Devil." And albeit one might learn that "repression" was not directed against the expression of sexual impulses as strongly as formerly thought, there was "repression" directed against the expression of anger. Further, the whole of the Puritan community was concerned, in a way which Americans today would consider extremely conservative and repressive, about the morals and virtues of each of its members.

It is no wonder, then, that depending on the current modes and trends in American values, at various times in our history Puritans have either been revered or reviled. As we have seen, the more rollicking Twenties condemned them, and the more serious Thirties began their rehabilitation. Because of this tendency, historians today are trying to get away from judging Puritans by contemporary standards. We are trying to rise above our tendency toward "presentmindedness," to show how Puritan attitudes fit in with the economic and political circumstances of the middle classes in the seventeenth century, and to understand why Puritan attitudes were reasonably appropriate to the needs of those classes in their time.

With this approach, some penetrating insights have emerged. The first comes from the historian Samuel Eliot Morison. In 1956 Morison argued that the alternative to a Puritanically-controlled intellectual life, given the conditions of seventeenth-century America, was not cool rationalism or vibrant humanism, but an intellectual vacuum, Morison writes:

> A humanist New England would doubtless have provided a pleasanter dwelling place, and a more sweet and wholesome stream to swell the American flood than a puritan New England. But . . . the mere physical labor of getting a living in a virgin country is so great as to exhaust and stultify the human spirit unless it has some great emotional drive. . . . The intellectual alternatives for New England were not puritanism *or* humanism, but puritanism *or* overwhelming materialism.[10]

Another particularly cogent insight emerges when contrasting the seventeenth-century Puritan family with its twentieth-century American counterpart. The Puritan family was at the same time a business, a school, a vocational institute, a church, a house of correction, and a welfare institution. Under those circumstances it was necessary, in the interests of a smoothly-running society, for Puritan governmental institutions to supervise and get involved with what we today would consider private matters. In the twentieth century, the factory, the government, the school, the cinema, etc., have taken over functions that were once consigned to the nuclear family; in our day, corresponding governmental "interference" would naturally seem too confining.

Finally, the historical profession's aim to abjure "presentmindedness" has led to a fuller understanding of everyday Puritan life than we have ever had before. New studies of almost every aspect of Puritan culture have emerged in the last twenty years, and now we also have one of the great interpretations of this scholarship by David Hackett Fischer in a rousing new book, *Albion's Seed: Four British Folkways in America*. Fischer studies Puritan folkways in detail in twenty-four different areas: Speech ways, Building ways, Family ways, Marriage ways, Gender ways, Sex ways, Child-rearing ways, Naming ways, Age ways, Death ways, Religious ways, Magic ways, Learning ways, Food ways, Dress ways, Sport ways, Work ways, Time ways, Wealth ways, Rank ways, Social ways, Order ways, Power ways, and Freedom ways. In this work, Fischer reinforces many of the old Puritan stereotypes, and acts the revisionist with regard to many others. (The book also includes an analysis of the cultures of the Quakers, the Cavaliers of Virginia, and the Backcountry settlers from the borderlands of North Britain). In my opinion, Fischer's book will come to be considered one of the great works on Colonial America.

In conclusion, whether or not one believes that the Puritans were too inhibited and somber for comfortable living, it is still important to recognize their significance in American history. Their spiritual dedication, their intellectual vitality, and their sense of mission have become a part of the "national character" of our middle classes. At its best, the Puritan legacy, as Ralph Waldo Emerson once wrote, prompts Americans toward "the pursuit of the vast, the beautiful, and the unattainable."

SELECTED BIBLIOGRAPHY

1. Breen, T. H. *Puritans and Adventurers*. New York: Oxford University Press. 1980.
2. Bremer, Francis J. *The Puritan Experiment: New England Society from Bradford to Edwards*. New York: St Martin's Press. 1976.
3. Demos, John. *A Little Commonwealth: Family Life in Plymouth Colony*. New York: Oxford University Press. 1970.
4. Fischer, David Hackett. *Albion's Seed: Four British Folkways in America*. New York and Oxford: Oxford University Press. 1989.
5. Miller, Perry. *Errand into the Wilderness*. Cambridge, Mass.: Harvard University Press. 1956.
6. _____. *The New England Mind: From Colony to Province*. Cambridge, Mass.: Harvard University Press. 1953.
7. _____. *The New England Mind: The Seventeenth Century*. New York: Macmillan. 1939.
8. Morgan, Edmund S. *The Puritan Dilemma*. Boston: Little, Brown and Co. 1958.
9. _____. *The Puritan Family*. Boston: Boston Public Library. 1956.
10. Morison, Samuel E. *The Intellectual Life of Colonial New England*. New York: New York University Press. 1956.
11. Perry, Ralph Barton. *Puritanism and Democracy*. New York: Vanguard Press. 1944.
12. Rutman, Darret B. *Winthrop's Boston: A Portrait of a Puritan Town*. New York: W. W. Norton. 1972.
13. Walzer, Michael. *The Revolution of the Saints*. Cambridge, Mass.: Harvard University Press. 1965.

The American Revolution: Model for Emerging Nations?

As a former colonial people and as the first major colony to achieve independence through revolution, one would expect most Americans to be sympathetic with the aims and aspirations of emerging twentieth-century nations. However, the opposite feeling is generally the rule. Americans find themselves strangely alienated by the turmoil of present-day revolutions. Indeed, Americans often have not only found themselves unsympathetic to colonial revolts but have sided with factions or elites that were attempting to inhibit democratic change and stamp out movements for reform.

Such an apparent contradiction in and deviation from America's own revolutionary past has caused certain historians to re-evaluate the turmoil of 1776. Disturbing questions inevitably emerge from this historical inquiry: does the American struggle for independence bear any resemblance to the revolutions of today? If so, why do Americans frequently find themselves opposed to today's national liberation movements? Is it because Americans have forgotten their history? Two prominent historians have recently focused on these questions: Richard B. Morris,[9] and Carl Degler.[3,4] Their answers differ dramatically. By surveying each of their arguments we should find ourselves more attuned to the importance of this issue.

Richard Morris emphatically believes that the American Revolution has served as a model for recent Third World revolutions. He notes that the American Revolution has determined much of the language of twentieth-century revolutionaries. Even our former antagonist, the Democratic Republic of Vietnam, felt itself compelled to justify its actions with a declaration very similar to that written by Thomas Jefferson in 1776.

Secondly, guerrilla warfare, so characteristic of twentieth-century colonial revolutions, was equally a part of America's struggle for independence. The aims of America in 1776 were to avoid climactic battles with a more powerful enemy, to stall for time while the British will to continue slackened, to withdraw when outnumbered, to conduct surprise counter-attacks, and to hope for some type of aid and support from a Great Power. The similarities with recent wars of national liberation are obvious and irrefutable, e.g. Cuba, Vietnam, Algeria, China.

Thirdly, Morris points to young America's conduct of foreign policy as exactly analogous to what is occurring in this century. The American nation had France as an ally during its fight for independence. However, as soon as the war was over, the new nation quickly moved to disengage itself from "entangling" ties with France, ties which might have embroiled America

"... I long to hear that you have declared an independancy—and by the way in the new Code of Laws which I suppose it will be necessary for you to make I desire you would Remember the Ladies, and be more generous and favourable to them than your ancestors. Do not put such unlimited power into the hands of Husbands. Remember all Men would be tyrants if they could." Abigail Adams in a letter to her husband, John, March 31, 1776.

in Europe's wars over the "balancing of power." In fact, America's quick embrace of isolationism, following the Revolutionary War, reminds one of emergent nations who coolly exploit the Cold War situation for their own advantage, and then proclaim neutrality and nonalignment—Nehru's India, Tito's Yugoslavia, Egypt today, etc.

Another similarity between the American experience and that of emerging nations is the existence of one-party politics. The two-party system has become such an integral part of the American domestic scene that Americans have forgotten those days when, for fifteen or sixteen years, the young American nation possessed only one party, the party of the Revolution. The opposition Tory party was smashed and dispersed, and until a national consensus was built the American people did not seem to desire a two-party system.

Lastly, Morris reminds Americans of the messianic zeal which was displayed during earlier revolutionary times, a zeal and sense of mission reminiscent of what many new nations are exhibiting today. In sum, Morris argues that if Americans truly understand their Revolution properly, they will better understand the colonial revolutions of the twentieth century:

> As the first great revolution of modern times, the American Revolution was both a war of decolonization and a movement of broad social change and reform. Waged to establish an independent nation, sovereign and equal with all the nations of the earth, it constituted at the same time a movement to support the rights of man, of all men, and women too. And, in that wider sense, the American Revolution, with its egalitarian overtones, has enormous relevance to the revolutions of the emerging nations of later times and, not least of all, to our own time. . . .[9]

Carl Degler disagrees. He argues that no one can study the American Revolution without noticing how different it was from the revolutions of today. First of all, Degler points to the "conservative" character of the American Revolution. The American revolutionary leaders were reluctant revolutionaries, Degler says. They were happy with their colonial life until the British government began, after 1763, to revise its imperial policy and to increase taxes. Americans revolted to keep things as they had been during the age of "Salutary Neglect." Degler points to American pamphlets that declared that the revolution would stop if only the British would cease their innovations in taxation and imperial policy. He emphasizes that Americans protested more or less peacefully for ten years before breaking away, clearly showing the conservative attitude of the majority.

There are also other differences. America had no long-established underground movements like those in twentieth-century colonial countries. Three-quarters of America's revolutionary leaders were established politicians in prerevolutionary days. This made the transition from colony to nationhood relatively simple and smooth. Degler notes that America was a "have," not a "have not" colony, as is the case with so many emerging nations today. The following facts are typical examples of the advantages America possessed: natural resources were abundant and easily accessible, the majority of the population owned their own land, three-fourths of the population were to some extent literate, most of the people had the vote locally, and there were no major divisive religious or cultural differences; the list could go on and on.

Degler's message, then, is that the American Revolution does not have a special relevance for the emerging nations of today. For them, the Chinese and Russian Revolutions have much more meaning and many more applicable lessons. Unlike these later revolutions, the American Revolution was narrowly political rather than broadly social. America's unique circumstances of isolation from Europe's entanglements and vast potential wealth enabled the "first new nation" to have an experience and a history which provides little relevance for Third World nations emerging from colonialism and extreme poverty in this century. The lesson here, for Degler, is that America's current foreign policy may be anachronistic if it is based on principles and ideals which are similarly irrelevant:

> In an age when America is a model for the whole world, it is important for us to remember that our history is irrelevant for most other peoples. If we do remember that then we will not expect other nations to follow our path and will save ourselves from disappointment arising out of misjudgment.

> . . . the burdens that our peculiar history place upon us as an international leader should not be ignored, or, as some would try to do, speciously transmuted into assets. Our history has neither fitted us for nor warned us of the international role that now we play.[3]

How does one reconcile these two approaches to a vital question of American history? Both authors may be correct, depending how one defines the scope of the American Revolution. If a historian focuses on the *tactics* of fighting a revolution, then the insights that Morris provides are illuminating. For the tactics of Americans during their struggle for independence are still useful and have been freely employed by twentieth-century nations. If a historian focuses on the *aims* of the American Revolution, that is, on the social goals that Americans set for themselves in 1776, then Degler's arguments are also revealing. As Degler has argued, social concerns and internal reforms were a secondary aspect of the American Revolution. To the extent that social or class conflict existed it was set aside, as all classes believed that their economic and political goals would be maximized by the removal of British rule.

This is in sharp contrast to twentieth-century struggles. Social concerns in these rebellions have been a priority; witness the great agitation for redistribution of wealth and for the removal of ruling elites. Further, Third World nations have strongly attacked the cultures and political legacies of the European countries which formerly dominated them. Compare this with America's post-revolutionary acceptance of British political traditions. There was no bitter attack against or rejection of the political ideals of the mother country. Rather, Americans argued that the British themselves were perverting and incorrectly interpreting their own parliamentary inheritance. The American slogans for equal representation and full civil liberties, all vital elements of modern social democracy, were later adopted and extended by the British themselves.

In conclusion, Americans are consistent with their early history when they manifest uneasiness and disagreement with the more radical social-democratic revolutions of today. As John Adams once remarked while comparing the American and French Revolutions: "Ours was resistance to innovation; theirs was innovation itself."

SELECTED BIBLIOGRAPHY

1. Bailyn, Bernard. *Ideological Origins of the American Revolution*. Cambridge, Mass.: Harvard University Press, 1967.
2. Brinton, Crane. *The Anatomy of Revolution*. Englewood Cliffs, N.J.: Prentice-Hall Inc., 1965.
3. Degler, Carl N. "The American Past: An Unsuspected Obstacle in Foreign Affairs." *The American Scholar*. Vol. 32, No. 2 (Spring 1963).

4. _____. ''The Challenge of the American Revolution Today.'' A Lecture delivered at De Anza Community College in honor of the Bi-Centennial of the American Revolution. 1976.

5. Fulton, Richard M., ed. *The Revolution that Wasn't: A Contemporary Assessment of 1776.* Millwood, N. Y.: Kennikat. 1981.

6. Maier, Pauline. *From Resistance to Revolution: Colonial Radicals and the Development of American Opposition to Britian, 1765–1776.* New York: Random House. 1972.

7. Martin, James Kirby. *Men in Rebellion: Higher Governmental Leaders and the Coming of the American Revolution.* New York: The Free Press. 1973.

8. Miller, John C. *Origins of the American Revolution.* Boston: Little, Brown and Co. 1943.

9. Morris, Richard B. *The Emerging Nations and the American Revolution.* New York: Harper and Row. 1970.

10. Wood, Gordon S. *The Creation of the American Republic, 1766–1787.* Chapel Hill: University of North Carolina Press. 1969.

1776: Was Unjust Taxation the Issue?

The Old Farmer's Almanac once carried the following humorous insight: "If Patrick Henry thought that taxation without representation was bad, he should see how bad it is with representation." I am sure that Americans, in their current mood of critical appraisal of taxation and bureaucracies, wholeheartedly agree with the gist of this quotation. So in light of our present-day tax protests, let us reconsider some of the perplexing questions associated with 1776. Was British colonial rule really that unfair? Was taxation without representation tyranny? Was taxation without representation un-American? Most of us will answer an unqualified and vocal "Yes!", but in each case we would be essentially incorrect.

In fact, British imperial practices were not totally unfair. Many advantages and benefits accrued to Americans under this system. The most obvious example was an assured market for colonial products. Also, under British auspices the colonies were paid "bounties" (cash subsidies) for key raw materials. From 1709 to 1774 the British Parliament paid Americans £1,438,702 in bounty payments for naval stores alone (i.e., lumber, masts, bowsprits, pitch, turpentine, etc.). These funds, it should be noted, came from the pockets of homeland English taxpayers (much to their chagrin). Further, between 1748 and 1763, £185,000 were granted in bounty payments to American indigo growers. These are but two of many examples of how the British imperial system was not totally unfair to the colonies. In general, it has been calculated that the burdens of colonialism, as regards the transatlantic trade, were proportionately higher in 1700 than they were in 1775. These statistics should give us some indication that taxation might not have been the key issue in the decision to revolt.

Was taxation without representation tyranny? Not according to the British unwritten "constitution" of that time. Many homeland Britons themselves were not "directly" represented in Parliament. This was due to aristocratic privileges and antiquated constituency boundaries. Rather, the majority of Britons were "virtually" represented, meaning that Members of Parliament, even if from different districts, always had the good of all Englishmen in mind. Though this policy of virtual representation seems unjust given the liberal standards of our time, during the eighteenth century it probably created the freest and most open political situation in the world.

The harshness of British rule should not be exaggerated when the American colonials are considered. On a per capita basis taxes in the colonies were five times greater in 1698 than they were to be in 1773. And in 1773 the taxes on homeland Britons were much higher than those on American colonials.

Well, perhaps taxation without direct representation was un-American? On the contrary, in Puritan Massachusetts, for instance, nonchurch members were taxed, though not represented in the legislature, and they were unable to vote in general elections. Further, throughout the colonies before the Revolution, the poor and unpropertied, though often unable to vote, were still taxed. Indeed, taxation without representation has been such an American tradition that it has continued into the twentieth century. Prominent examples are women, who were not given the vote until 1920 and yet were taxed; and Black Americans, who had to fight well into the 1960s for the right to vote, though they always found themselves on tax rolls. There is even the example of the Territory of Hawaii which did not have the vote for half a century until statehood was granted in 1959.

What was it then that caused such an uproar in 1776 and earlier, if it was not the burden of the taxes themselves? Far more important were the principles behind the taxation. Americans were incensed over the fact that the new British taxes levied after 1763 threatened their traditional rights as Englishmen. For instance, not only were the new taxes imposed without the consent of America's own directly-elected representatives, but American rights to a fair jury trial were also jeopardized. Specifically, infringements of the Sugar and Stamp Acts were to be settled in British admiralty courts. These courts were objectionable to the colonials for two important reasons: 1) they violated the colonials' rights to a trial by a jury of their peers, and 2) they put the burden of proof on the defendants, assuming that they were guilty until they proved themselves innocent.

Equally upsetting for Americans was the announced purpose of the new taxes: to pay the costs of British troops stationed in America. As the French and Indian "enemies" had been effectively contained by 1763, Americans believed that continued high troop levels in America were intended to intimidate the colonials themselves.

Eventually, British actions threatened even the colonials' cherished belief in legislative accountability. An example was the sudden announcement in 1772 by Governor Thomas Hutchinson that, henceforth, the British Crown rather than the Massachusetts legislature would pay his salary. Since control over the salaries of royal officials allowed colonial legislatures to exert a powerful hold on them, this development was disturbing. Later it was revealed that judges in Massachusetts, too, were to be paid by the British government.

It was this change in the principle of legislative accountability, plus colonial concern over the fate of their traditional rights as Englishmen, that caused so much of the discontent. Naturally, there was more than this behind the origins of the American Revolution. But these were some of the key concerns that lay behind the issue of taxation.

By 1776 American distrust of British rule had grown so large that Americans would not have accepted taxation *with* representation. Americans had simply outgrown their need for British parentage. The young colonies had matured beyond the confines of British rule. A rich ideology of republican self-government was sweeping the colonies, and the great concern was that continued British rule by an increasingly corrupt elite was beginning to pervert even the rich British democratic legacy. To maintain cherished ideals Americans believed they had to declare independence.

What, then, are the insights that can be garnered from the pre-Revolutionary period and applied to the taxation and bureaucratic situation of today? First, there exists a great American antipathy against paying taxes that go to maintain or enlarge government bureaucracy. This antipathy especially characterizes the feelings of America's business class. The great financier J. P. Morgan's comment immediately comes to mind here: "Anybody has a right to evade taxes if he can get away with it. No citizen has a moral obligation to assist in maintaining the government.''

Second, both in 1776 and in our time, taxation has been the rallying cry for the deeper problem of legislative accountability. As in colonial times, Americans today are upset with their diminishing control over a growing governmental bureaucracy; a bureaucracy which has become ever more cumbersome, inept and wasteful in recent years. In sum, protest against unjust taxation seems to be the symptom of a deeper malaise rather than the key issue itself. Of greater concern for most Americans is the status and vitality of their republican ideology and democratic traditions. Just as it was in 1776.

SELECTED BIBLIOGRAPHY

1. Alden, John R. *A History of the American Revolution.* New York: Alfred A. Knopf. 1969.
2. Brown, Robert E. *Middle-Class Democracy and the Revolution in Massachusetts, 1691–1780.* Ithaca, N.Y.: Cornell University Press. 1955.
3. Christie, Ian R. *Crisis of Empire.* New York: W. W. Norton Co. 1966.
4. Gipson, Lawrence Henry. *The Coming of the Revolution, 1763–1775.* New York: Harper and Row. 1954.
5. Middlekauff, Robert. *The Glorious Cause.* New York and Oxford: Oxford University Press, 1982.
6. Morgan, Edmund S. and Helen M. *The Stamp Act Crisis.* Chapel Hill: University of North Carolina Press. 1953.
7. Nash, Gary B. *The Urban Crucible: Social Change, Political Consciousness, and the Origins of the American Revolution.* Cambridge, Mass.: Harvard University Press. 1980.
8. Norton, Mary Beth. *Liberty's Daughters: The Revolutionary Experience of American Women, 1750–1800.* Boston: Little, Brown and Company. 1980.
9. Tuchman, Barbara W. *The March of Folly.* New York: Alfred A. Knopf. 1984

"*Though in reviewing the incidents of my administration I am unconscious of intentional error, I am nevertheless too sensible of my defects not to think it probable that I may have committed many errors. Whatever they may be, I fervently beseech the Almighty to avert or mitigate the evils to which they may tend. I shall also carry with me the hope that my country will never cease to view them with indulgence, and that, after forty-five years of my life dedicated to its service with an upright zeal, the faults of incompetent abilities will be consigned to oblivion, as myself must soon be to the mansions of rest.*" George Washington, Farewell Address, September 17, 1796.

Wherein Lies the Greatness of George Washington?

George Washington may be "first in war," and "first in peace," but it is doubtful today if Washington is "first in the hearts of his countrymen." To be sure, everyone, even the recent immigrant or the least historically-minded American, can identify Washington. Few Americans, however, can identify with him. He lacks the common touch which endears such men as Benjamin Franklin and Abraham Lincoln to students of history.

Perhaps the fault lies with American historians. For they have made Washington out to be so perfect and so lifeless that he seems to be more monument than man. And they have encircled him with such a host of suffocating myths that he has become a subject of dreariness and dullness to most Americans. Ralph Waldo Emerson once warned nineteenth-century historians about their excessive praise of Washington: "Every hero becomes a bore at last." Nathaniel Hawthorne, too, poked fun at the prevailing nineteenth-century image of Washington: "Did anybody ever see Washington nude? It is inconceivable. He had no nakedness, but I imagine he was born with his clothes on, and his hair powdered, and made a stately bow on his first appearance in the world."

Conceivably the fault for the deification lies not with historians, but rather with the circumstances of Revolutionary America. Washington was a living legend among his contemporaries. It is frequently admitted by historians that each age tends to search for a hero with which to identify. This was especially true of the Americans of the late eighteenth and early nineteenth centuries. They had just begun laying the foundations of independence, and they needed the inspiring confidence of a leader who could insure them that their new course of action, fraught with difficulties, was correct and just.

Deification was helped along, too, by the fact that the English-speaking world of the ensuing nineteenth century had about it an evangelical and didactic emphasis. As the historian Marcus Cunliffe has argued, it was a world "of tracts and primers, of Chambers's *Miscellanies* and McGuffey's *Readers,* of Samuel Smiles and Horatio Alger, of mechanics' institutes and lyceum lectures, of autograph albums and gift annuals. It *[was]* the age of Self-Help, Thrift, Duty, and Character."[3]

With this as a background, it is no wonder that Washington's awesome character was seized upon by moralists anxious to demonstrate a lesson. The end result was that Washington's personality was frozen into the icy contours with which we are familiar. It is this glacial image which has failed to evoke the love of present-day Americans. Unlike a Lincoln, or a Franklin, with whom we can identify, Washington remains aloof. His importance has been recognized, but it has not served to endear him to his countrymen.

Indeed, historians in the college classrooms of today often ignore Washington in favor of studying the Washington myth itself and how it evolved, rather than getting to know the man. As a result, as the historian Robert F. Jones has remarked: "For all the ink spilt in his name, few Americans know more about George Washington than a few stray facts and some stories, some true, some false, but all insignificant, about a cherry tree and a hatchet, dental problems, kneeling in prayer in the snows of Valley Forge and throwing a coin across a river."[6]

Washington is further ignored by modern historians in other ways. When the great ideas of Revolutionary America are studied, Washington is passed over in favor of the multi-faceted Jefferson. When the Revolutionary victory is focused upon, the incompetence of English generals gains the limelight. During the period of the Constitutional Convention, Madison as the "Father of the Constitution" is discussed. And during Washington's very own Presidency, the dramatic battle between Hamilton and Jefferson serves as the chief attraction.

Wherein, then, lies the greatness of Washington? In what did he especially excel? And what is his relevance for our own time? To best answer these questions, Washington's role in the three great achievements of Revolutionary America must be studied: the War of Independence, the Constitutional Convention, and Washington's Presidency under the new Constitution. For a quarter of a century, from 1775 to 1799, Washington stood at the forefront of these crucial events.

Regarding the American Revolution, Washington's brilliance as a military strategist has been debated since the early days of that great war. On the one side, critics have argued that Washington lacked military genius, and that his real contribution was his dedicated service as a noble symbol around which loyal patriots could adhere. The reasons for victory are attributed more to the efforts of other American generals, to the efforts of the Continental Congress, to the geographical obstacles which faced the British, and to the hesitancy and mediocrity of British generalship than to Washington's military expertise.

On the other side, the argument runs in exactly the opposite direction. Defeat, admirers insist, would have been inevitable if Washington had not been both a brilliant strategist and an able military tactician. Further, they argue, Washington possessed charismatic qualities which allowed him to shape and exploit the efforts of his subordinate generals and the Continental Congress. Indeed, two noted military historians, R. Ernest Dupuy and Trevor N. Dupuy, have argued that by 1781 Washington "had developed a competence worthy of favorable comparison beside Alexander at the Granicus, Caesar at the Rubicon, Hannibal at the Alps, Genghis Khan at the Great Wall, Frederick the Great at Prague, or Napoleon at Montenotte."[2]

A more prudent appraisal, however, emphasizes that Washington simply was not tested enough in battle to be accorded a place among the great military geniuses of all time. If the Revolutionary War had not been so characterized by "hit and run" tactics, if Washington had had the supplies, and the large armies of a Napoleon, then perhaps one could judge his greatness as a military commander with more certainty. The most that can be said is that Washington possessed the perfect disposition for the type of war he had to fight. Given the scarcity of supplies, the rivalries of the American states, the greenness of American troops, etc., Washington's patience, self-discipline, administrative abilities, willingness to work hard, faith in the American cause, and his incorruptibility were perfectly suited for the challenge at hand.

As Commander-in-Chief of America's Revolutionary Army, Washington is better compared to Dwight D. Eisenhower, another military administrator of exceptional abilities, than to the celebrated "fighting" generals of military history. Washington was never truly a military man. He recognized his importance as a symbol of the patriot cause. He recognized that oftentimes during the war force was a secondary factor, and that his army was equally an instrument of propaganda. His instinct guided him correctly toward the conclusion that the crucial battles in the American Revolution were in the arena of public opinion.

He made mistakes, especially at the battles of Long Island, Fort Washington, Brandywine and Germantown. He was not above being sensitive to criticism, or to shifting the blame for his errors onto others. But one must never lose sight of the fact that while other generals on both sides were being dismissed with predictable regularity, Washington held on to his position for eight long years. He adjusted his pugnacious military tendencies to fit the requirements of the moment. And, most importantly, he set for all Americans the supreme example of the "Disinterested Patriot." As a "Disinterested Patriot," he was a unique phenomenon in world history. Contrary to nearly all historical precedent, he retired after his great military successes to a private life of farming and business.

Washington set the pattern in America whereby military authority for generations would be subordinate to civilian authority. In spite of the encouragement of those around him after the Revolution, he resisted, in two famous instances, the temptation to set up a dictatorship. For Washington, victory in the Revolution also meant a victory for republicanism.

If Washington had failed, one can guess the alternatives for America. Maybe America would have fallen into the tragic cycle found in the Europe of the eighteenth century—the cycle of "wars, poverty, despotism, and corruption." If Washington had failed, conceivably the Revolution of '76 would have left a divided and embittered people subjected to a long and distressful history comparable to that of Ireland. Instead, Washington's success was a crucial element in America's success. As Jefferson observed: "The moderation and virtue of a single character has probably prevented this revolution from being closed as most others have been by a subversion of that liberty it was intended to establish."

Historians are in much more agreement regarding Washington's importance in the passage of the Constitution. Though Washington presided over the Constitutional Convention and signed the final document, his real influence was not inside the Convention in the drafting of the new document. Rather his influence was to be felt most strongly outside the Convention. The fact that Washington was even there at Philadelphia, and was in agreement with what was being done, did much to quell the suspicions of the public.

Like so many others, Washington had become disillusioned with the Articles of Confederation. From the beginning of America's struggle for independence Washington believed that any federal government had to be strong if the potential greatness of the new nation were to be realized. He saw the inefficiency of the Continental Congress during the Revolution, and how it could not significantly cope with the divisive rivalries of the thirteen states. He felt that the Revolution would have been over much sooner if only the Continental Congress had had the added power that was necessary. As America progressed after the Revolution, Washington became ever more convinced that the Articles of Confederation were not equal to the challenges facing the nation.

Not only did Washington believe that the Congressional branch of the government needed strengthening, but he also argued on behalf of a stronger executive branch. In fact, the probability that Washington was to be the new President eased the fears that many delegates had when a stronger executive office was fitted into the Constitution. Such was their confidence in Washington, that Convention delegates were content to leave vague the details of the new Presidential office for Washington to work out during the first term of his administration.

To summarize, it is doubtful if the Constitution would have been approved if Washington had not been such an integral part of the Convention process. Washington's attendance at Philadelphia, the fact that he presided over the Convention, the fact that he signed the finished document, and the probability that he would be the first President, were significant advantages for the Federalists who argued on behalf of the new charter of government.

Washington's contribution as America's first President has long puzzled historians. Few deny that Washington's legacy was rich and enduring, that the new U.S. government gained its legislative and executive precedents during his administration, and that he lent dignity and authority to the new Constitution. The debate revolves around the question of the extent to which Washington was the master of his own house.

Historians have wondered if Washington was the actual leader of his administration, whether he was a responsible executive making his own decisions, or if he was merely a figurehead, supplying the symbolic, ritualistic and mystical aspects of the office. Historians wonder if Washington was at his best as President. Many believe that the achievements of his administration were really the work of others, most notably Alexander Hamilton. Washington's friends kept quiet about his weaknesses, it is said, in order to exploit his prestige and to buy time until a pattern of rule settled around the new government. Washington was the only man in the nation who could have negated the fears that eighteenth-century Americans had over strong executive power. As the historian Forrest McDonald has remarked: "George Washington was indispensable, but only for what he was, not for what he did."[7]

This judgment of Washington is unfair. It is true that Washington was not a brilliant man. There were minds more facile and innovative than his. But it is a mistake to conclude that Hamilton and Jefferson were the guiding lights of his administration and that he concurred quickly with anything they proposed.

Though less intelligent perhaps than Hamilton and Jefferson, he was superior to both in his judgment, in his measuring of the abilities of other men, and in his dispensing of justice. Washington's was not the quick mind, but it was an energetic and disciplined one. Washington may not have been brilliant but he was steady and predictable. It was an achievement in itself to juggle the animosity that Hamilton and Jefferson had for each other in his very first administration.

Further, utilizing the historian Thomas A. Bailey's "absence-of-blunders" test, it is important to recognize that Washington made no important mistakes as President. This cannot be said of any other American President. Instead, Washington's eight years witnessed a list of achievements that another historian, J. A. Carroll, has numbered at not less than ten. According to Carroll, under Washington, the U.S. government:

1) gained its executive and legislative precedents
2) appended a bill of rights to the Constitution
3) established its credit at home and abroad
4) fostered manufacturing and encouraged commerce
5) survived a serious insurrection in the mountains of Pennsylvania
6) secured the transmontane frontier against Indian depredations
7) effected the removal of British troops from the Old Northwest

8) checked Spanish encroachments in the Old Southwest and obtained transit rights on the Mississippi
9) forged a policy for the disposition of public lands
10) and avoided involvement in the vortex of European wars.[2]

Such achievements only occurred because Washington was a diligent, systematic and gifted administrator. Washington was acutely cognizant of the importance of good administration in both setting precedents and in creating a smooth-working system of government. As he observed: "Many things which appear of little importance in themselves and at the beginning may have great and durable consequences from their having been established at the commencement of a new general government. It will be much easier to commence the administration, upon a well adjusted system, built on tenable grounds, than to correct errors or alter inconveniences after they shall have been confirmed by habit."

For the young Republic, then, Washington had become the "indispensable man." There was no better confirmation of this fact than the almost unanimous appeal by his Cabinet and the Congress that he consent to a second term as President. Washington himself had hoped to be able to retire after the first term. But such were the animosities of the emerging two-party system, and such were the challenges of foreign affairs that Washington was urged to postpone his retirement. Even Jefferson, the leader of the opposition party, was in the forefront of those who urged Washington to stay on. As Jefferson was to write to Washington: "The confidence of the whole union is centered in you. . . . North and South will hang together, if they have you to hang on."

In sum, Washington as President was more than a figurehead. He may not have been the originator of the most flamboyant aspects of his administration, but he had the ability to study hard the problems at hand, to trust strongly in his final decisions, and then to execute those decisions resolutely. As the political scientist Clinton Rossiter has so aptly summarized: "The most meaningful judgment one can make of his eight years is that he fulfilled the hopes of the friends of the Constitution and spiked the fears of its critics, and that in turning both these tricks with vigor and dignity he proved himself the best of all possible first Presidents."[9]

To conclude, a brief survey of Washington's part in the three key events of Revolutionary America can highlight his overall significance in American history. At each stage of his leadership, different qualities of his personal makeup were called to the fore. But the one constant that is found throughout is the superiority of Washington's character. Jefferson was right when he said that Washington's character was "in its mass, perfect, in nothing bad, in few points indifferent; and it may truly be said, that never did nature and fortune combine more perfectly to make a man great." This is not to say that Washington was infallible or that Washington was some kind of saint. But, politically, he was simply a symbol of the best that eighteenth-century America had to offer.

Yet, never has Washington's legacy been more neglected than at present. The reason for this is probably complex and elusive. But the historian Morton Borden has possibly come the closest to answering this ironic dilemma when he argued:

Washington is too rational for an age which has made a cult of the irrational; he is too much the heroic figure for an age which celebrates the anti-hero. The virtues and values for which he was once honored are under attack. Law and order, which Washington regarded as vital to the effective operation of democracy, is equated with repressive governmental controls. The moderation he preached and the practicality he endorsed are both rejected by young radicals and visionaries using the tactics of fear and violence. The patriotism he more than any other man symbolized is currently identified with nationalism and militarism. God is dead, some contemporaries declare, and so is the relevance of Washington.[2]

SELECTED BIBLIOGRAPHY

1. Billias, George Athan, ed. *George Washington's Generals.*   New York: William Morrow and Co. 1964.
2. Borden, Morton, ed. *George Washington.* Englewood Cliffs, N.J.: Prentice-Hall. 1969.
3. Cunliffe, Marcus. *George Washington, Man and Monument.*   Boston: Little, Brown and Co. 1958.
4. Flexner, James Thomas. *Washington: The Indispensable Man.*   Boston: Little, Brown and Co. 1974.
5. Freeman, Douglas Southall. *George Washington: A Biography* (completed by J. A. Carroll and M. W. Ashworth), 7 vols. New York: Kelley Inc. 1948–1957.
6. Jones, Robert F. *George Washington.* Boston: Twayne Publishers. 1979.
7. McDonald, Forrest. *The Presidency of George Washington.*   New York: W. W. Norton and Co. 1974.
8. Morgan, Edmund S. *The Genius of George Washington.* New York: W. W. Norton and Co. 1980.
9. Rossiter, Clinton. *The American Presidency.* New York: Time Inc. 1960.
10. Schwartz, Barry. *George Washington: The Making of an American Symbol.* New York: The Free Press. 1987.
11. Smith, James Morton, ed. *George Washington: A Profile.* New York: Hill and Wang. 1969.
12. Wills, Garry. *Cincinnatus: George Washington and the Enlightenment.* Garden City, N. Y.: Doubleday. 1984.

Did the Constitution Represent an Evolution of the Ideas of the Declaration of Independence?

One of the most rewarding endeavors for the historian is to choose a classic historical event and then to study that episode in extreme detail for relevant insights into human nature. Such an event is the meeting of the Philadelphia Convention of 1787. There the forces of controversy and creativity so coalesced that, in the words of British Prime Minister William Gladstone, "the most wonderful work ever struck off at a given time by the brain and purpose of man" emerged—the American Constitution.

If a work of genius is judged partly in terms of its durability, then indeed, the American Constitution fully deserves the praise that Gladstone accorded it. Today, it stands as the oldest written constitution in the world, having weathered seven major wars, one civil rebellion, six major depressions, and numerous lesser recessions. A document written for an agricultural nation of thirteen small states and four million people, huddled along the Atlantic Coast, has endured for two centuries and retains its relevance for an industrial, urban colossus stretching from the Atlantic to the Pacific and encompassing 250 million people.

But, alas, nothing is sacred to historians. A controversy rages over the meaning of the Constitution and the motives of the men who first composed it. The controversy can be separated into two general categories: those historians who believe that the Constitution was the work of patriotic statesmen who endeavored to preserve and protect the ideals of the Declaration of Independence; and those historians who believe that the Constitution was the brain-child of an elite group of wealthy, propertied men who aimed to carry out a conservative counter-revolution—a counter-revolution which eventually destroyed the egalitarian and democratic ideals of 1776.

The latter interpretation is almost invariably associated with the early-twentieth century work of Charles Beard, one of the greatest of America's historians.[1] According to Beard, America's Founders, upset with the highly democratic Articles of Confederation, set out to devise a charter of government that would better protect their economic holdings. He argued that the overwhelming majority of delegates to the Philadelphia Convention owned "personalty" in the form of public bonds and notes. Hence, a strong central government with key commerce, taxation, currency issuance, and banking powers would secure and enhance these securities.

Beard also argued that rigid property-holding requirements in the eighteenth century prohibited the masses from voicing their power and opinions. He stated that only one-fourth of the adult white men in the nation were involved in ratifying the Constitution, and that, in the end, no more than one-sixth of adult white men actually voted for the Constitution. Needless to say, women and blacks had no voice in this decision.

Beard's opinions, at first shocking when they appeared in 1913, came to dominate the historical literature dealing with the Constitution for the next thirty years. Such was the force of his argument that to this day almost all interpretations of the Constitution still take either a pro- or anti-Beard position.

As Beard's ideas were expanded upon by sympathetic followers, complementary premises were added to Beard's central argument. Soon it was argued that the Articles of Confederation was the true philosophical expression of the ideals and values of the Declaration of Independence. The post-Revolution problems of the young nation were no longer attributed to the weakness of the Articles themselves, but rather to the disorientation inherent in any post-revolutionary situation.

Pro-Beard historians also have emphasized the "conspiratorial" approach of the Founders: how they deviated from their initial orders to meet for "the sole and express purpose of revising" the Articles; how the meetings of the Convention were held in secret; and how a Bill of Rights was omitted from the original constitutional draft.

As for the ratification procedure itself, critics of the Constitution pointed out the irregularities of many of the state constitutional conventions, and how the convention at Philadelphia slyly bypassed the state legislatures in the first place by calling for "democratic" state conventions to rule on the validity of the new Constitution. Also emphasized was the vociferous disapproval of the Constitution by the majority of small farmers and artisans and the hard and bitter fight for its eventual acceptance.

In sum, Beard and those historians who have sympathized with his approach have argued that the Constitution was an undemocratic document with a series of special features. These included a system of checks and balances, an independent judiciary with the potential for judicial review, a strong executive with veto powers, indirect elections, etc. They were incorporated so that the mercantile, large landholding and public security-holding interests could be protected.

In marked constrast to the Beardian analysis are the views of historians who have argued that the Constitution was the work of noble and patriotic men, inspired by a continental vision. Rather than carrying through a conservative counter-revolution, these men wrote a charter of government that carefully balanced and preserved liberty and democracy. For these historians, Beard's conclusions do not offer a satisfactory explanation of the events surrounding the constitutional process.

For example, in *Charles Beard and the Constitution,* Robert E. Brown resolutely disputed Beard's conclusions point by point.[3] First of all, Brown criticized Beard's use of later Treasury Records as a valid indication of what securities the Philadelphia delegates owned back in 1787. Probably most of these investments were made after the Constitution went into effect. Further, Brown argued that the extensive availability of land allowed the majority of white adult males to be property owners, thereby enabling them to qualify for the vote in 1787.

Other historians strongly attacked the interpretation that the Philadelphia delegates acted conspiratorially. The fact that the Convention meetings were held in secret was simply to allow the delegates to freely voice their opinions without the effects of adverse publicity until the final document emerged for evaluation. In addition, the whole of the constitutional process involved a number of significant stages which required public approval and/or acquiescence. To be specific, state legislatures had to agree to send representatives to the Philadelphia Convention, to provide maintenance for those delegates, to set up an ad hoc convention to evaluate the proposal of a new Constitution, and to abide by that ad hoc convention's decision. At any point along the way, opportunities were available to protest and obstruct these developments.

Another historian, Cecelia Kenyon, has warned that it is a mistake to argue that the pro-Constitution forces, the "Federalists," decided upon a system of separation of powers and checks so as to protect their property rights.[9] In fact, the "Anti-Federalists," or opponents of the Constitution, wanted an even more extensive system of separation of powers and even more numerous and effective checks and balances. Kenyon also believes that it is a mistake to imply that the Anti-Federalists were more devoted to direct democracy and majority rule than the Federalists. In actuality, the Anti-Federalists exhibited *just* as little faith in democracy and human nature as *did* the Federalists. The real difference between the two factions, argued Kenyon, is that the Anti-Federalists believed that a republican government could exist successfully only in a relatively small territory and with a small and relatively homogeneous population. They did not share the Federalists' optimism that a republican form of government just might succeed even better in a large country. The Federalist argument here was that a minority faction would be less able to attain tyrannical power over a large country, with its widely dispersed and diverse interests.

Along this same line, Stanley Elkins and Eric McKitrick, in a particularly stimulating article, compared the ages of the main Federalist and Anti-Federalist leaders.[3] This comparison showed that, on the average, the Federalists were ten to twelve years younger than the Anti-Federalists. In Elkins's and McKitrick's opinion, it was this age difference which best emphasized their thesis that the Federalists were characterized by youth, energy and a national vision, whereas the Anti-Federalists were characterized by narrow, particularist, and localist sentiments.

There is no doubt that the debate over the motivations of the Founders and the nature of the Constitution will continue to rage. Whatever the opinions of the future, one thing is assured: the significance of the Constitution will always be recognized for it marks a distinct turning point in the course of American history.

There are some additional points that I especially want to emphasize, however. First of all, the beliefs, opinions and context of the eighteenth century must always be kept in mind. Given the accepted political theory and the accepted lessons of history of that time, it was assumed that the natural inclination of humans was to be selfish and contentious. The great fear was that liberty would be menaced by too much democracy, just as drastically as by too little. On the one hand, John Adams remarked: "Democracy never lasts long. It soon wastes, exhausts, and murders itself. There never was a democracy yet that did not commit suicide." On the other hand, the Founders also believed that liberty would be jeopardized from the extreme Right. They had not fought a king in a war for independence for nothing.

Their solution to the dilemma of good government was republicanism with its checks and balances, with its representative rule, and with democracy and aristocracy properly balancing each other. But, because of their prevalent distrust of human nature, their solution also encompassed an economic aspect. They endeavored to place control in the hands of those with a stake in society, men who owned property. Only those men were considered to be reliable and stable citizens. After all, this was an age when land was available to almost all white men with talent, drive and ambition.

Finally, as regards the argument that the Constitution was a departure from the ideals of the Declaration of Independence, one must recognize that a shift of emphasis had occurred between 1776 and 1787. In 1776 the situation required revolution; in 1787 it required reconstruction. The approach which was effective for one could not be effective for the other. The Constitution was a document which aimed to express the "sober second thought," the attitude of careful reflection.

In conclusion, it is always rewarding to study a classic historical event for its insights into human nature. In this instance, such was the realism of our Founders that Horace White, the nineteenth-century editor of the Chicago *Daily Tribune,* observed that the Constitution "is based upon the philosophy of Hobbes and the religion of Calvin. It assumes that the natural state of mankind is a state of war, and that the carnal mind is at enmity with God."[6]

SELECTED BIBLIOGRAPHY

1. Beard, Charles A. *An Economic Interpretation of the Constitution.* New York: Macmillan Company. 1935.
2. Bowen, Catherine Drinker. *Miracle at Philadelphia: The Story of the Constitutional Convention, May to September 1787.* Boston: Little, Brown and Co. 1966.
3. Brown, Robert E. *Charles Beard and the Constitution: A Critical Analysis of "An Economic Interpretation of the Constitution."* Princeton, N.J.: Princeton University Press. 1956.
4. Elkins, Stanley and Eric McKitrick. "The Founding Fathers: Young Men of the Revolution," *The Political Science Quarterly,* LXXVI, 2 (June, 1961).
5. Farrand, Max. *The Framing of the Constitution of the United States.* New Haven, Conn.: Yale University Press. 1913.
6. Hofstadter, Richard. *The American Political Tradition.* New York: Alfred A. Knopf, Inc. 1948.
7. Jensen, Merrill. *The Articles of Confederation.* Madison, Wisconsin: University of Wisconsin Press. 1940.
8. Kammen, Michael. *A Machine That Would Go of Itself.* New York: Alfred A. Knopf. 1987.
9. Kenyon, Cecelia M., ed. *The Antifederalists.* Indianapolis, Ind.: Bobbs-Merrill. 1966.
10. McDonald, Forrest. *Novus Ordo Seclorum: The Intellectual Origins of the Constitution.* Lawrence: University Press of Kansas. 1985
11. _____. *We The People: The Economic Origins of the Constitution.* Chicago: University of Chicago Press. 1958.
12. Main, Jackson T. *The Antifederalists.* Chapel Hill, N.C.: University of North Carolina Press. 1961.
13. Storing, Herbert J. *What the Anti-Federalists Were For.* Chicago and London: University of Chicago Press. 1981.
14. Wood, Gordon S. *The Confederation and the Constitution: The Critical Issues.* Washington, D.C.: University Press of America. 1979.
15. _____. *The Creation of the American Republic, 1776–1787.* Chapel Hill, N.C.: University of North Carolina Press. 1969.

Alexander Hamilton's Financial Wizardry: Momentous and Misunderstood?

Of all our Founders, Alexander Hamilton is the one who has been the least admired by succeeding generations of Americans. In many ways this is difficult to explain, for a rough sketch of his life reveals unparalleled accomplishment and dramatic intensity. The facts are these: he was an illegitimate child born in the British West Indies in 1755: he was orphaned at thirteen and became an aide-de-camp to General George Washington during the American Revolution at twenty-two; he was an ardent and persuasive advocate for the Constitution and finally was appointed Secretary of the Treasury by the age of thirty-four. All in all, Hamilton's legacy to the young American Republic was second in durability only to Washington's. It has taken until now for his accomplishments to be fully appreciated, yet among scholars dissenting voices still remain.

More specifically, it should be said that Hamilton's reputation in American history has gone through cycles. In his own time, he was an imposing and forceful figure, who, nonetheless, antagonized a goodly portion of his fellow politicians, and who was a major factor in prompting them to form an opposition party, the Democratic-Republicans. With the demise of his own party, the Federalists, and with the rise of populistic democracy during the Age of Jackson, Hamilton's reputation reached a low ebb.

At the end of the Civil War, Hamilton's star glittered again in the eyes of his countrymen, for those were dynamic times for American business and entrepreneurship. Yet, Hamilton's views were not unequivocally embraced. The rawness of the post-War industrial environment would not have been fully to his taste. As he once cryptically remarked: "I hate money-making men."

The early twentieth century was characterized by the rise of the Progressive Movement—an inspired, if somewhat naive, attack on the excesses of American capitalism. In such a climate the ideas of Hamilton were not particularly relevant. Perhaps the summation of the Progressive President Woodrow Wilson epitomized the feeling about Hamilton in that period: "A very great man, but not a great American."

Between the World Wars Hamilton was evaluated inconsistently. Hoover Republicans were generally favorable, but Roosevelt New Dealers saw in Hamilton's opponent, Thomas Jefferson, the perfect symbol for what they were attempting to achieve. Only since World War II has Hamilton's legacy come to be fully recognized. With our big, superintending national government, and with our strivings for a "realistic foreign policy," the times have been favorable for a deeper understanding of the Hamiltonian philosophy. Before elaborating on that philosophy, however, it might be instructive to study those criticisms of Hamilton which have so persistently impugned his character and reputation.

First of all, Hamilton's combative personality, his turbulent and explosive character, and his high-handed manner went far to rouse the fears and suspicions of his contemporaries and the rancor of subsequent historians. Whether arguing for the creation of a new constitution, or for the passage of his financial programs, his manner often detracted from his arguments. There always seemed to be a combination of respect and mistrust in those he addressed in those dramatic situations. He often raised doubts about his ultimate intentions. Many feared that Hamilton was aiming for the re-establishment of a monarchy in America, with George Washington as the king, and with himself as Prime Minister.

Second, his activist temperament mingled with a longing for military glory—a longing which stayed with him throughout his life. Among his post-Revolution cohorts this proclivity was bound to arouse suspicion. Hamilton displayed this tendency for military solutions in three crucial instances: the Newburgh Conspiracy of 1783, the Whiskey Rebellion of 1794, and the war-scare with France in 1798–1800.

Third, Hamilton's pessimistic views on democracy and on human nature seemed excessive even for his own time, and these ideas particularly have grated on American scholars through the years. Consider Hamilton's argument at the Constitutional Convention, an admonition which has been frequently quoted and criticized by historians:

> All communities divide themselves into the few and the many. The first are the rich and well born, the other the mass of the people. The voice of the people has been said to be the voice of God; and, however generally this maxim has been quoted and believed, it is not true to fact. The people are turbulent and changing; they seldom judge or determine right. Give, therefore, to the first class a distinct, permanent share in the government. They will check the unsteadiness of the second; and as they cannot receive any advantage by a change, they therefore will ever maintain good government. . . . Nothing but a permanent body can check the imprudence of democracy. Their turbulent and uncontrollable disposition requires checks.

Many questioned then, as they do now, Hamilton's preference for the rich, and the powerful. Hamilton's program was geared to the upper classes, and especially to the commercial and manufacturing men of those classes. This was disastrous in the long run for Hamilton, as ninety percent of Americans at that time were involved in farming. Hamilton never seemed to understand the common man—not his concerns, nor his fears, nor his hopes.

Further, there are two notorious instances when Hamilton leaked confidential information to a foreign power. The first was at the beginning of Washington's Presidency when Gouverneur Morris was dispatched to Great Britain to secure a favorable trade treaty. Hamilton's clandestine maneuvering deprived Morris of the one trump he had to play in his negotiations with the British—the threat of adopting high tariffs on British goods. Later, he behaved similarly when Washington dispatched John Jay to England to settle various controversial issues. Again, Hamilton's secret leaks deprived Jay of a major negotiating weapon—the possibility that the United States might join the Armed Neutrality against Great Britain.

Finally, there have been criticisms of Hamilton's hallowed economic policies. Here some historians argue that Hamilton was not a conservative in the proper sense of the word—devoted to love of country, religious faith, a common welfare, human dignity, the rule of law—but rather that he was an old-fashioned Tory of seventeenth century vintage. These historians argue that Hamilton was not farsighted in laying the foundation of a modern America, but rather that he harked back to restrictive and stagnant mercantilism.

Today these criticisms have been considerably softened as Hamilton's motives and thoughts have become clearer through years of careful study, and after the perspective of time has clarified his achievements. A brief narrative of his accomplishments and motivations will highlight the positive aspects of Hamilton's legacy.

Hamilton's whole life had been witness to the dangers to a nation and government which was not founded on durable, honorable, and stable financial practices. He had grown up on the Caribbean islands of Nevis and St. Croix; and he witnessed the unstable sugar economies of that region, and how a nation's debt ate away at both public and private initiative. He saw the wealth of those islands drained off because they lacked a diversified economy. During the American Revolution, as Washington's aide, Hamilton further saw how state and local jealousies, how the weaknesses of the Continental Congress, and how generals and soldiers more loyal to their states than to the national government, imperiled the American cause. During the period of the Articles of Confederation, he witnessed again the ill effects of a weak central government, without an effective judiciary or executive branch. He saw a government of fiscal incapacity and irresponsibility and how it failed to cope with the central economic challenges of the time.

Foreign-born, with no over-riding loyalty to any state, Hamilton was particularly atuned to the dangers of local and parochial rivalries and more apt to be a continentalist and ardent nationalist. He was bound to be especially concerned with the financial and economic foundations of any government.

Hamilton, therefore, was a major force in the chain of events leading to the Constitutional Convention. He was a key figure at the Annapolis Convention in 1786 and was one of the leaders in the call for a new convention to meet at Philadelphia in 1787. At Philadelphia, Hamilton was a prime mover in advocating abandonment of the Articles of Confederation in favor of a stronger charter of government and other drastic actions. At the Constitutional Convention, in fact, Hamilton gave a speech which, though considered reactionary by many of the delegates, did much to persuade them to deal more substantially with the issue at hand. After the Constitution was written, Hamilton made sure that his name was included among the original signers, and later he was one of the most important men in securing its ratification. He was the principal author of *The Federalist,* a compelling work extolling the virtues of the new Constitution and often acclaimed as America's outstanding work in politics. He was also the principal delegate who persuaded the New York delegation to ratify the Constitution.

When President Washington moved to set up his first administration, there was a consensus that Alexander Hamilton was the man best qualified to serve as Secretary of the Treasury, and best qualified to meet the problems and challenges which financially beset the new Republic. His series of enactments in this position were awesome. In all, Congress accepted six key proposals that were recommended by Hamilton: 1) that the public debt of the Revolutionary period be funded at par; 2) that the federal government assume the obligation to pay the Revolutionary debts of the states at par; 3) that Congress charter a national bank; 4) that a protective tariff be levied to stimulate industry and protect it against the dumping of foreign goods; 5) that the public lands be treated as a revenue source and sold at a good price; and 6) that an excise tax be enacted on distilled whiskey.

To gain a perspective on these proposals, one must consider the motivations of Hamilton. He was aiming to make American government viable. His proposals were practical; he understood and feared the consequences of any nation failing to get its financial and political house in order. He did not believe that the young Republic would survive without financial honor, and without establishing an aura of financial confidence.

For this reason, he also paid particular attention to gaining the support of men of wealth and position, and to intertwining their loyalty and economic interest with that of the new government. It is not necessary to suppose that an invidious preference for the wealthy was the motivating force here. Rather Hamilton believed that advancing the private enterprise of those who could increase national production would improve the welfare of all.

Further, Hamilton's policies were aimed at strengthening the central government and diminishing the long-entrenched attachment to the states. Consequently, he argued for a broad and liberal interpretation of the powers of the Constitution.

The only part of his program which did not pass Congress was his *Report on Manufactures*. In this *Report* Hamilton called for special legislation to protect and promote domestic manufacturing. He believed that America was two centuries behind Europe in its economic development. Because America lagged behind, the federal government must adopt means to protect infant industries from foreign competition. Hamilton was not a wholesale protectionist, however. Later on, as the American nation matured, Hamilton argued that protective measures could be removed and international competition encouraged. Until then, however, Hamilton believed that the American government should stimulate the development of a diversified economy. Without diversity, Hamilton feared, the American economy would not grow and flourish.

In addition, Hamilton loathed the idleness which he believed characterized too many Americans. Because of the richness of the soil, American farmers could with ease make a living, so that many were prone to laziness. By encouraging the development of a diversified economy, Hamilton argued that he would be creating an economic atmosphere which would inject energy and vibrancy into the American lifestyle.

In foreign policy, Hamilton deserves some recognition and praise. Though Hamilton did act underhandedly during the Morris and Jay incidents, he nonetheless grasped a fact of foreign policy that more heady patriots did not. Hamilton realized that good relations with Great Britain were imperative. The financial success of the new government depended upon it. When war broke out between England and France in 1793, Hamilton argued for strict neutrality, much to the chagrin of the pro-France populace in the U.S. The good sense of Hamilton's arguments was not lost on Washington, however, as he relied on Hamilton's ideas extensively in drafting his famous Farewell Address.

In conclusion, Hamilton remains one of the most controversial of America's Founders. Perhaps it was the humiliating circumstances of his birth and the early poverty of his childhood years that made him the most ambitious, romantic and turbulent of our early leaders. Perhaps it was his foreign birth that made him such a driving American nationalist, suspect of states' rights. The significance of these influences is admittedly conjectural. But it is clear that Hamilton addressed the key needs of the young nation. It was a time of crisis, and Hamilton offered the practical remedies which he believed would save the nation. Most historians agree that it was fortunate that Hamilton early got his way in these financial matters.

Historians will continue to debate, however, if Hamilton went too far in placing the "national interest" above the private interests of a basically agrarian people. After all, the national interest is an elusive concept to grasp, and one whose substance is difficult to determine. Further, as Professor Cecelia M. Kenyon has argued:

> The ethical priority of the individual and his welfare is the proper and ultimate end of government. To this end, the national interest is logically and ethically secondary; to this end, the national interest must stand in the relationship of means.

> Did Hamilton mistake the means for the end and tip the scale too far in the direction of the national interest? Did he give the national interest ethical priority over the demands of the individual?[4]

Hamilton might have quoted the words of his favorite poet, Alexander Pope, in rejoinder:

> For Form of Government let fools contest; Whate'er is best administered is best.

SELECTED BIBLIOGRAPHY

1. Cooke, Jacob E. *Alexander Hamilton: A Biography.* New York: Charles Scribner's Sons. 1982.
2. _____, ed. *Alexander Hamilton: A Profile.* New York: Hill and Wang. 1968.
3. Hacker, Louis M. *Alexander Hamilton in the American Tradition.* New York: McGraw-Hill Inc. 1964.
4. Kenyon, Cecelia M. "Alexander Hamilton: Rousseau of the Right," *Political Science Quarterly* (June 1958), Vol. LXXIII, No. 2, 161–178.
5. McDonald, Forrest. *Alexander Hamilton.* New York: W. W. Norton Co. 1979.
6. Miller, John C. *Alexander Hamilton: Portrait in Paradox.* New York: Harper and Bros. 1959.
7. Mitchell, Broadus. *Alexander Hamilton: A Concise Biography.* New York: Oxford University Press. 1976.
8. Padover, Saul K. *The Mind of Alexander Hamilton.* New York: Harper and Row, Inc. 1958.
9. Pancake, John S. *Jefferson and Hamilton.* Woodbury, N.Y.: Barron. 1974.

Was the War of 1812 Insignificant?

It is generally agreed that Americans are still somewhat disoriented, confused and distraught about the bitter legacies and deep divisions bequeathed by the Vietnam War. For the first time in our history, we seem to have lost that sense of purpose and mission which has so often characterized our nation in the past. In our preoccupation with the present and with ourselves, however, we forget that the Vietnam War was not the first war in which Americans were indecisive on the battlefield, nor the first war when public opinion was deeply divided. That "honor" belongs to the War of 1812, fought against Great Britain.

Indeed, it is hard to find an American war that ranks with the War of 1812 in terms of negative aspects. The War of 1812 was badly planned, badly financed, and badly fought. During the War, internal divisions were so extensive that many U.S. citizens blatantly traded with the enemy, and important political leaders from New England gathered at Hartford, Connecticut, in December 1814 to discuss the possibility of secession.

Perhaps the greatest insult to the significance of this War, however, was that more than 100 years had passed before historians began to critically analyze its causes and consequences. Instead, historians blandly accepted the indictments against the British incorporated in President James Madison's war message as sufficient explanation for the War. To review, Madison was caught in the middle of a European war that had raged almost continuously from 1803–1812, with the principal belligerents France and Great Britain. Both nations, intensely committed to victory, ignored the neutral rights of the young American nation. However, since Great Britain was the unrivalled naval power, it was the British who most severely threatened the sovereignty and prestige of the U.S.

Madison's first grievance against the British involved "impressment." This was the policy whereby Great Britain recovered any of its sailors who had abandoned the Royal Navy in favor of the better-paying American merchant marine. When they stopped ships, the British never claimed the right to impress verified American citizens, only British subjects. However, it was difficult for a sea captain in those days to tell a British citizen from an American one, and since sailors were so badly needed, British captains generally played it safe by allowing themselves the benefit of any doubt. What galled Americans was the fact that a British captain could, on the spur of the moment, determine the national identity of any man, and flagrantly overlook a nation's sovereign rights. In fact, the official record states that 6257 American men were unfairly impressed into service in the British navy.

Madison further complained about the British practice of cruising near American coasts and harrassing American commerce. There was also the problem with extensive British blockading practices, whereby neutral shipping was stopped just about anywhere on the high seas. In addition, Madison mentioned the Indian wars, then gaining momentum along the American Northwestern frontier, inferring that British instigation and British weaponry were responsible for this increased hostility. Finally, Madison was angered by the "Orders in Council," the Parliamentary laws which supposedly validated British commercial policies. Overall, these Orders in Council prohibited neutral trade with all enemy ports on the European continent, and subjected the goods of any nation that ignored the British blockage to seizure and confiscation. The losses of American merchants due to confiscation often ranged up to $60,000 per ship. In the key six months before the War broke out, approximately 100 U.S. ships were confiscated. Total confiscations between 1807 and 1812 numbered about 389. For all of these reasons, and the fact that British infractions had been blatantly carried on for at least nine years, Madison decided to petition Congress for a declaration of war. Congress, after a heated debate, agreed with Madison and war was officially declared on June 18, 1812.

It was only after World War I, when the disillusionment with the results of that War was at its height, that historians also became more critical of Madison's reasons for war. Certain key events and issues did not seem to square with the traditional explanation of the causes of the War of 1812. For example, the War of 1812 had been declared by a Jeffersonian-Republican Administration. However, while Jeffersonian-Republicans were historically representative of the interests of small farmers, they were notably less responsive to the grievances of the manufacturing and mercantile interests of the American Northeast. Further, the Northeast, supposedly the section most adversely affected by British maritime practices, staunchly opposed the War and went so far as to plan the infamous Hartford Convention. Finally, news of the repeal of the Orders in Council reached America just as war was being declared. Yet Madison did not stop the War. If the Orders in Council were of such importance as a cause, why were not immediate peace negotiations begun?

Historians noted these contradictions and began their search for causes elsewhere. In their studies they noted that the most vociferous agitation for war came from Congressmen representing the South and the West. As they probed deeper, many historians came to the conclusion that expansionistic desires and economic concerns were the real causes for Southern and Western belligerence. Expansionist designs were particularly aimed at Canada and Florida. Canada was controlled by Great Britain at that time and Florida was part of the Spanish Empire. Hence, a war against Great Britain and its ally, Spain, offered the opportunity for acquiring Canada and Florida, two rich prizes. The West, it was discovered, was also suffering from the effects of an economic depression. Westerners blamed the British blockade, and British interference with the fur trade, for the West's economic problems. Again, war seemed an answer to this predicament.

In sum, "revisionist" historians in the 1920s and 1930s rejected the traditional explanation that Madison's declaration of war was based on concern for maritime rights and national prestige. Instead, these revisionists argued that the South and the West allied with each other and supported war as a means to gain the rich lands of Canada and Florida, to end the economic depression which plagued the West, and to get at the source of their problems with the Indians.

In the 1950s and 1960s the pendulum swung back and historians were once again arguing that maritime issues were the key ones leading to war. A closer study of voting patterns, economic trends, prices of farm products, the status of the western fur trade, and the status of Indian relations with American frontiersmen and farmers convinced the vast majority of 1950s

46

and 1960s historians to reject the hypothesis that sectional interests were the primary factor in the decision for war. A detailed study was made of exactly who did, and who did not vote for war in the Congress of 1812. Though the most flamboyant and adamant "War Hawks" came from the South and the West, it was argued that the vote divided more exactly along party lines rather than sectional ones.

Regarding the repeal of the Orders in Council, various documents and private papers seemed to reveal that Madison did indeed use that opportunity to open peace negotiations. However, the British would not negotiate on the issue of impressment, so Madison decided to continue with the War. Impressment, after all, was the most long-standing of the American grievances, and the first one mentioned in Madison's war message.

Revisionist historians were also accused of misreading the Congressional debate dealing with the acquisition of Canada and Florida. The revisionist argument that western desire for Canada and Florida was a key cause of the War was disputed. Rather Congressional agitation for these two areas, it was argued, was intended for tactical purposes. Military success in Canada, for instance, could be used at the bargaining table in exchange for British concessions on their maritime policies. As these historians emphasized, there were still plenty of western lands left to be occupied without the possession of Canada and Florida.

The issue of the Indian menace was also played down. Though the Indian problem was certainly of primary concern to Westerners, the areas most affected were Mississippi, Indiana, Illinois and Michigan, territories which still had no vote in Congress.

The most intriguing thesis put forward by a historian in the 1950s and 1960s was Roger H. Brown's in 1964.[1] Brown argued that Americans saw British aggression as a test and a challenge aimed at the heart of their young Republic. The issue to be decided, in American eyes, was whether a government based on the principles of republicanism and representative government could summon up enough "unity of purpose and firmness of will" to function effectively "in the jungle of international life."[1] Hence, Brown concluded that the insults of the British commercially, their interference with American trade and neutral rights, and their infringement of American sovereignty were of such importance to national prestige that, fearing for the viability of the republican experiment, war was declared.

The most recent historical studies have taken a startlingly new departure; they argue that the English position was right all along and that accommodation with England would, in fact, have been in the best interests of the United States. Instead, the argument continues, Republican foreign policy was so blinded by excessive hatred of England that it did not accurately assess the true requisites for U.S. security, nor did it accurately assess the true dangers that a Napoleonic victory would entail. Napoleon was the real threat to U.S. long-term security. A Napoleonic victory with its aspirations toward universal empire, could have placed the U.S. in grave jeopardy along both its Canadian and Spanish borders. Maintaining the balance of power in Europe was therefore vital to the U.S., and given Napoleon's objectives, that meant the maintenance of English domination of the seas. All that the U.S. could have wanted from its early nineteenth-century foreign policy—commercial prosperity, retirement of the national debt, territorial expansion, limited military spending, and national security—would have been better served by a rapprochement with England and a policy of aggressive opportunism vis-a-vis France and Spain.

The latest studies have even questioned the validity of the U.S. position on impressment and on neutral rights. Regarding impressment, the U.S., it is now argued, was wrong not to recognize that there were far more British sailors in the U.S. merchant marine than there were U.S. sailors in the Royal Navy. If the U.S. had done more to restrict the use of British deserters, perhaps the English would have been more flexible toward U.S. demands. In 1803 and 1804, England agreed to a partial repudiation of impressment, only to be rebuffed by the Jefferson Administration, which believed that time was on the American side, and that a better agreement could be had by a policy of delay. Again, in the Monroe-Pinkney Treaty of 1806, which Jefferson refused even to submit to the Senate, the British were amenable to easing impressment as a matter of practice, if the broader principle were overlooked. Is it any wonder, then, these modern historians argue, that the English came to believe that the U.S. must be secretly pro-French, and hence should be treated as an enemy?

There is strong criticism, too, regarding the U.S. position on neutral rights. Jefferson and Madison wanted acceptance of the principle that merchant ships flying the American flag were immune to forcible seizures if they were not carrying illegal cargoes. This principle, however, was not accepted by any Great Power at that time. Besides, from a practical point of view, restrictions under the British Orders in Council and the Rule of 1756 prohibited U.S. trade only with the European mainland. Americans could still trade with Great Britain and its possessions, and with French and Spanish possessions in America. In point of fact, three-fourths of U.S. trade would still be allowed. As the U.S. had only become the carrier of the European trade because the Napoleonic Wars had swept the French, Dutch and Spanish shipping from the seas, could not the English be expected to inhibit this ersatz trade with their mortal enemy?

The following quotations give the student of this controversy an idea of how significantly some present-day historians have shifted ground from the arguments of the past. Note the following comments on impressment:

> In truth, the solution to the manifold aggravations over impressment lay mainly in American hands. Had the United States made efforts to remove the large number of British sailors in the employ of American shippers, it is quite likely that the British would have reduced substantially, and perhaps even eliminated, the oppressive practice of which the United States complained. American municipal regulations, enforced by the national government, that imposed penalties on shippers who employed British subjects, alongside a system for providing papers of American citizenship with stringent precautions against forgery, which the existing system of "protections" clearly lacked, could have virtually eliminated the problem.[10]

And again on neutral rights:

> Britain's claim to restrict a neutral trade forbidden to the neutral in time of peace was based on the contention that only by doing so might it effectively bring the war to Napoleon. Britain's armies were small in number; its main contribution to the defeat of the Napoleonic empire, to say nothing of its security against conquest, necessarily rested on its supremacy at sea. The American claim, if recognized, would have severely weakened Britain's principal weapon and sharply compromised its rights as a belligerent. The interest for which the United States contended, by contrast, was of a lesser weight. The carrying trade, to be sure, was immensely profitable. . . . But the pursuit of this trade reflected no compelling necessity; the happiness and prosperity of the Union, though they assuredly depended on commerce in some measure, did not rest on America becoming the carriers for all the world, and it would be absurd to pretend otherwise.[10]

This is the current status of the historiographical debate surrounding the origins of the War of 1812. What is particularly noteworthy is that while the causes of the War of 1812 have been hotly debated, there has been an almost unanimous consensus on the positive effects of the War.

First, the War of 1812 marked the full realization of American independence. Even though Americans had won their political independence in 1783, their national destiny was still being decided by events in Europe. The great war between Britain and France was just one example among many. However, with the War of 1812, 200 years of colonialism officially came to an end. The focus of American government turned westward, not eastward across the Atlantic. The key problems and concerns in the next century would be internal, not external. Top priority was to be given to westward expansion and growth.

Second, American modernization and industrialization were thrust forward by the War. During the War, and in the years immediately preceding, Americans had learned to rely on their own manufacturers, for British and French products were unavailable. This development proved to be a tremendous economic stimulus to American manufacturing and domestic business growth. Madison's traditionally agrarian party was forced to adjust its thinking to the realities of a more modern and technologically progressive America.

Finally, the War reinvigorated America's sense of mission and vindicated the strength of republicanism as a viable form of government. At a crossroads in history, the American system of government summoned up the resolution and the sustained energy necessary to survive and advance.

Perhaps there are insights to be gained from all this as to how the Vietnam War will be treated by future American historians. We have seen in the instance of the War of 1812 how the causes of wars remain debatable through the years as the pendulum of opinion swings back and forth. What is much less debatable are the effects of wars. As with the War of 1812, the Vietnam War has speeded up technological, economic and social trends, and has forced a re-evaluation of institutions and forms of government. Would Americans today be better off forgetting the divisions and the antipathies of the immediate past for a realistic appraisal of the challenges of the future?

SELECTED BIBLIOGRAPHY

1. Brown, Roger H. *The Republic in Peril: 1812.* New York: Columbia University Press. 1964.
2. Caffrey, Kate. *The Twilight's Last Gleaming: America vs. Britain, 1812–1815.* New York: Stein and Day. 1977.
3. Coles, Harry L. *The War of 1812.* Chicago: University of Chicago Press. 1965.
4. Horsman, Reginald. *The Causes of the War of 1812.* Philadelphia: University of Pennsylvania Press. 1962.
5. McDonald, Forrest. *The Presidency of Thomas Jefferson.* Lawrence: University Press of Kansas. 1976. (Though McDonald's book emphasizes the Jefferson Presidency, there is much material relevant to later Republican foreign policy during the Madison Presidency.)
6. Perkins, Bradford. *Prologue to War.* Berkeley: University of California Press. 1961.
7. Pratt, J. W. *Expansionists of 1812.* New York: P. Smith Co. 1925.
8. Risjord, Norman K. "1812: Conservatives, War Hawks, and the Nation's Honor," *William and Mary Quarterly,* 3rd ser., XVIII (1961), 196–210.
9. Stagg, J. C. A. *Mr. Madison's War: Politics, Diplomacy, and Warfare in the Early Republic, 1783–1830.* Princeton, N. J.: Princeton University Press. 1983.
10. Tucker, Robert W. and David C. Hendrickson. *Empire of Liberty: The Statecraft of Thomas Jefferson.* New York and Oxford: Oxford University Press. 1990. (Again, though the Jefferson Presidency is emphasized, Republican foreign policy to the War of 1812 is significantly discussed.)

Come all ye sons of freedom
Come all ye brave who lead 'em
Come all who say God speed 'em
   And sing a song of joy!
To Jackson ever brave,
Who nobly did behave—
Unto Immortal Jackson,
The British turn'd their backs on,
He's ready still for action,
   O Jackson is the boy.

Jackson Is the Boy, popular song in 1815.

The Indomitable Andrew Jackson: Symbol of an Age?

The so-called Age of Jackson, roughly the years from 1815–1850, was one of the great eras of change and reform in American history. This period witnessed the beginnings of a number of humanitarian crusades. Among them were the abolitionist movement, the womens' rights movement, and the determined drive for educational, prison and hospital reform. In these years constitutional and political changes were equally significant. The right to vote was extended in most states to all white males over twenty-one years of age regardless of property holdings. The first really broad-based, two-party system emerged. And the nominating convention became a fixed tradition in the realm of presidential politics. Finally, the era was crowned by the acknowledged existence of a hero: the powerful figure of Andrew Jackson. Jackson was the most popular President since George Washington. He even challenged Washington's heralded military reputation by displaying vigorous military leadership during the War of 1812, culminating in his famous victory at the "Battle of New Orleans."

Amidst these scenes of progress and triumph, however, existed deep pockets of poverty and misery. This first great age of urbanization and expanding wealth simultaneously saw the appearance of major slums, the cruelest period of Indian dispossession, and the burgeoning power of Southern slaveholders. Because of these vivid contrasts the Age of Jackson ·has intrigued and attracted a legion of historians and provided many historical interpretations. The aim of this essay is to explain the traditional interpretation regarding this period of history and then to discuss current opinions.

The first task is by far the easiest for, in general, historians during the first fifty years of the twentieth century portrayed both the age and the man in very positive terms. For these scholars the election of Andrew Jackson to the Presidency in 1828 was an important historical turning point. First of all, it was argued that Jackson's victory marked the rise of the "common man" to new political, social and economic importance in American national life. Jackson brought the first "rags to riches" story to the Presidency; he was the first President not to come from the old Virginia or Massachusetts establishments. He was the first President who had not had experience as either Vice-President or as Secretary of State. In the highly laudatory biographies of the early 1900s, Jackson was depicted as the first President who truly represented the "people" against the special interests, the forces of democracy against the forces of aristocracy. The example most often used to support this contention was Jackson's veto of the recharter bill for the Second Bank of the United States.

Jackson was also characterized as a great nationalist. His aggressive foreign policy, his stand against the secessionist tendencies of South Carolina during the Nullification Crisis, and his role during the War of 1812 were cited as examples of Jackson's intense patriotism. Therefore, Jackson's years of political power were seen as a time of rising democracy and inspired nationalism. They were described as a period when financial monopolies were brought into line with the best interests of the nation, a time when the average person was accorded not only a new equality of opportunity but also a new equality of respect.

During the last two decades, however, many historians have been busy challenging this traditional interpretation. A number of historical schools of opinion have emerged, making the debate surrounding the Jackson years one of the most complicated in all of American historiography.

One school in opposition to the traditional interpretation has been called the "Entrepreneurial" school. These historians reject the argument that the basic struggle of the 1830s was between classes, between the poor and the aristocrats. What was really taking place, they insist, was a battle between two sets of capitalists, those with established wealth and power, and those "on the make." As for the poor, they were equally forgotten by both these privileged groups. In the Entrepreneurial interpretation, for instance, Jackson's famous fight against the Second Bank of the United States was not a battle between the forces of freedom and the forces of monopoly, as it was traditionally portrayed, but rather a power play between the financial interests of the old wealth situated in Philadelphia, and the newer financial wealth centered in New York.

Another group of historians in opposition to the traditional school is the "neo-Conservatives." It is their contention that Americans were not divided by ideological and class concerns as commonly espoused, but rather united by a consensus founded upon republican beliefs and liberal attitudes. Neo-Conservative historians in their research find a middle-class rather than a lower-class orientation to the Jacksonian movement. In the view of this historical school, the conflict of the era centered around personalities and political issues and not around economic disparities.

Some historians have gone even farther and have questioned whether "Jacksonian Democracy," as a label, properly fits the decade of the 1830s at all. These historians believe that the era was too heterogeneous to warrant a simple characterization, and that the fabled equality of opportunity, traditionally emphasized, was not a prominent feature of that decade. Thus, a number of historians today doubt whether "Jacksonian Democracy" ever existed.

What historical trends can be derived from this complicated situation? Despite the extensive research, there are few satisfying answers when it comes to Jacksonian America. Like other historians, I favor certain hypotheses, but almost any modern approach to the period involved reveals a paradox.

On the one hand, I have found that Jackson's popularity among most historians is ebbing. On the other hand, Jackson is becoming more and more firmly entrenched as a symbol for his age. How is this so? Simply because the same qualities which are anathema to many present-day historians were qualities highly revered by Jackson's own generation. Let me explain.

Jackson's intense hatred of Indians, his high-handed actions against foreign powers, and his military bearing were esteemed and cheered by his fellow Americans. Jackson embodied, in extreme form, the cultural attitudes of his time. Both the hopes and the fears of his generation found their expression through him. In other words, the social tensions which were widely shared by all Americans in the 1830s appeared in Jackson's personality. Hence, the aggressiveness of his responses and personality complemented the deeper psychological needs of the nation.

Americans in those years were passing through a time of significant turmoil and rapid change. They were the first generation of Americans to face the tribulations of urbanization and modernization. As a result, they were faced with a tremendous challenge. Could they retain their spiritual bravura, their unique national character, which had presumably been fostered by a rural setting, if that setting was being transformed? Could America's cherished political and cultural traditions withstand the onslaught of progress?

Such a challenge raised extreme tensions amidst all the opportunities, hopes and expectations of the 1830s. Jackson, by far the strongest chief executive up to that time, easily became the mirror and the focus of the anxieties and aspirations of his generation. Jackson offered emotional stability to a nation of people who were dynamic and fired with ambition, on the one hand, and fearful of where they were going, on the other. He served as a symbol to reaffirm the young nation's self-confidence and to restore its sense of national destiny. That age, then, unquestionably revelled in their hero of the "Battle of New Orleans," their Indian fighter par excellence, their first "log cabin to the White House" President.

However, today, Jackson's violent, often unpredictable, temperament is not highly revered. Many historians are seeing the age and the man for the illusions that they were. These scholars are recognizing that an age which succumbed to violence and aggressiveness as an answer to confusion and dilemma was to learn a hard lesson—that violence, in the long run, is counterproductive and generates results which are least expected. Though the vigorous personality of a strong President seemed to bring together men and women of diverse interests, beneath the surface were the stresses and divisions which soon led to the Civil War.

Finally, on the question of whether or not Jacksonian Democracy was a myth or a reality, feelings are mixed. Each of the current assessments have an importance and a relevance. As emphasized, this period in American history witnessed the first major period of industrialization, urbanization and modernization. Hence, America reflected the same combination of opportunity mingled with anguish that England had gone through earlier in its transition from the age of feudalism to the age of capitalism. There were those Americans who were able to adjust to the transition from an agrarian to an urban life and were able to make more money and gain a greater amount of success, or a greater voice in the government, than ever before. Simultaneous with this rapid change, the middle class rose in power and in prominence. There were those, however, who were unable to adjust and found themselves languishing in a poverty unheard of in the days when rural life dominated.

So depending upon one's approach to history, this period offers a multitude of interpretations. The neo-Conservative will find a growing middle class and an American consensus emerging. The Entrepreneurial school of opinion will find new capitalists on the rise. Others may find immense distress among the poor and question if the American ideals of democracy and equality existed at all.

Perhaps the one certainty about the Age of Jackson is that, as time passes, and as the research techniques of historians become more refined, interpretations will continue to be quite diverse. And the conclusions regarding Jacksonian America will probably remain the least satisfying of any in American historiography.

Postscript: Given the centrality of Andrew Jackson to Chapters 10, 11, and 12, it is perhaps mandatory at this point to organize a brief character and personality sketch of the "Hero of the Battle of New Orleans."

The first feature which strikes this writer in Jackson's personal makeup was his indomitable determination and willpower. This resolve and tenacity were particularly seen in the War of 1812, when Jackson simply refused to lose. The tougher the circumstances, the tougher Jackson became. Jackson had the ability to thrive in the face of adversity, the power to gain strength in the face of misfortune. This steadfastness was harnessed to an unflagging energy, making Jackson more than a formidable opponent; it made him unstoppable.

This fortitude was also lashed to a deep, complex need to dominate. Jackson could brook no disagreement that remotely resembled a threat to his authority or position. This was true of Jackson throughout his life. We will see it in his determined handling of the Cherokees; his playmates saw it first hand in Jackson the little boy. His childhood play speaks volumes of this need to dominate; a bit of gibberish accompanied his merriment—"Set the case: you are Shauney Kerr's mare, and me Billy Buck; and I should mount you, and you should kick, fall, fling and break your neck; should I be to blame for that?" This need to dominate made Jackson the first to defy superiors or violate rules if he considered the circumstances to warrant it.

Another element of his personality was his temper—it was mean, vicious, and savage. Though Jackson was willing to allow personal animosities to end if his opponent gave ground, if his opponent would not cave in, Jackson nurtured his hatred, kept it alive, and was dogged in its application. Jackson always interpreted his difficulties to be the result of a personal animus against him. He thought in conspiratorial terms, on the lookout for human machinations behind any of his personal setbacks. This unsavory tendency made Jackson overbearing and irascible. Jackson, a fierce guardian of his name and reputation, possessed a need for revenge. His temper could flash in an instant, and decline just as quickly. But he was remorseless in his goal of getting even if he considered himself slighted.

Yet, Andrew Jackson was charismatic. He exuded authority, confidence, magnetism. Supremely cognizant of his abilities and talents, Jackson took on a father-like image to those who acquiesced to his will; a father who could be ceaseless in his devotion and care, farsighted in his wisdom, strict and stern in his discipline, and sure in his grasp of right and wrong.

Jackson was a man of limited education, but his mental capacity was formidable nonetheless. He possessed genuine intellectual abilities, and one can see his strength intellectually in his written statements and speeches. Though often ungrammatical, with numerous errors of spelling and syntax, Jackson's phrases convey powerful eloquence and an impassioned forcefulness.

Jackson was not thwarted by his limited education because he acted from instinct and intuition rather than from knowledge or information. For the most part, his instincts were tremendously attuned to his era so as to give him an unexampled power over his contemporaries.

Jackson's intellectual makeup also incorporated a profound honesty and an exemplary courageousness. Jackson was a man of scrupulous integrity. He was decisive, and forthright. He spoke without fear or hesitation.

In sum, Jackson was an awesome, puzzling figure. Awesome because Jackson's demonic nature bordered on the superhuman in its power. Puzzling because his personality was a bundle of contradictions and variances. James Parton, in a justly famous sketch, outlined the immense problems facing the biographer attempting to delineate the essential Jackson:

He was one of the greatest of generals, and wholly ignorant of the art of war. A writer brilliant, elegant, eloquent, without being able to compose a correct sentence, or spell words of four syllables. The first of statesmen, he never devised, he never framed a measure. He was the most candid of men, and was capable of the profoundest dissimulation. A most law-defying, law-obeying citizen. A stickler for discipline, he never hesitated to disobey his superior. A democratic autocrat. An urbane savage. An atrocious saint.[5]

Whatever the final characterization by contemporaries or historians, balance or moderation have not been aspects of the picture. Andrew Jackson's personality was forceful, dominating, fearsome.

SELECTED BIBLIOGRAPHY

1. Benson, Lee. *The Concept of Jacksonian Democracy.* Princeton, N. J.: Princeton University Press. 1961.
2. Davis, Burke. *Old Hickory.* New York: Dial Press. 1977.
3. Latner, Richard B. *The Presidency of Andrew Jackson: White House Politics, 1829–1837.* Athens: University of Georgia Press. 1979.
4. Meyers, Marvin. *The Jacksonian Persuasion.* Palo Alto: Stanford University Press. 1957.
5. Parton, James. *Life of Andrew Jackson.* 3 volumes. Boston: Houghton Mifflin Co. 1888.
6. Pessen, Edward. *Jacksonian America.* Homewood, Ill.: Dorsey Press. 1978.
7. Remini, Robert V. *Andrew Jackson.* 3 volumes. New York: Harper and Row. 1977–1984.
8. Schlesinger, Jr., Arthur M. *The Age of Jackson.* Boston: Little, Brown and Co. 1945.
9. Ward, John W. *Andrew Jackson: Symbol for an Age.* New York: Oxford University Press. 1955.

"We wish to remain on the land of our fathers. We have a perfect and original right to remain without interruption or molestation. The treaties with us, and laws of the United States made in pursuance of treaties, guaranty our residence and our privileges, and secure us against intruders. Our only request is, that these treaties may be fulfilled, and these laws executed." Memorial of the Cherokee Nation to Congress, August 21, 1830.

The Trail of Tears:
A Different View After 150 Years?

This summer marks the 153rd anniversary of "The Trail of Tears." On June 6, 1838, the notorious forced removal of the Cherokee Indians began. From their native lands in the American Southeast (western North Carolina, northern Georgia, northeastern Alabama and eastern Tennessee), they were transported 800 miles to a newly designated Indian Territory beyond the western boundary of Arkansas. Herded into stockades, boxed like animals into railroad cars and forced to walk the last leg, an estimated 4000 of 18,000 Cherokees died en route.

Apologists for Andrew Jackson, the president whose inflexible determination was most responsible for the removal decision, still exist. Scholars usually marshal the "context-of-the-times" argument in defense of Jackson. Such a perspective enjoins the student of American history to keep in mind the beliefs, opinions and possibilities of a nineteenth-century world. Rampant imperialism and assuredness of white superiority were relatively unquestioned tenets in Western society. Even a comparative approach spanning the seven continents (where indeed have native peoples received their due?) seems to narrow the realistic alternatives truly available for the leaders of that time.

Many scholars sympathize with the predicament Jackson outlined in a message to Congress dated December 3, 1833:

> Those tribes cannot exist surrounded by our settlements and in continued contact with our citizens. . . . They have neither the intelligence, the industry, the moral habits, nor the desire of improvement which are essential to any favorable change in their condition. Established in the midst of another and superior race and without appreciating the causes of their inferiority or seeking to control them, they must necessarily yield to the force of circumstances and ere long disappear.

The removal issue was interlaced with constitutional, political and legal complexities. Legally the Cherokees had federal treaties recognizing their lands—Treaty of Hopewell (1785), Treaty of Holston (1791), Treaty of 1819. But the state of Georgia, the most adamant for immediate Indian relocation, also had a federal treaty—the Compact of 1802—promising Cherokee lands in return for Georgia's relinquishment of claims in western territories (now Alabama and Mississippi).

Politically and constitutionally the national argument over states' rights versus centralism was heating up as South Carolina was explicitly challenging the high tariffs recently passed by

Congress, and was implicitly fearing what a strong central government might do in the future regarding slavery. Jackson was concerned that South Carolina remain isolated, and that Georgian discontent not strengthen the states' rights position.

Jackson had the fierce will of American frontiersmen to consider. Besides the perennial desire for more cotton lands, gold had been discovered in Cherokee territory. Whatever ideals and principles on behalf of the Indians might have existed, they would have been difficult to uphold in the face of the secular materialism of the white majority.

In fact, Jackson's arguments mirrored exactly those of this frontier majority. For Jackson, Indians in their tribal state were children—cruel, vicious children—who had to be dealt with firmly and sternly. Indians could not be reasoned with, they could not be depended upon to keep their promises, they could not discipline themselves to be truly reliable in their oaths. Indeed, their promises were merely deceptions—attempts to momentarily lull whites into complacency before sneak attacks were undertaken.

The source of the Indians' weakness of character in their natural state, according to Jackson, was that they possessed too much land. Their ownership of millions of acres allowed them to indulge in a lifestyle predetermined to promote uncivilized behavior. Their wanderings and their indulgences were bound to get them into trouble with the civilized, settled, and progressive whites. If the Indians were more restricted in their lands, however, they would be forced to re-evaluate and remedy their errant ways. They would come to see more readily the superiority of white cultural achievements. Seizure of Indian land, then, was in their best interest. Indeed, removal altogether was even better. It would allow the Indians more time to readjust, free from the pressures of white encroachment.

Jackson believed that he knew what was best for the "real" Indian. He felt he had a special rapport with them. The obstacle to the "real" Indians embracing wholeheartedly Jackson's sensible argument of removal was the "half-breed" Indian. In Jackson's mind, it was the "half-breed" who schemed and argued selfishly for himself without a thought as to what was best for the whole tribe. These beliefs of Jackson's were nearly universal among westerners. Jackson also believed himself to be completely free of racial prejudice toward Indians—after all, he befriended many Indians, he adopted an Indian orphan, and he sanctioned marriages between Indians and whites. Jackson convinced himself that he aimed to preserve the real Indians' heritage with the program of removal.

Jackson further believed that the treaty-making precedent with the Indians was wrongheaded and dangerous. He argued that the Indians had no sovereign rights which Congress was bound indefinitely to preserve. It was a danger to the security of the United States itself to allow an independent sovereignty within its borders. Not only would this principle be a centrifugal force in an already difficult federal experiment, but there was a military danger besides, the danger that some powerful foreign nation might utilize Indian sovereignty to promote secessionist tendencies within the U.S. Jackson's March 4, 1817, letter to President-elect James Monroe neatly summarized his attitudes:

> If they [the Indians] are viewed as an independent nation, possessing the right of sovereignty and domain, then negotiating with them and concluding treaties, would be right and proper. But this is not the fact, all Indians within the Territorial limits of the United States, are considered subject to its sovereignty, and have only a possessory right to the soil, for the purpose of hunting and not the right of domain, hence I conclude that Congress has full power, by law, to regulate all the concerns of the Indians.

In sum, removal would protect the Indians in the future; it would serve as a means of safeguarding tribal integrity from white laws. Jackson offered promises that the Indians would be sovereign in the West once and for all. Jackson emphasized these points in his message to the American people—his Farewell address of March 4, 1837:

> This unhappy race . . . are now placed in a situation where we may well hope that they will share in the blessings of civilization and be saved from the degradation and destruction to which they were rapidly hastening while they remained in the States; . . . the philanthropist will rejoice that the remnant of that ill-fated race has been at length placed beyond the reach of injury or oppression, and that the paternal care of the General Government will hereafter watch over them and protect them.

Was Jackson right? Did removal save the Cherokees? The Cherokees today have a tribal identity, a living language and three government bodies—The Cherokee Nation East, the Cherokee Nation West and the Original Cherokee Community of Oklahoma.

The reality, Jackson's critics contend, is that Cherokee survival was in spite of federal policies. Cherokee titles to Southwestern lands were never secured. Trade routes to the Southwest and the Pacific Ocean cut through the Cherokee territory, and by the 1840s the westward flow of white emigrants made a mockery of Indian sovereignty. Within a decade of the Trail of Tears, plans were afoot in Congress for yet another relocation.

Complicating the issue morally, and in direct contradiction to Jackson's December 3rd message, was the fact that in the 1820s the Cherokee Nation made the decision to "Americanize" much of their culture. To be specific, the Cherokee Nation had embarked on a decade-long renascence which effected a profound cultural transformation. In their conscious strategy of perfecting the necessary techniques for political autonomy and of developing the requisite economic base for self-sufficiency, the Cherokee people entered an era of cultural "take-off" that was to carry them to the threshold of the modern world.

A survey of the political changes introduced in this period will serve as a harbinger of the types of changes in other areas. Indeed, politically, the Cherokees effected not less than a governmental revolution. At least 115 laws were passed between 1817 and 1828, laws which culminated in the adoption of a written constitution on July 26, 1827, patterned after that of the U.S. With their constitution, the Cherokee Nation became a tripartite republic. The legislative branch consisted of a bicameral legislature—the National Committee served as the upper house, the National Council as the lower house—representative of eight newly-created districts. Judicially, the Nation was divided into a three-tier system, also based on the eight districts. District courts handled all criminal cases, excepting murder, and all civil cases involving less than $100. Circuit courts handled murder cases and all civil cases involving more than $100. At the top of the judicial system was the Superior Court (later renamed Supreme Court) which heard appeals from the lower courts. A judge, marshall, and local council were empowered to enforce the laws in each district. There was a circuit judge for every two districts. The Executive branch of the government was made up of the following six key officers: Principal Chief, Second Principal Chief, Speaker of the Council, President of the National Committee, Clerk of the National Council, and Clerk of the National Committee.

By 1828, then, the political transformation seemed complete. While the U.S. government was decreasing its assistance, the Cherokee Nation had evolved an honest and efficient government of civil liberties, jury trials, and written laws. Almost miraculously, the Cherokee Nation, within a mere generation, had gone from a decentralized, town-oriented government to a centralized, national system of rule. They established a permanent capital—New Echota—with three main public buildings and the gridwork planning for future development. They were handling treaty negotiations with confidence—consistently rebuffing the U.S. Government in its attempts between 1822 and 1828 to get more Cherokee land. They held a nation-wide election campaign in 1828 to fill the offices of the new constitution, a campaign wherein both mixed-bloods and full-bloods gained the fulfillment of significant participation. In sum, their political survival seemed well-assured.

The economic changes were equally dramatic, and at the heart of this economic transformation was a steady population growth. Between 1809 and 1825, for example, the Cherokee population increased by 7000 people, this despite the tremendous array of adversities that faced the Nation in this period—war, emigration, famine, sickness, and white pressure and animosity. Population growth itself was reflective of a dynamic, essentially coherent, cultural situation. Along with greater numbers of people, was a steady growth in other areas of economic development: the numbers of sheep and hogs had doubled between 1809 and 1825; the numbers of slaves [the Cherokees had regrettably adopted the farming policies of the surrounding whites] had almost doubled; farm production increased; and the number of Cherokees daily acquiring white skills was increasing. A traveler through the Cherokee Nation at this time would witness a criss-crossing network of toll roads, mills and blacksmith shops, inns and commercial ferries, and virtually no Cherokees living by hunting alone.

Complexity extended to other areas of Cherokee culture. After 1822, Cherokee pride was greatly enhanced when Sequoyah discovered a means of writing the Cherokee language. His eighty-six symbols of a Cherokee syllabary could be learned with relative ease by anyone who spoke Cherokee, and his method of writing soon became for the traditionalist community a code to air their opinions and to give outlet to their feelings. By 1825, the majority of Cherokees could read and write. The Cherokee Nation had indeed crossed a major dividing line in their progress toward modernization. The *Cherokee Phoenix*, their bilingual newspaper, began publication on February 21, 1828. A year later, the words *and Indian Advocate* were added to its masthead, reflective of both increased pride, and the growing Cherokee belief that they had become the rightful spokesman for all the Indian nations who were fighting against removal.

Simultaneously, the number of children attending missionary schools was growing. By 1826, there were eighteen mission schools in the Cherokee Nation. Christianity, (especially after 1830 when a native ministry was created by the Baptists and Methodists), became a means for more and more Cherokees to promote their self-esteem. Christianity offered on a personal level the self-worth that political and economic revitalization were offering on a national level. Christianity gave to individual Cherokees another option in their goal of personal fulfillment in a changing and difficult world. By 1830, Christianity had combined with Cherokee nationalism to provide a more vital means for Cherokees to control their inner lives and their future. Flush with the excitement of this educational and religious progress, the Cherokee people organized literary, temperance and benevolent societies. They established libraries. Plans were made for a museum and a national academy. In all these ways they hoped to win acceptance from the white majority. They were mistaken in their suppositions. Prejudice triumphed over Christian principles.

Even the favorable Supreme Court ruling, written by Chief Justice John Marshall, in the famous case of *Worcester v. Georgia* could not save the Cherokees. Marshall's opinion, delivered on March 3, 1832, was a forthright vindication of the Cherokee position. Marshall argued that Georgia's extension of state law over the Indians was unconstitutional: "the settled doctrine of the law of nations is, that a weaker power does not surrender its independence—its right to self-government, by associating with a stronger, and taking its protection. [The Cherokee Nation is] a distinct community, occupying its own territory, with boundaries accurately described, in which the laws of Georgia can have no force, and which the citizens of Georgia have no right to enter, but with the assent of the Cherokees themselves, or in conformity with treaties, and with the acts of Congress."

Unfortunately for the Cherokees, legal loopholes abounded and made the Court's decision meaningless. Technically the Federal Government could not enforce the Supreme Court's decision until the Georgia state judge refused *in writing* to comply with the Court's order. There was no provision in the existing legislation to remedy the problem if a state court declined to acknowledge *in writing* its refusal to obey the order—a course of action which the state of Georgia decided to take. Besides, the Supreme Court adjourned before there was an opportunity to report Georgia's intransigence. Therefore, Jackson did not have the legal authority to move against Georgia. Until the Supreme Court issued a writ of *habeas corpus* or summoned Georgia state officials before it for contempt, the President was legally powerless to act. The pugnacious statement attributed to Jackson by Horace Greeley—"Well, John Marshall has made his decision: *now let him enforce it!*"—is apocryphal. More exactly, Jackson observed: "the decision of the supreme court has fell still born, and they find that they cannot coerce Georgia to yield to its mandate."

Whatever one's position on Jackson's policies, this 153-year anniversary is worth remembering. Ethnic rivalries and confrontations constitute one of the greatest challenges facing our nation today. Looking dispassionately at the results of ethnic conflict in the past perhaps will insure a greater measure of wisdom in the future.

It is true that oppressed minorities have existed in every society, and that defeated peoples have suffered at the hands of invaders throughout recorded history. But this Cherokee example is a much rarer occurrence. It is the story of a whole people forced to abandon their native land; cut off from the roots of their cultural identity. Such a story, comparable to the Babylonian captivity of the Jews, will always attract social attention and scholarly concern.

This is especially so in a nation of our professed ideals—devotion to the inalienable rights of the individual. Furthermore, our whole nation was at fault. The American people of the time failed to respond to the spectacle of injustice; they failed to live up to the demands which democracy made upon its citizens.

Recalling the Trail of Tears is also an antidote to illusory thinking. Historical good fortune and material success have seemed to many Americans a providential sign of special innocence and virtue, a liberation from the sin which so characterizes other nations. The treatment accorded the Cherokee Indians reminds one of the universality of guilt in our morally ambiguous world.

What was said about the Spanish in Chapter Two of this book may equally apply here. By winning on the one side, Jacksonian Americans lost on the other. By not recognizing the true dignity of the Indian they diminished their own humanity.

SELECTED BIBLIOGRAPHY

1. Dippie, Brian W. *The Vanishing American.* Middletown, Conn.: Wesleyan University Press, 1982.
2. Drinnon, Richard. *Facing West.* Minneapolis: University of Minnesota Press. 1980.
3. Foreman, Grant. *Indian Removal.* Norman: University of Oklahoma Press. 1932.

4. Goodwin, Gary. *Cherokees in Transition.* Chicago: University of Chicago, Department of Geography. 1977.
5. Green, Michael D. *The Politics of Indian Removal.* Lincoln: Nebraska University Press. 1982.
6. Horsman, Reginald. *Expansionism and American Indian Policy.* East Lansing: Michigan State University Press. 1967.
7. McLoughlin, William G. *Cherokee Renascence in the New Republic.* Princeton: Princeton University Press. 1986.
8. Phillips, Ulrich B. "Georgia and States' Rights." *Annual Report of the American Historical Association.* 1901.
9. Prucha, Francis Paul. *The Great Father.* 2 vols. Lincoln: University of Nebraska Press. 1984.
10. Satz, Ronald N. *American Indian Policy in the Jacksonian Era.* Lincoln: University of Nebraska Press. 1975.

12

What Is the Challenge of Women's History? Jacksonian America as a Case Study*

There is a virtual revolution going on in the area of Women's History, a revolution which is transforming the historical profession, and which promises to carry forward into the social mores of American society. The effects are therapeutic, productive, and essential.

This challenge of Women's History is especially relevant to the "traditional" male historian. Most traditional male historians have had a tendency to measure the great turning points in the past by looking at the key wars, conquests, revolutions, religious transformations, or at changes in political administration. What these historians have failed to realize is what works nicely for the history of men does not necessarily work for the experience of women. In the past, women have generally been excluded from the decisive realm of political, military, and religious decision-making. Hence, any focus on those exclusive spheres necessarily jeopardizes a faithful rendition of women's role in history. In fact, great turning points in history which mark progress in the lives of men, might have an opposite, negative effect on the lives of women.

Jacksonian America, as we noted in Chapter 10, is an important instance when historical developments advanced the relative position of most white men in society. It added to their economic opportunities, their liberties, and their social standing. It was one of the great eras of male achievement and advancement.

But for women, the so-called Age of Jackson had an opposite effect. During this period the status of women deteriorated dramatically. Increasingly the boundaries of women's existence were focused on the home. They were given the responsibility for raising the children, but they were warned not to become involved with "unwomanly" and "unnatural" activities, such as an independent career in the business world. Domestic concerns were said to be the proper role for women. The ideal woman, sequestered in the home, was to be "pious and pure, fragile and weak, submissive and domestic, passive and unintellectual." This ideological development, labeled the "Cult of True Womanhood" by historians, and this domestic role, labeled the "Woman-Belle ideal," caused American women to be confined to a narrow, stifling lifestyle.

This sexist ideal had not been the rule in Colonial America. In seventeenth and eighteenth-century America, women made significant headway in establishing a place for themselves in the

*The constraints of space force me to focus almost exclusively on the experience of white women in this essay. However, the reader should take special note that there is no way to properly illuminate American women's history without also paying careful attention to the experience of all American women, regardless of color or class.

63

"We hold these truths to be self-evident: that all men and women are created equal; that they are endowed by their Creator with certain inalienable rights; that among these are life, liberty, and the pursuit of happiness. . . .—Whenever any form of Government becomes destructive of these ends, it is the right of those who suffer from it to refuse allegiance to it, and to insist upon the institution of a new government. . . . Such has been the patient sufferance of the women under this government, and such is now the necessity which constrains them to demand the equal station to which they are entitled." Seneca Falls Declaration of Sentiments and Resolutions, July 19 and 20, 1848.

workaday world. Indeed, survival depended on the contribution of each and every member of the colonial community. Labor was scarce, and human qualities such as initiative, fortitude, and technical skills were highly valued in any person, regardless of sex.

Moreover, Colonial America was a pre-industrial world. Unlike the nineteenth century, the work place was not separated from the home, and women labored alongside their husbands engaging in tasks both highly valued in the home and in the market place. There was a reciprocity in Colonial marriages that was later lost. Working together, men and women could better appreciate the contributions, limitations, and difficulties of the other.

Obviously, not all women in Colonial America worked. Nor did they attain full equality with men. But the unique conditions in the New World earned women more rights than were granted them by English law. And since so many made vital contributions to Colonial society, women who confined their activities to the home knew that their decision evolved from specific personal circumstances, not from supposed inherent inferiorities in the sex, or from an ideology which implied that females could only be effective within the home's secure boundaries.

However, an important retrogression in the status of women came as Americans approached the nineteenth century. Students of historical modernization have long noted that the period between approximately 1780 and 1830 was a time of significant transformation. It was in this period that America witnessed the beginning of rapid intensive economic growth, the start of sustained urbanization, and the marked change toward increased mechanization. The velocity of these changes has to be particularly emphasized. For example, in the area of American urbanization, while farmers in 1800 outnumbered city dwellers by a ratio of 15 to 1, by 1830 the ratio had declined to slightly less than 10.5 to 1. In 1850 it was only 5.5 to 1.

Such a transformation would cause any generation of Americans severe psychic anxieties. The unplanned expansion of cities, the lack of adequate public services, the pervasiveness of poverty and crime, the increasingly heterogeneous population, the growing lack of community cohesion, and the atomization of the family became hallmarks of that era. This generation of Americans felt especially anxious and insecure, and sought even more vigorously for stability and unifying beliefs, for they saw themselves as the inheritors and interpretors of a precious past. They were the first generation entrusted with the legacies of the Revolutionary era. In their hands was the task of preserving the traditional goals and ideals of agrarian America from the ravaging effects of material prosperity and physical expansion. The old ideals of an agrarian utopia seemed strangely irrelevant in the new times. Nonetheless, Revolutionary ideals were too embedded to be jettisoned completely. So the task became one of adjusting these agrarian ideals to the new realities.

A search was begun for a new philosophy which could ease the tensions and uneasiness of the times. A philosophy was sought that could ease any guilt that might be associated with this materialistic age so closely juxtaposed to a recent past that was thought to be idealistic and self-sacrificing. What better way to perpetuate the pastoral ideal, to maintain nostalgic visions of spartan village life, to ease the lacerated feelings of males grasping for fame in a new business world, than by focussing on the home and especially on women's role in that home!

The home became the haven where original ideals were to be nurtured. The responsibility for preserving the lessons of the past, for maintaining the democratic legacies of Revolutionary America was relegated to American women. Women came to serve as the ballast upon which men could base their unsteady voyage in an urbanized, mechanized world. Further, imputing women with innately inferior qualities strengthened male self-esteem. The levelling tendencies of Jacksonian America, the vicissitudes of a whirlwind economy created so much uncertainty that it is not improbable to reason that defining women as inferior beings helped to give unsure males a fixed standard to ease the doubts they had about themselves.

While men, then, during the Jacksonian era made key gains, the relative status of women plummeted. A composite of myths surrounded women that fettered their energy and activity, that denied them their worth as autonomous beings, that deprived them of a sense of personal identity, and that inhibited them from becoming a complete individual. Women came more and more to be depicted as "toys," "ornaments," and "embellishments" to enhance the position of men. A woman's life did not have any independent meaning or purpose without relation to a man. Increasingly women came to be defined only in reference to a man; either as daughter, sister, mother, or wife.

Two important points need to be added here. First of all, the image of a delicate female at home, happily and completely occupied with household and family, did not reflect the reality of the lives of a majority of women in Jacksonian America. It did not take into account the many thousands of urban and rural working women. It has been estimated that from two-thirds to three-fourths of the total number of factory workers in the first half of the nineteenth century were women. The failure to recognize these women naturally inhibited any organized attempts they made to ameliorate their condition. Nor did the myths of true womanhood accurately describe middle- and upper middle-class women, the one segment of society they were supposed to describe. Because of the housing shortage during these years, boardinghouse living and apartment living in hotels were the reality for a great many middle-class women. This fact alone deprived a substantial number of women of a home of their own and the opportunity of making a contribution in the sole sphere of activity that was open to them. In the boardinghouse or the hotel, domestic tasks were taken over by hired employees. The result was the "useless lady." These "useless ladies" might have found some compensation for their lonely despair if they were assured that their presence at home at least enriched the lives of their husbands. But the imperatives of livelihood and the availability of urban recreational activities combined to keep men away from home for long periods of time. Men's absence, as a result, only served to underscore the hollowness of women's existence.

A second point to note is that, so far, Jacksonian women have been depicted in this argument as passive agents, solely reacting to the domineering ideology of men, and not actively determining their own condition. This is somewhat of a wrong impression. The restrictiveness of the "Woman-Belle ideal" would soon drive women out of the home to work in benevolent societies aiming to help humankind, and then to the formation of organizations aimed to improve their own condition. The women's rights movement of the nineteenth century was soon to be launched.

Other women fought for autonomy within the family. For many women there was a clever strategy behind the cunning ambush of blushes and fainting spells. If man claimed the pleasure of fame, education, and riches, there was another way of striking back at that "tyrant" of the household: he could be mothered. Many women were able to capitalize on the fragile male ego, and to use the Victorian strictures about their sexuality to force men into an intriguing dual role of master and child.

To conclude, one clear intention of this essay is to relate that the traditional male historian of today is finally appreciating just how much patriarchal values have distorted the depiction of the past, and how much women have been portrayed merely as marginal contributors to human progress. Why should war and politics have more significance than, for example, child-rearing practices? Traditional male historians now realize that women have been treated as a great "monolith," placed in the home, caring for their husbands and their children, or they have been discussed in relation to philanthropic activities, but, throughout it all, no class, ethnic, social, or economic differences have been noted.

A second key emphasis of this essay is to show how the usual depiction of Jacksonian America just will not do as a valid interpretation of American history in the early nineteenth century. What is needed is a melding of the traditional story with the new insights of Women's History.

It is just such a blend of the two stories which evokes a modern parallel to the Woman-Belle ideal and the Cult of True Womanhood. One wonders if today's search for stability and surety during rapidly changing times has rekindled in the 1990s a reluctance to accept the liberated woman and her true place in American society.

SELECTED BIBLIOGRAPHY

1. Berg, Barbara J. *The Remembered Gate: Origins of American Feminism.* New York: Oxford University Press. 1978.
2. Chafe, William H. *Women and Equality: Changing Patterns in American Culture.* New York: Oxford University Press. 1977.
3. Cott, Nancy F. *The Bonds of Womanhood: "Woman's Sphere" in New England, 1780–1835.* New Haven: Yale University Press. 1977.
4. _____ and Elizabeth H. Pleck. *A Heritage of Her Own: Toward a New Social History of American Women.* New York: Simon and Schuster. 1979.
5. Degler, Carl N. *At Odds: Women and the Family in America from the Revolution to the Present.* New York: Oxford University Press. 1980.
6. Friedman, Jean E. and William G. Shade, editors. *Our American Sisters: Women in American Life and Thought.* Boston: Allyn and Bacon. 1976.
7. Lerner, Gerda. *The Majority Finds Its Past: Placing Women in History.* New York: Oxford University Press. 1979.
8. Melder, Keith E. *Beginnings of Sisterhood: The American Woman's Rights Movement, 1800–1850.* New York: Schocken Books. 1977.
9. Ryan, Mary P. *Womanhood in America.* New York: Franklin Watts. 1979.
10. Welter, Barbara. *Dimity Convictions: The American Woman in the Nineteenth Century.* Athens, Ohio: Ohio University Press. 1976.

13

John C. Frémont:
A Barometer of American Attitudes?

Historical reputations can be a barometer of public attitudes. In periods of nationalistic fervor, historical figures possessing animal vigor and qualities of daring are in ascendance. During periods of caution and restraint, a nation prefers its past heroes to have displayed subtlety in leadership. For example, in the jingoistic years 1894–96, twenty-eight books on Napoleon were published in the United States as compared to none in the conflict-weary year of 1879. (I would wager that interest in the forcible and ardent Henry VIII was on the rise during the Margaret Thatcher years in England; while that of the wily, procrastinating Elizabeth I was in decline.)

For Americans, John C. Frémont might well be a future barometer—a measure of how Americans feel about themselves and the world. Criticism of this swash-buckling explorer reached an apogee in the 1870s and 1880s when memories of the Civil War and frontier violence exhausted the public's patience with yet another aggressive, buccaneering historical figure. Currently, historians are about evenly divided in their judgments of Frémont's legacy. It may be instructive to see which way the scales tip in the decades ahead.

Frémont was definitely in tune with the spirit of his age. Expansionism was in the air and the nation felt its destiny lay in extending its boundaries to the Pacific. One can capture this feeling of "Manifest Destiny" by looking at a map of the United States in 1840. Mexico held vast territories in the southwest and west, and the British were joint occupants of a vast territory in the northwest. Given the American belief in the superiority of their institutions, and given the confidence generated by a historical experience of repeated successes, Americans were primed to lionize anyone who would be a part of conquering, opening, and taming those mysterious western territories. To Americans of the 1840s, that was exactly what Frémont achieved.

At a time when there were still no reliable maps of the Far West, Frémont led two expeditions which explored and mapped even more of that territory than the famous Lewis and Clark expedition. The first expedition along the Oregon Trail to South Pass in the Rockies covered over 2000 miles. The second expedition to Oregon, along the eastern side of the Cascades and the Sierra Nevada, then across the Sierra Nevada into California by way of Carson Pass, and then back home again, covered more than 5000 miles (my rough calculations).

All of Frémont's explorations were scientifically organized and meticulously recorded. Traveling these distances under the most difficult of conditions, Frémont was fastidious in his temperature recordings, soil and water testings, astronomical calculations, and even in his collection of plant specimens. Then, to complete his scientific approach he put his findings into Government Reports that became classics in the literature of exploration. Frémont's reports became the most widely read descriptions of the American West of that time. Not only were the routes, flora, fauna and geology of these lands depicted, but instructions were included for the proper season of travel, the supplies and equipment to take, and the location of waterholes and grass for livestock. Information was provided on the many Indian tribes encountered and the best method of treating them according to their mores. In short, he put the Western dream into words, and then made that dream seem more accessible to a generation of prospective emigrants.

Born an illegitimate child, with a possible life of shame, scorn, defeat, and obscurity, he fought the ignominy of his birth, struggled relentlessly, and became a magnificent survivor. Without a degree from West Point, he became the outstanding officer in the Army Topographical Corps. Without the secure foundation of a respected family life, he became a hero of his age.

It was Jessie Benton Frémont who most succinctly summarized the impact of her husband's legacy: "From the ashes of his campfires have sprung cities."

Western exploration was not an enterprise for the timid and the weak. It required of a man the ultimate in ability to endure deprivation and hardship. Frémont himself possessed an incredible endurance, an astounding energy. He had the stamina and drive to struggle against near impossible odds. More importantly, he possessed a natural ability to lead men and to draw from them boundless loyalty. At the time of his second expedition, Frémont was only thirty years old.

Frémont's third expedition, one year later, was even more eventful. Crossing the continent again, over the Sierra Nevada mountains into California, Frémont temporarily turned his back on exploration to prompt the Bear Flag uprising and to help in the conquest of California during the ensuing Mexican-American War. Frémont's energy, strong will, and belief in action were welcomed by the equally audacious Commodore Robert F. Stockton. Between them there existed the belief that what was good for America was surely good for the *californios** (and the world for that matter), and the fall of California into American hands was a by-product of their bravura. Though Frémont was court-martialed by the U.S. Army for his failure to follow a subordinate role to the late-arriving General Stephen W. Kearny into California, Frémont remained a romantic symbol of conquest for the average American. On his return to Washington, D.C., from California, he was met most everywhere by cheering throngs of people. Insubordination was not a very serious offense in the America of the 1840s. One could argue that President James Polk's pardoning of Frémont was a foregone conclusion.

The years ahead for Frémont were no less dramatic. Fourth and fifth expeditions were planned and executed; Frémont was to be one of the first two Senators from California; he was the first candidate of the newly-created Republican Party for the Presidency in 1856; and he served as a major general in the Civil War.

Despite this, his later years were a struggle with poverty and public disrepute. He died at the age of seventy-seven, largely forgotten, in a meager hotel room in New York City.

Present-day historians who are critical of Frémont find this sad end to the Frémont story quite predictable. They particularly emphasize the impulsive, unstable, erratic aspects of Frémont's personality. They grant him his flamboyance, but feel it was commingled with irre-

---

Californios, persons of Spanish or Mexican heritage whose place of birth or residence was California. The term has been used particularly in relation to the period from c. 1830 through the U.S. conquest in 1846.

sponsible and obsessive behavior. The result was accomplishments tarnished by impatient opportunism and inconsistent adventurism.

His impetuosity surfaced on his very first expedition. On the return leg of the trip, he decided to have his men shoot the rapids of the flooded Platte River in a collapsible rubber boat rather than take the time to unload their baggage and make the crossing more slowly and cautiously. The boat eventually capsized, strewing materials, men, and crucial records along and in the river. Through sheer luck the records were later retrieved downstream. During the second expedition, he made the rash decision to cross the Sierra Nevada in mid-winter, a feat that had never before been attempted, and a course of action which greatly endangered the lives of his already exhausted and footsore men. The expedition barely made it across. Here, critics argue, was a foolhardy option chosen more for the sake of personal glory than for regard for his men. This risk-taking was to have a disastrous result on his fourth expedition when he drove his men into the San Juan mountains of the Rockies during one of the worst winters in memory. One-third of his expedition died; an isolated group escaped death only by resorting to cannibalism.

Critics are no less censorious of Frémont's behavior in California. They believe that California might have been brought peacefully into the Union had it not been for Frémont's filibustering activities during the Bear Flag revolt. Frémont later claimed to have had secret authorization for his aggressive behavior. However, no evidence has ever surfaced to support Frémont's claims. Rather, Frémont instigated a resistance to the American takeover: by antagonizing Mexican authorities; by raising the American flag and making a show of force on Hawk's Peak (now Frémont's peak); by spreading spurious anti-Mexican rumors among the American immigrants; by instigating the Bear Flag Revolt; and by advising Stockton to issue a bombastic and offensive proclamation to the *californios*. The two key Mexican leaders of California, Colonel José Castro in the north and Pío Pico in the south, had announced that resistance to the Americans was hopeless, and both had left for Mexico soon after the outbreak of the Mexican-American War. There was no reason for Frémont and Stockton to alienate the *californios*, for most *californios* had not been satisfied with Mexican rule. Moreover, Frémont's filibustering was completely illegal. If the Mexican-American War had not subsequently erupted, the Bear Flag Revolt might very well have been California's "Alamo." Critics argue that Frémont was fortunate that news of the war brought responsible men to the fore with valid instructions to act.

The historian John Hawgood goes even further in his condemnation of Frémont's California legacy by inserting a literary critique: "The Bear Flag Revolution would undoubtedly not have bulked so large in history . . . but for the attempts to tamper with the record by John C. Frémont . . . and by his gifted wife. . . ."

Civil War historians have generally been equally uncomplimentary of Frémont's leadership as commander of the Department of the West. In August of 1861 he placed Missouri under martial law and issued the first emancipation proclamation. Lincoln was aghast. The President had been gingerly handling the slavery question because of his need for the support of the Border States. Frémont's actions caused mutiny in Missouri and threatened to jeopardize the careful balance that Lincoln was trying to preserve. Frémont even went so far as to object to Lincoln's order to modify his proclamation so as to make it conform with Congress's Confiscation Act of August 6, 1861. When Frémont compounded his defiance with serious military losses in the battles of Springfield, Missouri, and Wilson's Creek, Lincoln had no choice but to dismiss him from the western command. Frémont eventually resigned his commission in the Union Army on June 4, 1864.

From this survey of the literature on Frémont, one can see that Frémont was not only one of the most controversial figures in California history, but one of the most controversial figures in the history of the United States. There were few incidents in his life that did not cause disagreement in his own time and that do not cause bewilderment to biographers and historians today.

Whether there will be a future consensus on Frémont is hard to tell. But one thing seems certain—Frémont will probably never settle in the very first rank of American heroes. The truly great men and women of America's past can be made to sparkle whichever way you look at them.

SELECTED BIBLIOGRAPHY

1. Brandon, William. *The Men and the Mountain: Frémont's Fourth Expedition.* New York: William Morrow & Co. 1955.
2. Dillon, Richard. *Humbugs and Heroes: A Gallery of California Pioneers.* Garden City, N.Y.: Doubleday. 1970.
3. Egan, Ferol. *Frémont: Explorer for a Restless Nation.* Garden City, N.Y.: 1977.
4. Frémont, John Charles. *Memoirs of My Life.* Chicago and New York: Belford, Clarke & Co. 1887.
5. Jackson, Donald and Mary Lee Spence. eds. *The Expeditions of John Charles Frémont.* Urbana: University of Illinois Press. 1970 and 1973.
6. Nevins, Allan. *Frémont: Pathmarker of the West.* 2 vols. New York: Frederick Ungar Publishing Co. 1939 and 1955.
7. Smith, Henry Nash. *Virgin Land: The American West as Symbol and Myth.* Cambridge, Mass.: Harvard University Press. 1950.

The Black Experience Under Slavery: Accommodation, Resistance or Revolution?

No issue dominates the history of early nineteenth century America like the problem of slavery. By then, slavery was already an "ancient" institution in the U.S. The American nation had developed along with, and in many ways because of, chattel slavery. Politically, the question of slavery served as the focus of the North-South conflict. Economically, slavery was important both as an essential labor force for the South and in terms of absolute monetary value—an estimated $2 billion in 1860. Socially, it was looked upon by white Southerners as an essential element in their control of the black race. Ethically, slavery raised the thorny question of whether it could be justified on moral grounds. And constitutionally, slavery created a problem because of its ambiguity; while it was clear that Congress had no power to deal with slavery in the states, the power of Congress was less clear regarding the Western territories.

Given this significance and diversity, historians have studied slavery from a number of different perspectives and far more extensively than any other nineteenth century dilemma. For instance, much debate has been focused on the historical origins of slavery in America. Perhaps the outstanding work on this issue has been historian Winthrop Jordan's *White Over Black*.[7] In a particularly brilliant first chapter, Jordan traces American racial attitudes back to their beginning in Elizabethan England. Jordan discusses how the African's color, religion and cultural life contributed to a set of negative first impressions for the English. Jordan even examines the effect that the extraordinary animal life of Africa had on the development of English attitudes. Jordan is careful to remind the reader that English prejudices about blacks reveal next to nothing about the realities within Africa or the truth about its peoples. Rather English prejudices were an indication of the fears and anxieties that Englishmen had about themselves and about their own nation.

Another historical approach which has generated much debate centers on the two questions which will be the focus of this essay: What was slavery really like? And how did slaves react to their peculiar situation? What makes this controversy doubly interesting is that the answers have varied markedly through the years.

The first major interpretation to dominate the twentieth century historical scene came after World War I and was associated with the writings of historian Ulrich B. Phillips.[9] Phillips argued that the Southern plantation was a benevolent and paternal institution, wherein Southern slave-owners generally behaved with fatherly concern toward their slaves. It was Phillips, in

"That man over there says that women need to be helped into carriages, and lifted over ditches, and to have the best place everywhere. Nobody ever helps me into carriages, or over mud-puddles, or gives me any best place! And ain't I a woman? . . . I have borne thirteen children, and seen them most all sold off to slavery, and when I cried out with my mother's grief, none but Jesus heard me! And ain't I a woman? . . . Then that little man in black there, he says women can't have as much rights as men, 'cause Christ wasn't a woman! Where did your Christ come from? Where did your Christ come from? From God and a woman! Man had nothing to do with Him." Sojourner Truth, Address to the Ohio Women's Rights Convention, 1851.

74

fact, who reinforced the "Sambo" image of black people as smiling, deceitful, irresponsible, happy and lazy—as grown-up children. Dealing with such people, argued Phillips, required a firm, but gentle, paternal hand.

Slavery was a dying institution, continued Phillips. Slavery could only thrive in the cotton South, where black people physically were best suited to the South's humid, hot weather. Therefore, he argued that slavery had reached its "natural limits" by 1860. It logically followed for Phillips that the Civil War was a tragic, unnecessary war. The real culprits behind the Civil War were narrow-minded, self-righteous Abolitionists. They were the ones who exaggerated slavery's abuses; they were the ones responsible for creating the uproar which pushed the nation off its moderate course.

It is interesting to note that Phillips was writing immediately after a war (World War I) which the generation of the 1920s and 1930s considered to be an unnecessary and tragic mistake. He was also writing at a time when great numbers of blacks, recruited by agents for steel mills, stockyards, etc., made their way North, and Northerners found themselves having to adjust to these new neighbors and new social conditions. It was in the first phases of this adjustment that Northern whites found themselves strangely susceptible to what had formerly been considered uniquely Southern attitudes and prejudices. It might be added that Phillips was a Southerner by birth, who had himself moved North and who had suffered through the pangs of adjustment to "Yankees."

The next major book on these aspects of slavery came out in 1956 and it was written by Kenneth M. Stampp.[11] Stampp took issue with Phillips on almost every point. First of all, Stampp argued that slavery was a profit-oriented system, a capitalistic institution which was flourishing, not dying at the time of the Civil War. For Stampp, Phillips could not be further from the truth when he argued that slavery was a paternal and benevolent system. For Stampp, slavery was a systematic method of controlling and exploiting labor. Stampp pointed out that masters demanded from their slaves a long day of hard work and managed by whatever means to get it. He also emphasized the cruel, harsh and evil aspects of the plantation system: the slave diet, the breakup of marriages and families, and the condition of slave dwellings, etc. Finally, Stampp argued that black people were not the smiling, child-like, docile creatures that Phillips described. Rather they were rebels—resistance fighters. Stampp made mention of the numerous slave revolts to prove his point. After carefully studying the private diaries and letters of numerous plantation owners, he stressed how Southerners lived in terror of the possibility of these revolts.

Again, we should note how Stampp's writings reflected contemporary events. The 1950s were characterized by an active Civil Rights movement. It was a time when much larger numbers of Black Americans actively protested against the discrimination and injustice that they were suffering. It was also the period after World War II when, from the American point of view, a necessary war had been fought against the forces of tyranny, brutality and immorality. Hence, it was natural for Stampp to see the Civil War as another necessary war.

In the 1960s, still another significant approach to the problem of slavery was offered by the historian Stanley Elkins, who borrowed heavily from the discipline of psychology, and presented a thesis which took issue with almost all of Stampp's conclusions.[2] Elkins argued that Stampp was so preoccupied with countering Phillips that he had lost his objectivity. Elkins's contention was that Phillips was reasonably right about the Sambo image, but for the wrong reasons. That is, Phillips explained black behavior as representative of racial and cultural inferiority. Instead, Elkins used insights from his study of psychology to argue his point.

For example, Elkins stated that Stampp was wrong on the issue of slave insurrections. Those that occurred, pointed out Elkins, were few and unsuccessful. In fact, slave rebellions were invariably led by free blacks, for those were the blacks who had contact with the idea of freedom and who could, therefore, identify with freedom-fighting. How could a slave organize a rebellion around an abstract right that he had not experienced, asked Elkins?

Further, Elkins concurred with the Sambo stereotype by explaining that black slaves became "accommodationists" under the stressful conditions of slavery. The master-slave relationship was one of utmost authority on the one side and utter dependence on the other. As a result, a childlike attachment to the master was the resultant psychological adjustment on the part of the slave.

The 1970s and 1980s have been fertile years for new judgments about slavery. There are historians today who, through the use of computers, have transformed data-gathering techniques. Now complex archival material, obscure census records, innumerable local and regional statistics, climate conditions, food availability, etc., have been programmed on computers and the results are often quite enlightening.

One of the best of the modern writers on slavery is John Blassingame.[1] Blassingame notes that most of the historians involved in the dispute over the nature of slavery have been white and "liberal." Because a liberal-white perspective has predominated, there has been the tendency on the part of these historians to see blacks solely as passive participants and as victims and never as creative participants in a complex social process. The historian Elkins, especially, is criticized for this oversight. Further, grave doubts have been expressed as to the reliability of Elkin's psychological interpretations. Blassingame argues that white historians have to ask another question besides: "What was done to the slaves?" They have to ask: "What did the slaves do for themselves and how did they do it?"

If historians would ask such questions, argues Blassingame, they would find out that slaves led a rich cultural and family life that was kept hidden from their white masters and was confined to their slave quarters. Blassingame emphasizes that slaves had a number of other significant relationships in their lives besides the one with their masters. Because of this social diversity, slaves were able to preserve much of their self-esteem. Hence, while much controversy has been expended on whether slaves were Sambos or rebels, a more basic fact has been ignored—"there was a great variety of personality types among slaves." Depending on his circumstances, and depending on what he wanted, an individual slave, at any given time, would act the part of any three of the personality types Blassingame discusses: Sambo, rebel or Jack.* In truth, continues Blassingame, the image of docility was a sham and a mask to hide the slave's true feelings and thoughts.

While the slave was customarily obedient and deferential to his master, this was not necessarily an innate character trait. He went through the ritual of deference in some cases because he recognized that it was mandatory for his survival. In most cases, he went through

*Blassingame offers the following thumbnail sketch of Jack:
Jack worked faithfully as long as he was well treated. Sometimes sullen and uncooperative, he generally refused to be driven beyond the pace he had set for himself. Conscious of his identity with other slaves, he cooperated with them to resist the white man's oppression. Rationally analyzing the white man's overwhelming physical power, Jack either avoided contact with him or was deferential in his presence. Since he did not identify with his master and could not always keep up the facade of deference, he was occasionally flogged for insubordination. Although often proud, stubborn, and conscious of the wrongs he suffered, Jack tried to repress his anger. His patience was however, not unlimited. He raided his master's larder when he was hungry, ran away when he was tired of working or had been punished, and was sometimes ungovernable. Shrewd and calculating, he used his wits to escape from work or to manipulate his overseer and master.[1]

the ritual the way that most men perform habitual acts: with little thought about their symbolic significance. Besides, the deferential posture was not the only one the slave assumed. At the same time that he was deferential to his master, he also interacted with other human beings on other levels; he viewed poor whites with contempt, enjoyed the love, respect, and companionship of his family; thought of himself as superior to besotted, licentious masters; won praise, inspired admiration, acquired status, found companionship, obtained sexual gratification, dominated others, and played and relaxed in the quarters. Most importantly, he had a great deal of time free from observation by whites.

The resiliency of the slave was such that the infrequent occasions when he went through the ritual of deference were not sufficient to blot out the numerous other roles he played. . . . The typical slave used his wits to escape from work and punishment, preserved his manhood in the quarters, feigned humility, identified with masters and worked industriously only when he was treated humanely, simulated deference, was hostilely submissive and occasionally obstinate, ungovernable, and rebellious.[1]

Possibly the best representative of current attitudes about slavery is Herbert Gutman.[6] Gutman, too, argues that slaves were more influenced by their own culture and by their own very special kinship and family ties, than by their relationship with whites. Therefore, he painstakingly delineates the enlarged kinship groups, and the elaborate extended families that slaves created when faced with the limitations of slave life. He concludes that there were distinct slave feelings, beliefs and institutions which were passed from generation to generation that were more important than how the slaves were treated by their owners.

In his epilogue, Gutman leaves his readers with a penetrating thought. He does not believe that slavery was responsible for the current characteristics found in many black families, particularly the absent-father, mother-centered pattern. Rather he argues that the most damage to the black family has occurred since emancipation and is associated with income levels. The most important clue to the problem for black families today is the job picture for the black male, claims Gutman. The rate of black family breakup between 1950 and 1970 is far out of proportion to that of other Americans, he emphasizes, and it is a myth that this tragedy stems from slavery and cannot be eradicated by economic and social reforms.

Gutman's insights probably come closest to explaining present-day economic and unemployment trends among black Americans. (See page 192 for relevant statistics on this matter). In fact, here is an instance where research in a historical subject contains an immediate relation to current social problems. In this case, it should also serve as a forewarning. Though technological challenges presently seem to be the most pressing, historical perspective lends credence to the premise that social problems are the most persistent and the most difficult to solve.

SELECTED BIBLIOGRAPHY

1. Blassingame, John W. *The Slave Community: Plantation Life in the Ante-Bellum South.* New York: Oxford University Press. Revised and Enlarged Edition. 1979.
2. Elkins, Stanley. *Slavery: A Problem in American Institutional and Intellectual Life.* Chicago: University of Chicago Press. 1959.
3. Fogel, Robert W. and Stanley L. Engerman. *Time on the Cross: The Economics of American Negro Slavery.* Boston: Little, Brown and Co. 1974.
4. Fredrickson, George M. *White Supremacy: A Comparative Study in American and South African History.* New York: Oxford University Press. 1981.

5. Genovese, Eugene. *Roll, Jordan, Roll*. New York: Pantheon Books. 1976.
6. Gutman, Herbert G. *The Black Family in Slavery and Freedom*. New York: Pantheon Books. 1976.
7. Jordan, Winthrop D. *The White Man's Burden: Historical Origins of Racism in the United States*. New York: Oxford University Press. 1974.
8. Litwack, Leon F. *Been in the Storm So Long: The Aftermath of Slavery*. New York: Alfred A. Knopf. 1979.
9. Phillips, Ulrich B. *American Negro Slavery*. Baton Rouge: Louisiana State University Press. 1966. (First edition, 1918).
10. _____. *Life and Labor in the Old South*. Boston: Little, Brown and Company. 1929.
11. Stampp, Kenneth M. *The Peculiar Institution*. New York: Alfred A. Knopf. 1956.

Were the Abolitionists Reformers or Fanatics?

One of the perennial criticisms of the study of history has been that it often seems irrelevant to contemporary events. In fact, this criticism is unfair. Historians, though they are immersed in a study of the past, are also strongly influenced by the present. The weight and urgency of contemporary events determine not only the subject matter which is chosen for research, but the approach to that subject matter. The result is an interpretation or an analogy which frequently proves to be quite timely and relevant. The predominant problem, in truth, is that historians oftentimes are too imprisoned by the present in their conclusions. The result is that many interpretations prove to be ephemeral and dubious. On the other hand, it is also true that the added perspective of time and experience work to offer a keener and more perceptive understanding of the past. The passage of time allows long-range trends to emerge and the enduring lessons of history to be more clearly visible.

A subject which possibly best reveals both the pro's and con's of the historical dilemma is the study of Abolitionism. To review, Abolitionists were those mid-nineteenth century reformers (ca. 1830–1860) who agitated for the immediate abolition of slavery. They were adamantly against compromising with the Southern slaveholder and opposed to the gradual and indirect methods of earlier anti-slavery protestors. Interpretations of Abolitionism have varied through the years since the Civil War, but for our purposes a focus on the insights of the last fifty years will be sufficient.

During the 1940s and 1950s there was seldom a good word said on behalf of the Abolitionists. They were variously described by historians as irresponsible fanatics, self-righteous and dangerous demagogues, and gullible and narrow-minded idealists. They were criticized for their inflexible attitudes and for their propensity for bringing difficult social questions into the realm of personal morality. Because they had a tendency to view problematic issues as strictly "right or wrong," they were blamed as one of the key causes of the Civil War. Their fanaticism, it was argued, made compromise with the South impossible. Because of the Abolitionists, the Civil War, which might have been avoided if a breadth of view and a balance of judgment had been displayed, became inevitable and irrepressible.

The 1940s and 1950s were, in general, years when Americans were proud of the sacrifices they had made and the progress they had attained. World War II had been fought and won with a seemingly unselfish attitude. And, after the War, Americans were equally proud of the philanthropic attitude that they had demonstrated in the rebuilding of Europe and Japan through such efforts as the Marshall Plan. It was natural that the satisfaction that was felt by Americans with their system of government would be projected onto their study of history. Historians generally believed that the American system of government had about it a certain "pragmatic" genius, in that positive internal reform was always possible through peaceful and legal means. Since the Abolitionists used extra-legal means to attain moral ends, and because they were incapable of exhibiting patience with the workings of a democratic system, they were severely condemned.

The buoyancy and optimism of the 1950s quickly came to an end in the 1960s. The Vietnam War, which grew larger and larger despite vigorous protests, caused many Americans to question the cherished traditions of the past. Many came to believe that a faceless and heartless group of bureaucrats was running the government in callous disregard of the real needs of the American people. The assassinations of the Kennedys and Martin Luther King, Jr., and the possible coverups involved, caused many Americans to believe that their society and government might very well be fundamentally unsound.

During the tumultuous "Sixties" historical scholarship began to reflect this change and concern. All aspects of America's past were restudied and re-evaluated and no conclusions were more intriguing than those associated with the Abolitionists. The "new" opinion was more sympathetic, and historians of the 1960s apologized for the Abolitionists' emotional atittudes and uncompromising stances. Instead, they stressed the enormous cruelties of the institution of slavery. In fact, it became popular to state that extremely evil institutions were the cause of extreme and militant responses. It was further argued that a gradual and piecemeal approach to slavery was not sufficient for its eradication. The Abolitionists, it was said, faced a nation which was flawed at its center by slavery and racism. The Abolitionists had to treat slavery as a moral issue; they had to attack with a sense of immediacy; and they had to militantly assault existing institutions. Any other approach, any less effort, would serve to perpetuate slavery, an institution which historians in the 1960s saw as a strong capitalistic enterprise which could not be restructured without the use of force.

Abolitionists, then, emerged in the 1960s with a new dignity and with a new importance. Liberal historians, in particular, felt a real admiration for the idealism of the Abolitionists. Caught up in the moral fervor of the Civil Rights movement of the early 1960s, these historians saw the Abolitionists as forerunners of the twentieth-century Movement. As Tilden G. Edelstein argued: "In times of social injustice it may be the inactive individual, not the reformer, who is mentally disturbed."[2]

With the end of the Vietnam War and with the new attitudes of the mid-1970s and 1980s, it was natural that interpretations of Abolitionism would change. As Americans "recharged their batteries" after the emotional and psychological stress of the 1960s, as they entered the post-atergate years with a healthy sense of skepticism, a new consensus began to appear. It is still too soon to tell the exact outlines of this new opinion as it relates to Abolitionism. But some aspects are now clear.

A clearly positive historical judgment of Abolitionism is not emerging. Too many negative characteristics of the Abolitionist movement remain questionable for present-day historians to extend unqalified praise and acclaim. For instance, there is the fact that though white Abolitionists were intensely anti-slavery, they were not pro-black. The great majority of white Abolitionists refused to employ or associate with blacks. Very few regarded the black man and woman as equal to whites. Rather they accepted the white supremacy doctrines of their time. The immorality of slavery was what bothered them. The issue of blacks as people was ignored.

One can understand how difficult it was for the Abolitionists, given the prominent beliefs of their age, to make a leap of faith and expect that some day, given an environment of freedom, the slavery-stunted black people would "catch up" with whites. In a way, one can understand why the Abolitionists were unable to transcend the basic parameters of their society's beliefs about racial differences. Indeed, Abolitionists may deserve credit for opposing slavery despite their inability to care about black people. Nonetheless, more and more historians today are finding it difficult to overlook these unfortunate attitudes.

Secondly, historians have begun to focus less and less on those Abolitionists who remained outside political channels in their protest, in favor of those who worked within the system. New studies have appeared emphasizing the accomplishments of those Abolitionists who joined the "political anti-slavery movement" which gained momentum after the 1840s. It was these more moderate Abolitionists who were responsible for the formation of the Liberty Party in 1839. The Liberty Party's platform, which simply called for an end to slavery, was too radical for the time, so it was eventually supplanted by the Free Soil Party and the broader platform of "Free soil, free speech, free labor, and free men!" It was this Free Soil Party which provided the impetus for an even newer creation in 1854—the Republican Party.

The anti-slavery agitators who finally found a home in the Republican Party were those who abandoned the doctrine of immediate emancipation. Their position, however, protested slavery's expansion. Anti-slavery Republicans were willing to allow slavery to continue in the South, but they were adamantly against its growth into the West. Their platform can be described as a type of "containment" policy—the elimination of slavery through the restriction of it.

What should be noted is how the historical approach that began in the mid-1970s reflects the currently popular mood. How often we have witnessed the radicals of the 1960s recognizing the value of working within established political channels in the 1970s and 1980s. It is natural that today's historians would focus on those protestors who did the same in the past.

In conclusion, considering the excitement generated by differing historical opinions these past fifty years, maybe the English historian A. J. P. Taylor's insight is the most apt after all: "Events are well enough in their way; what historians write about them is much better."[11]

SELECTED BIBLIOGRAPHY

1. Dumond, Dwight L. *Antislavery: The Crusade for Freedom.* Ann Arbor: University of Michigan Press. 1961.
2. Edelstein, Tilden G. *Strange Enthusiasm: A Life of Thomas Wentworth Higginson.* New Haven, Connecticut: Yale University Press. 1969.
3. Filler, Louis. *The Crusade Against Slavery, 1830–1860.* New York: Harper and Row. 1960.
4. Kraditor, Aileen. *Means and Ends in American Abolitionism.* New York: Pantheon Books. 1969.
5. Kraut, Alan M. ed. *Crusaders and Compromisers: Essays on the Relationship of the Anti-slavery Struggle to the Antebellum Party System.* Westport, Conn.: Greenwood. 1983.
6. McPherson, James M. *The Struggle for Equality: Abolitionists and the Negro in the Civil War and Reconstruction.* Princeton: Princeton University Press. 1964.
7. Perry, Lewis and Michael Fellman, ed. *Antislavery Reconsidered: New Perspectives on the Abolitionists.* Baton Rouge: Louisiana State University Press. 1979.

8. Quarles, Benjamin. *Black Abolitionists.* New York: Oxford University Press. 1969.
9. Sewell, Richard H. *Ballots for Freedom: Antislavery Politics in the United States, 1830–1860.* New York: Oxford University Press. 1976.
10. Sorin, Gerald. *Abolitionism: A New Perspective.* New York: Praeger Publishers. 1972.
11. Taylor, A. J. P. *From Napoleon to Lenin.* New York: Harper and Row, 1966.
12. Walters, Ronald G. *The Antislavery Appeal: American Abolitionism after 1830.* Baltimore: John Hopkins University Press. 1977.

Why Does Lincoln Deserve
His Heroic Rank?

Mark Twain once observed: "It isn't what they don't know that hurts people, it's what they do know that isn't so." This quotation is always important for Americans to remember, as our history is filled with myths and misperceptions. But Mark Twain's words ring particularly true when we approach the question of Abraham Lincoln's significance in American history. Lincoln is a President whom historians consistently rate as the greatest among all American Presidents. Yet, if Americans, in general, were queried as to the exact reasons behind Lincoln's greatness, they would most probably give the wrong answers.

The most typical response would mention Lincoln as the "Great Emancipator," the friend of blacks, the President who fought hard and succeeded in freeing the slaves. This stereotype, it turns out, is manifestly untrue. Lincoln's personal policy regarding emancipation was quite different from what eventually emerged as official policy. First of all, Lincoln believed that the states should be responsible for freeing the slaves, rather than the federal government, and that the process of emancipation should be handled gradually, over a number of years, lasting until 1900 if necessary. Secondly, he argued that the slaveholders should be compensated for their financial losses as a result of emancipation. Finally, he believed that the freed blacks should then be "voluntarily" colonized abroad—either to Africa, Haiti, Panama, etc. It was a bitter blow to Lincoln when his personal policy failed to gain either Congressional or popular support.

In the end, it was domestic and foreign pressures that forced Lincoln to issue the Emancipation Proclamation. By 1863 Lincoln recognized that, for a number of reasons, a public proclamation of emancipation would aid the Northern war effort. However, his executive pronouncement had to be carefully worded so as not to alienate pro-Union Southerners, particularly those residing in the "border" states fighting on the Union side. Accordingly, the proclamation freed the slaves only in the rebellious Confederate states, where Lincoln, in actuality, did not have any authority. Those slaves in the pro-Northern slave states of Maryland, Delaware, Kentucky, West Virginia and Missouri were not affected by the Emancipation Proclamation. No wonder the London *Spectator* was prompted to remark: "The principle is not that a human being cannot justly own another, but that he cannot own him unless he is loyal to the United States."

Lincoln's greatness is definitely not associated with any special popularity in his own lifetime. His very election to the Presidency split the nation and prompted the Southern states to

"If we could first know where we are, and whither we are tending, we could better judge what to do, and how to do it. We are now far into the fifth year since a policy was initiated with the avowed object and confident promise of putting an end to slavery agitation. Under the operation of that policy that agitation has not only not ceased, but has constantly augmented. In my opinion, it will not cease until a crisis shall have been reached and passed. 'A house divided against itself can not stand.' I believe this Government can not endure permanently half slave and half free." Abraham Lincoln, The House Divided Speech, June 16, 1858.

secede. His actions at Fort Sumter precipitated a civil war. As the War progressed, his Presidential conduct brought division to his own political party. Lincoln chafed at any restraint imposed upon his executive powers and, as a result, undertook many actions unilaterally. For instance, he called out the state militias, expanded the regular Army and Navy, spent monies, suspended the writ of habeas corpus, and authorized military arrests and trials of persons not under military jurisdiction. All of this he did without waiting for Congressional approval. These actions alienated many and it was not long before the Democratic Party fully broke with Lincoln and developed a platform with the idea of a "negotiated peace" as an alternative to Lincoln's war policies. His own Republican Party almost failed to nominate him for a second term because of the opposition he aroused.

Nor is there unanimity on Lincoln's abilities as a military tactician. Some historians have been critical of Lincoln's military thinking and his interference with the selection of key generals. Those who disagree with these historians must admit, nonetheless, that there is no major historical consensus regarding Lincoln as a great strategist or as a military genius.

Where, then, is there unanimity of opinion? And why is Lincoln consistently considered our greatest President? It was his stand against the expansion of slavery and against the idea of popular sovereignty that is the key to understanding Lincoln's significance in American history. Three key issues emerged in the years before the Civil War: the issue of slavery itself, the question of whether slavery should be allowed to expand into the territories newly acquired from Mexico, and the problem of the future status of black people in a white-dominated American society. In each of these areas Lincoln was the first major politician to offer an alternative to the position of the South and to the position of Northern Democrats, led by Senator Stephen Douglas of Illinois.

The issue of slavery itself was particularly divisive. Political and economic, as well as ethical considerations made this problem nearly impossible to resolve. In the great debates with Lincoln in 1858, Stephen Douglas reflected an attitude of indifference to slavery. Douglas believed that slavery would survive only in areas of the nation where cotton could be grown. Lincoln disagreed vehemently. Lincoln foresaw the use of slavery in factories, in mining, in lumbering, etc., and in the long run, he feared, it could become a grave threat to the freedom of all American workers.

Hence, Lincoln was strongly against allowing slavery to spread. He agreed that the federal government had no right to severely curtail slavery where it already existed, but he would not agree to its extension. What Lincoln, in effect, was calling for was a policy of "containment;" i.e. the extinction of slavery through its restriction. Lincoln wanted Americans to recognize that a policy of popular sovereignty (where the question of slavery would be resolved by a popular vote in each new state) might allow slavery to expand to national proportions.

With regard to the future status of black people, most Americans were frankly racist. In fact, during the debates, it was Douglas's ploy to try to associate Lincoln with Abolitionism and with the idea of social and political equality for black people. As was seen by Lincoln's personal policy regarding emancipation, he, too, was a racist; and in the debates he spoke out against social and political equality for blacks. However, Lincoln also added that he would in no way deny the humanity of black people. He would not agree with Douglas that slaves were merely chattel property. Lincoln argued that blacks were technically equal under the rights of the Declaration of Independence.

Anything that argues me into . . . the idea of perfect social and political equality with the negro is but a specious and fantastical arrangement of words by which a man can prove a horse-chestnut to be a chestnut horse.

But Lincoln continued:

I hold that . . . there is no reason in the world why the negro is not entitled to all the rights enumerated in the Declaration of Independence—the right of life, liberty and the pursuit of happiness. I hold that he is as much entitled to these as the white man. I agree with Judge Douglas that he is not my equal in many respects, certainly not in color—perhaps not in intellectual and moral endowments; but in the right to eat the bread without leave of anybody else which his own hand earns, he is my equal and the equal of Judge Douglas, and the equal of every other man.

Notice the limitations of Douglas's vision and understanding in his answer to Lincoln.

The signers of the Declaration of Independence never dreamed of the negro when they were writing the document. They referred to white men, to men of European birth and European descent, when they declared the equality of all men. . . . When Thomas Jefferson wrote that document he was the owner, and so continued until his death, of a large number of slaves. . . . Now, do you believe—are you willing to have it said that every man who signed the Declaration of Independence declared the negro his equal, and then was hypocrite enough to continue to hold him as a slave. . . . And yet, when you say that the Declaration of Independence includes the negro, you charge the signers of it with hypocrisy.

I say to you, frankly, that in my opinion this government was made by our fathers on the white basis. It was made by white men for the benefit of white men and their posterity for ever.

In effect, Lincoln was calling for the continued union of democracy and nationalism as a solution to the problems facing Americans in the 1850s and 1860s. There were strong nationalistic sentiments in the hearts of most Americans in those years. The nation was expanding westward with feelings of patriotism, superiority and aggression. Lincoln wanted to ensure that this expansion continued to be accompanied by a liberal code of laws and institutions.

Throughout much of the Western world in the 1850s and 1860s the forces of traditionalism and nationalism were allowed to triumph over the ideals of liberalism and democracy. One need only look at the actions of Bismarck in Germany, Cavour in Italy, Napoleon III in France, even Disraeli in Great Britain. Each acquiesced to economic and imperialistic pressures and, to varying degrees, sacrificed constitutionalism and democracy in their own countries or in newly acquired territories. Lincoln was the sole exception. This fact, more than anything else, earns Lincoln the accolades of American historians.

In addition, perhaps no nineteenth-century American retains his relevance for today's American as well as Abraham Lincoln. A key to this relevance is a statement the sixteenth president used in his poetic second inaugural address: "With firmness in the right, as God gives us to see the right, let us strive on to finish the work we are in."

Lincoln was remarkably modern in this comment, for he realized that human beings can rarely know if they are acting exactly correctly in the great political and social crises of their lives, but that they must do their very best anyway. Lincoln possessed the intellectual depth and awareness to be skeptical about his conclusions, especially during the critical years of our tragic Civil War, but he retained the courage to act decisively nonetheless. He did not allow his doubts to immobilize him or deter him from vigorous and effective action. As a result, Lincoln is an inspiration to present-day historians in a way that other great, but self-righteous, historical figures can never be.

In fact, Lincoln provides a welcome contrast to the political crusaders who have plagued the world's politics in our recent past—men and women who have believed themselves to be the special children of Providence and who were, therefore, rigid, intolerant and unquestioning.

Indeed, Lincoln's pre-eminent stature becomes clear when juxtaposed with the spiritual confusion which has beset the minds of history's crusaders. Lincoln was able to look at his world of North versus South without the dangerously deceptive myths of innocence and special virtue. He was able to retain a remarkable detachment and objectivity as he coped with a morally ambiguous world. We see this once again in his second inaugural speech:

> Both [the North and the South] read the same Bible, and pray to the same God; and each invokes His aid against the other. It may seem strange that any men should dare to ask a just God's assistance in wringing their bread from the sweat of other men's faces. But let us not judge that we be not judged. The prayers of both could not be answered—that of neither have been answered fully.

When Lincoln resorted to Biblical analogies or quoted Scripture, it was with a recognition that both sides in the great challenge that he faced had sinned. He discerned the pretensions of both the North and the South, and he emphasized the universality of guilt. A perfect example was his speech on March 30, 1863, which called for "a day of national humiliation, fasting, and prayer":

> May we not justly fear that the awful calamity of Civil War, which now desolates the land, may be but a punishment, inflicted on us, for our presumptuous sins, to the needful end of our national reformation as a whole People?

Lincoln had before him the example of John Brown, the fanatical abolitionist who did divide the world into neat categories of right and wrong, good and evil, innocence and guilt. Lincoln saw the political impossibility of Brown's sacred goal—the eradication of evil. Lincoln saw, as Brown did not, that when a national leader applies political means to effect social ends, or resorts to the use of political power to attain even a lofty goal such as liberty, evil is implicated automatically into the process. In the end, Brown's spiritual sickness was to destroy what he wanted to preserve, and it was to strengthen what he wanted to deny.

How often have we read about political leaders who were caught up in a preconceived idea so that they refused to re-evaluate their policies in light of new developments or unique circumstances? How often have we seen unwelcome facts sacrificed on the altar of a predetermined idea? Political crusaders have abounded in history, with their advisers who dared not counter with unwelcome options. These crusaders looked at their world in fixed patterns of good and evil, innocence and guilt, praise and blame. They viewed compromise as a type of contamination of self, not recognizing that true virtue lies, especially in a nuclear world, in never allowing one's moral judgments to jeopardize the pursuit of peace.

How often has the crusader's all-or-nothing approach to the world led to irreparable violence even in our own time, a violence made more terrible and destructive because it was associated with fanatic moral rigidity?

How many of our world leaders today preach and judge rather than listen and understand; how many exhibit a confusion of morality with moralism?

At a time when the resurgence of patriotism around the world seems to carry with it an obligation to hate one's enemy; when the prevailing attitude in foreign policy appears to be that it is better to be feared than loved; and when it is often judged to be a disgrace when one has to compromise with one's adversary—we would all do well to remember Lincoln.

In Lincoln, the historian has a statesman who did not need to maintain himself with self-righteous convictions and who did not need to believe that his side was solely decent and the enemy surely evil. Lincoln possessed the requisite humility, doubt and wisdom to explore important alternatives, and then he invoked the necessary courage to pursue those alternatives.

During the Civil War, at an official reception, Lincoln had occasion to refer to the Southerners rather as erring human beings than as foes to be exterminated. An elderly lady, a fiery patriot, rebuked him for speaking kindly of his enemies when he ought to be thinking of destroying them. "Why, madam," said Lincoln, "do I not destroy my enemies when I make them my friends?"

In conclusion, when we get our heroes out of focus and when we forget the reasons for their greatness, it is only a matter of time before those heroes will be removed from their hallowed places and lost, in a meaningful way, for succeeding generations. Something more is lost, however. A nation that loses its pride in its heroic past will also lose its faith in the future and its faith in the goodness of humankind. And it is just this type of optimism and faith in humankind which is a requisite for a healthy democracy.

SELECTED BIBLIOGRAPHY

1. Current, Richard N. *The Lincoln Nobody Knows.* New York: Hill and Wang. 1958.
2. Donald, David. *Lincoln Reconsidered.* New York: Alfred A. Knopf. 1947.
3. Fehrenbacher, Don E. *Prelude to Greatness: Lincoln in the 1850s.* Palo Alto: Stanford University Press. 1962.
4. Handlin, Oscar and Lilian. *Abraham Lincoln and the Union.* Boston: Little, Brown and Co. 1980.
5. Oates, Stephen B. *Abraham Lincoln: The Man Behind the Myths.* New York: Harper and Row, Publishers, 1984.
6. _____. *With Malice Toward None: The Life of Abraham Lincoln.* New York: Harper and Row. 1977.
7. Potter, David M. "Civil War." In C. Vann Woodward, ed., *The Comparative Approach to American History.* New York: Basic Books. 1968.
8. Sandburg, Carl. *Abraham Lincoln,* 6 vols. New York: Harcourt, Brace and World, 1926–1939.
9. Thomas, Benjamin P. *Abraham Lincoln.* New York: Random House, Inc. 1952.

Could the South Have Won the Civil War?

At first glance the answer to this question might appear quite elementary. Given the numerous advantages that the North had at the beginning of the Civil War, it seems almost inevitable that the Confederate cause was doomed to fail. For instance, consider the following assets that the North had compared to the South. There were twenty-three Northern states to eleven Confederate; the population of the North was more than twice that of the South; the amount of money in Northern banks was more than four times that of Southern banks; the value of real and personal property in the North was more than three times that of the South; and the value of annually manufactured products in the North was more than ten times that of the South. Further, the North possessed three-fourths of the nation's railroad mileage, almost all of the registered shipping and the great edge of having the skilled workers and technological expertise to administer and develop this overwhelming industrial predominance. In addition, the industrial and urban North benefited through having the type of economy that would flourish under nineteenth century wartime conditions, whereas the agricultural South possessed the type of economy that would be devastated by war.

It is surprising, then, that most American historians have argued that the South could, indeed, should have won the Civil War. These historians recognize the advantages that accrued to the North, but emphatically counter that the South had certain assets which more than compensated for the North's economic and industrial superiority. The most important advantage was that the South did not need to conquer the North in order to win. The South only needed to stand on the defensive, utilizing its geographical barriers—rivers, mountains, swamps—as successive lines of fortification until the North wearied and decided to end the fight. History has often witnessed the lighter, smaller foe defeating the heavier, larger opponent. It was not unreasonable to expect the South to win given the interior lines of communication, the long and deeply indented coastlines, the vastness of Southern territory (almost as large as all of Western Europe), and the many excellent generals at Confederate disposal.

Why, then, according to traditional accounts, did the South lose? The answer that is presented most often is that the South, in giving full reign to its particularist, localist and individualistic ideals, made a number of disastrous political decisions which dissipated their assets and opportunities and insured defeat. One example was the Southern failure to enforce a national taxation law and choosing instead to finance the War through borrowing and the policy of "impressment." Impressment meant that Southern army agents were allowed the power to confiscate necessary war commodities whenever and wherever the need arose. It was a most capricious policy because farmers and producers near the scene of military fighting would find their goods continually impressed, while those farmers and producers in outlying areas stood a good chance of retaining their goods. In the end, less than five percent of Southern revenue was raised by taxes. Borrowing and impressment were the main Southern alternatives, and inflation, as a result, was rampant. This lack of taxation policy is just one example in the economic sphere of the Southern insistence upon their individual and states' rights. But such particularistic, localistic and individualistic attitudes also inhibited coordinated Confederate efforts in the shipping and railway industries, too. One might look at Northern economic policies for a contrast. Though the North proved reluctant at first to raise taxes to finance the War, nonetheless, before the War was over, twenty-one percent of the Union's income came from taxation. As for its shipping and railway industries, the Union government initiated a number of innovative expedients whenever necessary to coordinate these vital aspects of modern war.

Southern particularism was also manifested in the area of internal security. An excessive concern for local rights inhibited Confederate leaders from clamping down on internal dissension. Though the South was plagued by a more severe disloyalty problem than the North, Jefferson Davis was reluctant to resort to the implementation of martial law, the suspension of the writ of habeas corpus or to the application of strict censorship. For example, not a single newspaper was closed down in the South during the Civil War despite the fact that many were intensely critical of Confederate leadership. This should be compared with the Northern record of curtailing the rights of approximately 300 newspapers at various times during the War. Lincoln, when necessary, was quick to suspend the writ of habeas corpus and declare martial law. As the historian George M. Frederickson has warned:

> This contrast (between the North and South) can scarcely be attributed to a greater southern devotion to civil liberties. Prewar critics of slavery had learned how narrow the limits of southern tolerance could be. The southern majority did not object to the forcible suppression of unpopular individuals, groups, and opinions, but its strong commitment to localism made it reluctant to see such powers exercised by a central government. [4]

To be sure, no nation serious about maintaining a life-and-death struggle can tolerate the freedoms usual in peacetime.

Further, the Confederate government was equally lax in compelling individual Southern states to coordinate their efforts for the common cause. There were innumerable examples where Southern state governments refused arms, men, even food and clothing though the needs of the Confederacy demanded it. Just one example of how jealous Southern states were of their rights and goods was a situation which developed during the last days of the War. While Lee's army was literally fighting in rags, North Carolina was holding in its warehouses 92,000 uniforms, along with thousands of blankets, tents and shoes. Though North Carolina was the center of the South's cotton industry, the production of its mills was reserved almost exclusively for North Carolina regiments.

The North provides a marked contrast. Lincoln was able to integrate the efforts of his war governors. And he was even able to reach out and tap the efforts of the opposing party, the Democrats, on behalf of the Union cause.

Other Southern political decisions, though not directly related to a particularist, localist or individualist doctrine, were equally diastrous. The most conspicuous was what has been called the "King Cotton" delusion. This was the South's fallacious supposition that without cotton there would be massive unemployment abroad and, to alleviate rioting and suffering, Britain and

France would be impelled to intervene in the Civil War on behalf of the Confederacy. Therefore, instead of buying a fleet of blockade runners and exporting its most valuable product to Europe for vastly important supplies and munitions, the South voluntarily kept all of their cotton at home. This "King Cotton" diplomacy was tremendously shortsighted. Not only did it fail to take into account the cotton surplus in European warehouses in 1861 and the complexities of European diplomatic affairs at that time, it also failed to adjudge the importance of Northern wheat to European nations.

There was also the failure to adopt some type of a conscription policy that would apply to black slaves—almost forty percent of the Confederacy's manpower resources at the beginning of the War. Since slaves were viewed as a type of property by the Confederate Congress, the allocation of this vast manpower reserve was left to the whim and discretion of individual slave-holders. The argument here is not that the Confederacy should have put blacks into uniform. Such a step would have shaken the foundations of slavery. Rather blacks could have been conscripted into a mobile and flexible labor force ready at one time or another to construct or maintain railroads, build fortifications, work in factories—in other words, to be available to move as rapidly as possible to those areas of the Southern war effort which most needed their labor.

Finally, Civil War historians have traditionally pointed out that the election of Jefferson Davis was also a mistake politically. Davis, it has been argued, was inadequate as the Commander-in-Chief of his nation. He lacked the charisma and the political acumen necessary for success. It is said that Davis never thought in terms of overall strategy, as did Lincoln. Rather, he troubled himself with the insignificant details of battle, details that would have been better left to his field generals.

In sum, though historians have traditionally recognized the major economic differences between the two warring sections, they consider political misjudgments to be the key to ultimate Southern defeat. More recently, however, "revisionist" historians have taken a completely different approach to this question of the South's potential for victory. They argue that the War was a mismatch from the very beginning, and they object to answering the question: "Why did the South lose the War?" Instead, they insist that the proper question should be: "How did the South hold out so long?"

There was only one way that the South could have won, contend these revisionists, and that was by pursuing guerrilla tactics. However, to try and conduct guerrilla warfare and still maintain control of their vast slave population would have been an impossible task. Hence, the Confederate government had to accept the confrontation on the North's terms and fight the type of industrial war for which the South was so inadequately prepared.

Revisionists reason that the South held out so long because its government successfully adopted a type of "state socialism" with which to defend itself. Indeed, revisionists maintain that the South in many ways became more centralized, organized and nationalized than did the North. Not only was a new national government created in the midst of wartime pressures, but new centers of industrial production were established in every Confederate state where none had existed before. Revisionists admit that this modernization process was destroyed when the South was eventually defeated. But they implore their readers not to ignore the great industrial, economic and social accomplishments of the South during the Confederacy period.

One revisionist, an Italian historian, Raimondo Luraghi, has intriguingly compared the state socialism implemented by the South in the Civil War to that of China after World War II.[6] Like China, argues Luraghi, the South found itself in the predicament of having to fight a modern war, on the one hand, while maintaining an aversion toward developing the industrial capitalism necessary to win that war, on the other. The only way that the South could survive this dilemma, without subsidizing the rise of a capitalistic class or creating a bureaucratic elite, was to institute a policy of state socialism carried out by the army. In this way the Southern experience, states Luraghi, foreshadowed that of China, and allowed the South to progress along the path of modernization without embracing alternatives for which it had immense distaste.

This, then, is the outline of one of the newest of historical controversies. Traditional interpretations emphasize that the South could have won, while revisionists believe that the Confederate government performed miracles enough by holding out as long as it did. Given the polarity of these two views, it is difficult for us to definitively take one side or the other in this argument. However, there is some common ground between these two schools of thought; and this agreement focuses on the excruciating choice facing the South. To fight for the old cherished principles of states' rights, slavery, and cotton meant losing the War. To industrialize, centralize, and nationalize meant losing the future. As historian Frank Vandiver has aptly concluded: "Southerners tried to slip the choice, to fight both ways, and lost both the war and the future. But they saved a legend."[12]

SELECTED BIBLIOGRAPHY

1. Catton, Bruce. *The Centennial History of the Civil War*   (three volumes). Garden City, N.Y.: Doubleday and Co. 1961–1965.
2. Donald, David, ed. *Why the North Won the Civil War*. New York: Macmillan Co. 1963.
3. Foner, Eric. *Politics and Ideology in the Age of the Civil War*. New York: Oxford University Press. 1980.
4. Fredrickson, George M. ed. *A Nation Divided: Problems and Issues of the Civil War and Reconstruction*. Minneapolis: Burgess Publishing Co. 1975.
5. Hattaway, Herman and Archer Jones. *How the North Won: A Military History of the Civil War*. Urbana: University of Illinois Press. 1983.
6. Luraghi, Raimondo. *The Rise and Fall of the Plantation South*. New York: Franklin Watts. 1978.
7. McPherson, James. *Ordeal by Fire: The Civil War and Reconstruction*. New York: Alfred A. Knopf. 1982.
8. Parish, Peter J. *The American Civil War*. New York: Holmes and Meier Publishers. 1975.
9. Potter, David M. *Division and the Stresses of Reunion, 1845–1876*. Glenview, Ill.: Scott, Foresman and Co. 1973.
10. Roland, C. P. *The Confederacy*. Chicago: University of Chicago Press. 1960.
11. Thomas, E. M. *The Confederacy as a Revolutionary Experience*. Englewood Cliffs, N. J.: Prentice-Hall Inc. 1971.
12. Vandiver, Frank E. *Their Tattered Flags: The Epic of the Confederacy*. New York: Harper and Row. 1970.

Why Is Reconstruction a Revisionist Battleground?

The era of Reconstruction is probably the most controversial of all periods studied in American history. Whereas the Civil War is popularly characterized in terms of heroes, ideals and greatness, the age which followed it is portrayed as villanous, corrupt and venal. With almost virtual unanimity American historians today see Reconstruction as an age of failure. There have been two main schools of interpretive thought regarding Reconstruction: the traditionalists and the revisionists. An examination of the basic premises of each school will, in part, explain why the era has been cast so negatively.

The traditional interpretation of Reconstruction evokes images of bitterness, partisanship and vengeance.[1,5,6] In a period where reconciliation was needed to heal the wounds of war and a mood of harmony was needed between the newly-reunited sections of the nation, narrow political concerns instead won the day and hatreds were begun that were to last for generations. At first, according to the traditional version, it seemed as if the transition from war to peace would be made smoothly and gently. Abraham Lincoln, in his infinite wisdom, was moving to enact a just and fair program of reunification. Though thwarted in many instances by a group of revenge-seeking Northern Congressmen, dubbed the Radical Republicans, Lincoln nonetheless seemed on the verge of implementing a compassionate program, best epitomized by his own words: "With malice toward none and charity for all."

With Lincoln's tragic death, however, a second chapter of the traditional interpretation began. In this chapter, the figure of President Andrew Johnson came to the fore. It was Johnson, during the Congressional recess of 1865, who put Lincoln's mild plan for reunion into operation, a plan which proved to be a striking success. Southerners were quickly brought back into the Union and showed their willingness to let bygones be bygones by organizing efficient local governments and dealing fairly with the newly-freed black slaves.

Chapter three opened with the Radical Republican attack upon Johnson's supposedly reasonable implementation of Lincoln's program. Motivated by hatred, revenge and the prospect of political power and economic profit, these Radicals launched a vicious assault on Johnson's reconstructed Southern governments. More disastrously, they refused to seat the newly-elected Southern Representatives and Senators, moved to impeach Johnson himself, and took the Reconstruction process into their own hands.

Andrew Johnson had the unenviable task of succeeding the martyred Lincoln. The following is a stanza from "O Captain! My Captain!", Walt Whitman's tribute to the fallen Lincoln.

O Captain! my Captain! our fearful trip is done,
The ship has weather'd every rack, the prize
    we sought is won,
The port is near, the bells I hear, the people all
    exulting,
While follow eyes the steady keel, the vessel
    grim and daring;
But O heart! heart! heart!
    O the bleeding drops of red,
        Where on the deck my Captain lies,
            Fallen cold and dead.

The traditionalists believe that the Radical program was characterized by one mistake after another. The South was put under military rule for ten years. Innocent and loyal white Southern voters were disfranchised when a stiff and unfair ("iron-clad") oath of allegiance was required of them. Illiterate blacks were prematurely given a disproportionate share of the political power and came to dominate Southern politics with the help of unscrupulous Northern adventurers, the "carpetbaggers," and Southern turncoats, the "scalawags." Not surprisingly, the result of such rule was corruption and misspent monies running into the millions of dollars.

A fourth chapter dealt with the eventual "redemption" of the Southern states. Decent Southern whites, their patience exhausted by the orgy of misgovernment and violence and stimulated by a feeling of desperation, drove the blacks, the carpetbaggers, and the scalawags from office. Through the organization of vigilante groups like the Ku Klux Klan and motivated by a need for self-defense, the South was finally returned to a condition of "home rule." In 1877, President Rutherford B. Hayes formally completed an agreement with white conservative Southern leaders whereby federal troops were withdrawn from the South and these Southern leaders finally were given control over their own destinies.

Thus, the traditional interpretation portrays the era of Reconstruction as an "Age of Hate." The natural political legacy of this hatred was a solidly one-party South for generations. The social legacy was embittered racial relations between blacks and whites. And the economic legacy was decades of impoverishment for millions of Southerners.

This traditional version of the Reconstruction story dominated American historiography until the late 1920s. Then a movement toward "revision" began which has continued into our own time and has, in fact, come to dominate today's historical scene. Completely revised is the old view of a courageous Andrew Johnson loyally implementing Lincoln's plan. Instead, revisionists reveal an inept politician who bungled terribly at crucial moments in the Reconstruction process. Highlighted, too, by revisionists is Southern white obstructionism. Encouraged by Andrew Johnson, Southern whites enacted "black codes" immediately after the War as a means of re-enslaving blacks. In another show of stubborness they also sent to Congress, for the 1865 session, former Confederate military and political heroes as their representatives. It was only after this show of defiance that the Radical Republicans moved to take control of the political levers of power.

Revisionists also point to numerous myths in the old version of the story. The first myth deals with the length of time that Reconstruction lasted. The traditional view describes the period of Radical domination as lasting from 1867–77, but in actuality the length of time varied from state to state. Two Confederate states, Tennessee and Virginia, never experienced true Radical governments at all. As for the rest, at varying times each of them saw control return to conservative white Southern forces, with only three states having Radical control lasting the full ten years.

The second myth involves the idea of military rule. Never was the South put under a harsh brand of military rule. One needs only to compare the treatment of the South after the Civil War with comparable instances in world history to see how leniently the South was treated. Not one political prisoner was ever executed. Jefferson Davis was kept in prison for only two years and then set free. Robert E. Lee, the Confederacy's military chief, was never imprisoned or mistreated. Presidents Lincoln and Johnson during the first year of peace spent most of their time dealing with matters of amnesty and pardon. All in all, no more than 20,000 troops were ever stationed throughout the South, with only two garrisons having more than 500 soldiers.

The third myth is that of white disfranchisement. The statistics here are quite revealing. In the worst phase of disfranchisement, when delegates for the postwar constitutional conventions were chosen, and in the ensuing election to choose the first postwar representatives, it is estimated that 150,000 out of approximately 630,000 eligible white Southerners were disbarred from or chose not to take the required oath of allegiance. Those who did take the oath were duly registered and voted. Thereafter, the nature of the franchise was left to the Southern states themselves and in the following elections eight of the eleven Confederate states placed no legal obstacles whatever in the way of white registration.

The fourth myth is that of black domination. At the height of black influence, no black held the position of governor in any state; only one black was a member of a Southern state supreme court; and, excepting Louisiana and South Carolina,* blacks were always a minority in either the state legislatures or in the constitutional conventions. Further, there were very few black Congressmen. Blacks usually held local positions when they held office.**

Finally, we come to the myth of corruption. It must be admitted here that there were misspent monies in the Radical governments. It has been estimated that the six Radical governments embezzled or absconded approximately half a million dollars each. But the important fact about this statistic is to remember the context of the times. The post-Civil War decades were characterized by corruption throughout the U.S. The three million misspent dollars attributed to the Radical governments should be balanced against the 100 million that Boss Tweed allegedly swindled from the New York public treasury during this same period. Further, the Radical malfeasance should be balanced against the general mood of private greed at the expense of public good which occurred at this time and which prompted the historian Vernon L. Parrington to label this era as the "Great Barbecue" in American history.

In sum, the old literature had nothing good to say about Radical Reconstruction. The new literature, on the other hand, revises the numerous myths and also points out that there was some progress, particularly in the areas of education and social reform. For instance, the first public educational system in the South was established by the Radical governments. Secondly, tremendous progress was made in the area of prison reform, in the treatment of the mentally disabled, and in similar such areas of social concern. Finally, the newly-written Southern state constitutions remained solid examples of achievement, as did the two amendments, the Fourteenth and Fifteenth, which Radical initiative added to the American Constitution.

A logical question appears at this point: if the traditional view of Reconstruction was so flawed, why did it come to so dominate American historiography? One can understand why Southerners obdurately held to the traditional view, but why did Northerners also accept the many myths and misperceptions? To answer this puzzling query, it is important to remember that between 1880 and 1930, American cities, especially in the North, witnessed a tremendous immigration from foreign lands. Northern whites, basically of Western European stock, watched

---

*Louisiana and South Carolina stand out as exceptions because both had large and old cities, New Orleans and Charleston, where a great number of free blacks who had some education and experience outside slavery resided in the antebellum years.

**The reason why the extent of black influence was to be so greatly exaggerated by white Southerners was their belief that blacks were not yet prepared to have the vote, let alone to hold political office. However, one must remember that thousands of Southern whites were illiterate, yet still enjoyed political privileges. But perhaps the best refutation of the anti-vote argument was presented by Reconstruction Congressman George W. Julian: "By no means would I disparage education, and especially political training; but the ballot is itself a schoolmaster. If you expect a man to use it well you must place it in his hands, and let him learn to cast it by trial. . . . If you wish to teach the ignorant man, black or white, how to vote, you must grant him the *right* (Julian's emphasis) to vote as the first step in his education."

with fear the "intrusion" of millions of Eastern and Southern Europeans and other "undesirables" into their cities. They especially feared the negative effects on American society and American democracy that this rapid influx might bring. In the eyes of Northern whites, these "illiterate" foreigners threatened to pervert America's unique destiny. Subconsciously, establishment Northerners, particularly scholars and historians, found themselves in sympathy with antebellum Southern white prejudices toward blacks and other "outsiders." Northern academe, therefore, accepted and developed a historical interpretation of the Civil War and Reconstruction which concurrently resolved the prejudices they were experiencing. In essence, the "traditional" historical interpretation of Reconstruction rationalized for these scholars nativistic prejudices which would normally have been proscribed. Later, because of World War I, these prejudices and fears were further stirred. For World War I not only stimulated an intense feeling of patriotism on the part of Americans, but it also produced the tendency to define a true patriot as an "older stock" American, thereby excluding "newer immigrants" from Southern and Eastern Europe. The result was that the 1920s saw the solidification of the traditional interpretation of Reconstruction, support for the movement for immigration restriction, and the resurgence of the Ku Klux Klan in the South and its spread into the North.

In conclusion, one can see from the perspective of modern times that there was not really anything so very radical about Radical Reconstruction. Once all the myths are recognized, we see that Northern and Southern whites were very quick to abandon their moral values and social concerns (particularly regarding the future equality of black people in American society) in order to get back to the business of getting ahead in everyday life.*

Reconstruction, however, remains a story of failure. Even recognizing the myths, there is unanimity that the age was one of missed opportunities, and one of dashed expectations. The question remains why? Was it because the politically expert Lincoln was removed and the politically inexperienced Johnson became President? Was it because of the studied intransigence of Southern whites? Was it because of the enervating effects of a national belief in white superiority? Was it because of the inherent weaknesses of a federal system of government? Or was it a failure to adjust hallowed economic beliefs to the poignant reality that newly-freed blacks needed preferential treatment? These are the questions that remain to be answered regarding the most tragic of eras in the American past. It is not too much to expect that many of these issues will be resolved in the near future now that so many myths have been cleared away.

*To understand how truly "conservative" Reconstruction was, one must remember that the really radical idea of the time, and the most dynamic, was rejected as out of hand: Thaddeus Stevens's proposal that each freed black family be provided forty acres and a mule. Instead, black people were freed without any economic basis upon which to sustain their freedom. American politicians did not recognize the need for a full governmental commitment to the plight of black people. Though Congress, in March 1865, did create the Bureau of Refugees, Freedmen, and Abandoned Lands to aid emancipated slaves, its efforts to ease the worst burdens of Southern blacks were temporary, inadequate and often grudging. American politicians did not recognize the need for sustained preferential treatment so that black people could gain a solid economic foundation upon which to build later civil and social rights. In the end, the only preferential treatment that was given was in the form of charity or philanthropy, a slender need in the face of American racial prejudice.

SELECTED BIBLIOGRAPHY

1. Bowers, Claude G. *The Tragic Era: The Revolution after Lincoln.* Cambridge, Mass.: The Riverside Press. 1929.
2. Brock, W. R. *An American Crisis: Congress and Reconstruction.* New York: Harper and Row. 1963.
3. Castel, Albert. *The Presidency of Andrew Johnson.* Lawrence: Regents Press of Kansas. 1979.
4. Donald, David. *The Politics of Reconstruction.* Baton Rouge, La.: University of Louisiana Press. 1965.
5. Dunning, William A. *Reconstruction: Political and Economic, 1865-1877.* New York: Harper and Brothers. 1907.
6. Fleming, Walter L. *The Sequel of Appomattox.* New Haven: Yale University Press. 1919.
7. Foner, Eric. *Nothing But Freedom: Emancipation and its Legacy.* Baton Rouge: Louisiana State University Press. 1983.
8. _____. *Reconstruction: America's Unfinished Revolution, 1863–1877.* New York: Harper and Row. 1988.
9. Franklin, John Hope. *Reconstruction: After the Civil War.* Chicago: University of Chicago Press. 1961.
10. Gillette, William. *Retreat from Reconstruction, 1869–1879.* Baton Rouge: Louisiana State University Press. 1980.
11. Patrick, Rembert W. *Reconstruction of the Nation.* New York: Oxford University Press. 1967.
12. Stampp, Kenneth M. *The Era of Reconstruction.* New York: Alfred A. Knopf. 1965.

What Is the Significance of the Frontier in American History?

On a hot July day in 1893, a young Wisconsin historian delivered a paper to members of the American Historical Association, gathered at the Chicago World's Fair, entitled: "The Significance of the Frontier in American History." While the "Darling of the Nile," Little Egypt, was serving as the main attraction to scores of visitors, Frederick Jackson Turner, then only thirty-one years old, was challenging his contemporaries in the historical profession as regards their predominant theories about American history.[6]

Specifically, Turner was reacting against the "germ theory" of American history popularized by his own professor, Herbert Baxter Adams. According to Adams, the seeds of American democracy could be traced back to the forests of medieval Germany. It was there that Teutonic tribes harbored democratic ideals until they were carried to Great Britain and developed, finally to be transmitted to America. Wherever there was Anglo-Saxon stock, Adams argued, the seeds of democracy were present and only needed to be nurtured to grow.

Turner countered the germ theory by pointing out that the roles of free land and the environment were more significant than the European heritage or the Teutonic ideals in explaining the American past. For Turner, the frontier, the West, was the key determinant in understanding the national character of Americans. The existence of the frontier, he argued, created an arena wherein unique American characteristics were developed. The wilderness, the savageness of the West, constantly forced Americans to reevaluate, to readjust, and to reinterpret their ways of living and their cultural traditions. These adjustments occurred over and over again as people moved farther and farther west. When someone completely "European" in his culture landed upon America's shores, what would emerge after a period of encounter with "the frontier" was someone who had learned to change and adjust; a new person, an American.

Turner listed a number of prominent effects of the frontier experience. First of all, the frontier promoted the development of a certain sort of "democracy." This occurred because the availability of land worked against the entrenchment and perpetuation of aristocratic distinctions. The West offered a seeming equality of opportunity, and the rigorous life which it required promoted an equality of respect among those who lived there.

Along the same line, the frontier promoted individualism. Self-reliance was at a premium in the West, and was reinforced by an abundance of natural resources. The frontier freed a person from the strictures of social controls; in fact, the American's tendency was to become anti-social. Politically, such individualistic feelings would encourage the development of the American version of "democracy."

Turner further argued that the West, by stimulating mobility among Americans, also increased nationalistic feelings. The opportunities for movement, and movement itself, worked to destroy feelings of localism. This unsettling of the population, plus the vast potential for internal trade offered by the West, worked irresistibly to promote nationalism.

In addition, Turner introduced the "safety-valve" concept. This is the idea that the West served as a harmless outlet for many of the discontented and unsuccessful in the cities. Because of the existence of the West, the argument went, America always offered an opportunity for its urban poor, or at least the most enterprising and ambitious among them, to have a second chance at success. Hence, America never fully developed the class resentments characteristic of Europe, nor did any strong labor or socialist party develop to complicate the political scene.

Finally, Turner argued that the West stimulated the development of certain intellectual or behavioral patterns in the American personality. As Turner himself put it in his eloquent prose:

> That coarseness and strength combined with acuteness and inquisitiveness; that practical, inventive turn of mind, quick to find expedients; that masterful grasp of material things, lacking in the artistic but powerful to effect great ends; . . . that dominant individualism, working for good and for evil, and withal that buoyancy and exuberance which comes with freedom—these are traits of the frontier. . . .[6]

It was not long before Turner's hypothesis replaced the germ theory as the key causal explanation of American development. Soon, however, it was Turner's time to come under attack. The years between 1920 and 1940 saw the highpoint of this criticism. Those years of rapid modernization, urbanization, and then depression, encouraged more elaborate economic interpretations of the past. For that generation of historians, Turner's frontier hypothesis seemed colossally oversimplified.

Some of the new studies focused upon the oversimplifications and the overstatements inherent in Turner's theory. Turner's tendency to make the grand generalization, without including supportive facts, was criticized. Further, critics noted that Turner's use of certain terms was ill-defined: e.g., he used the terms "West" and "frontier" interchangeably, causing imprecision in meaning and expression.

Many historians especially attacked the idea that the frontier was the main source for "American democracy." A rigorous comparison was made between the constitutions of western states and those of eastern states. It was found that the western states were basically imitative of the law and institutions already established in the east. In some cases, eastern constitutions were more "democratic" than western ones.

Further, critics accused Turner of ignoring the great "democratic" philosophers and jurists of the past. What about the immense contributions of men like Locke and Hobbes, Montesquieu and Milton, Coke and Blackstone, and a host of others, critics asked? Indeed, what about the contributions of the ancient Greeks and the republicans of ancient Rome? As one historian remarked, Turner placed too much emphasis on real estate, and not enough on state of mind.

Closer study, Turner's critics argued, also showed that the safety-valve concept was invalid. Costs were prohibitive for the poorest in the cities to ever make the trek out West. Though land in the West was often cheap, it was never free, and the most unsuccessful of the urban proletariat were rarely able to emigrate. In fact, just the opposite occurred. The cities served as a safety-valve for poverty and failure in rural areas. For every man or woman who migrated from the city to the country, there were twenty that moved the other way, from the country to the city.

These, then, are the pro's and con's of Turner's famous frontier hypothesis. Quite obviously both sides of the argument have merit, so where does one draw the line in this matter? The following is the approach that I have used to clarify the issue.

First, one must recognize that geography and environment act less as a *creator* of cultural behavior than as a *selection* process upon that behavior. In other words, geography sets certain limits to human behavior, but it does not determine which alternatives within those limits will be pursued. Land is passive; it is people who are active. For instance, compare the German immigrants in Colonial America with the English. Both peoples settled in Pennsylvania, Maryland, and Virginia, but their farming methods, crops, and labor systems differed markedly. The Germans preferred the clay loams in heavily forested areas, while the English chose the light, sandy soils of the uplands. The English girdled the trees, and farmed by merely scratching the soil amidst the stumps, while the Germans cleared the land thoroughly and plowed deeply. The English allowed their livestock to roam freely, but the more careful Germans built their barns with precision and enclosed their animals. Finally, the English took readily to tobacco farming and avidly became slaveholders, whereas the Germans were reluctant slaveholders, and more often stuck to farming the familiar wheat.

As this example shows, the free land offered many opportunities, but the way those opportunities would be developed depended on the cultural attitudes, and the technology, that men and women brought with them. It was to this extent that the frontier had a significance in American history; it *conditioned* the decisions that were to be made, but it did not *determine* them.

Recent scholarship, however, may force historians to discard the Turnerian model altogether. New work in social history, environmental history, urban history, women's history and Indian history is displaying how simplistic, even how ethnocentric, sexist, and racist the Turner approach really is. The heroes in the Turner story were English-speaking white men. The setting was agrarian; the story was the development of democracy in the relatively well-watered Midwest. Invisible in this approach, however, were crucial actors on the Western stage: Indians, Hispanics, French Canadians, Asians and women. Also invisible were activities in the areas of mining, urban development, commerce, finance, railroad building, and territorial government. Neglected, to, were the desert and mountain arenas.

Patricia Nelson Limerick's *The Legacy of Conquest: The Unbroken Past of the American West* has attempted to synthesize this modern research into a new model, and she currently has the historical profession applauding. Limerick's thesis is well-stated in her title. Looking at the West as a *place* ("the West in this book will generally mean the present-day states of California, Oregon, Washington, Idaho, Utah, Nevada, Arizona, New Mexico, Colorado, Kansas, Nebraska, Oklahoma, Texas, Montana, Wyoming, North Dakota, and South Dakota and, more changeably, Iowa, Missouri, Arkansas, and Louisiana"), rather than a *process* (as did Turner), Limerick sees "conquest" as the unifying theme of Western history, and she sees it as a conquest that has created far more problems than solutions, a conquest with a legacy of persisting challenges. "Conquest" is straight-forwardly defined by Limerick as "a contest of property and profit accompanied by a contest for cultural dominance." With this definition Limerick emphasizes the "boom-and-bust" nature of Western development, with its few winners and many losers.[3]

She also underscores the mining experience as most reflective of the manner of conquest in the West: "Mining set a mood that has never disappeared from the West: the attitude of extractive industry—get in, get rich, get out."[3] One sees that mood in the reoccurring "rushes" in Western history whether in farming, ranching, oil, synfuels, or high tech. It is a myth, argues Limerick, that the Western story was one of freedom, opportunity, abundance, and success. The reality was conflict, unintended consequences, and complexities. Further, Turner was wrong to state that the frontier was closed in 1890. Such a date omits too much influential twentieth-century history and omits too many significant people.

For Limerick, then, there is a moral burden for the West that is comparable to that of slavery in the South—that is, the grave injustice that an invading nation did to both native peoples and to the environment. And like most conquest the rewards have begun to unravel, especially in the areas of environmental deterioration, and in the cultural resurgence of those minorities once thought to be defeated, i.e. Indians and Hispanics.

Limerick has truly written an exciting book and in the face of critical reviews, she has emphasized that she still stands by "the four reasons" that led her to attempt this synthesis:

1) My mother and father had raised me to find it impolite, indeed, intolerable to exclude people from conversations in which they deserved to join. . . . And that pattern of thought, structured right into the word "frontier," meant in practice that "frontier" was inevitably an Anglo-centered concept, pushing Indian people, Hispanic people, and Asian people to the periphery. Turnerian history, or frontier history, either excluded minority people, or pushed them to the edge of significance, and that was, according to my parents' rules of manners, intolerable. It was, moreover, inaccurate—flattening and distorting the complexity of the American West. . . .

2) I was made equally uncomfortable by the common notion that a Great Divide separated the nineteenth-century West and the twentieth-century West. . . .

3) I wanted to narrow the widening gap between "sophisticated, scholarly history" and "readable, simplified, popular history." If you cannot express your findings in terms that an intelligent freshman can understand, I have long felt, then you haven't yet figured out those findings. . . .

4) I wanted to make mainstream American historians stop declaring western American history to be a dead or dying field. . . .[9]

For some historians, Limerick's arguments, in comparison with the optimism and buoyancy of Turner's are disillusioning. As Donald Worster has pointed out: "The West . . . was always supposed to be the primary scene of our national success; like General Motors or Walt Disney, it was supposed to make us proud. To turn that supposition completely upside down, to convince serious readers that the West has been a failure too, and one from which we can learn profound insights about ourselves, is a very large order."[9] Limerick has a ready answer for this lament: "I don't think I am a glum or disillusioned person, and I don't think this is a glum or disillusioned book. I think it is realistic, and whatever illusions it destroys, were illusions we did nto need anyway."[9]

Whether or not Limerick's work will come to be as seminal as Turner's is open to debate. But her imagination, literary skill and daring are now being hailed by most historians.

SELECTED BIBLIOGRAPHY

1. Billington, Ray A. *America's Frontier Heritage*. New York: Holt, Rinehart and Winston. 1966.
2. _____, ed. *The Frontier Thesis: Valid Interpretation of American History?* New York: Holt, Rinehart and Winston. 1966.
3. Limerick, Patricia Nelson. *The Legacy of Conquest: The Unbroken Past of the American West*. New York and London: W. W. Norton and Co. 1987.
4. Smith, Henry Nash. *Virgin Land: The American West as Symbol and Myth*. Cambridge, Mass.: Harvard University Press. 1950.
5. Steffen, Jerome O. *Comparative Frontiers: A Proposal for Studying the American West*. Norman: University of Oklahoma Press. 1980.
6. Taylor, George Rogers, ed. *The Turner Thesis*. Lexington, Mass.: D.C. Heath and Co. 1972.
7. Turner, Frederick Jackson. *The Frontier in American History*. New York: Henry Holt and Co. 1921.
8. Webb, Walter Prescott. *The Great Frontier*. Cambridge, Mass.: Harvard University Press. 1952.
9. Worster, Donald, and Susan Armitage, Michael P. Malone, David J. Weber, and Patricia Nelson Limerick. "*The Legacy of Conquest* by Patricia Nelson Limerick: A Panel of Appraisal." *The Western Historical Quarterly*. Vol. 20, No. 3 (August 1989).

U.S. HISTORY SINCE 1877

☆

The fate of the country . . . does not depend on what kind of paper you drop into the ballot box once a year, but on what kind of man you drop from your chamber into the street every morning.

Henry David Thoreau

☆

How Did Southern Populists Respond to Industrial America?

It is naive to draw dramatic historical parallels between the economic, political and social dilemmas of one generation and those of another. Yet, now it seems auspicious for Americans to study the successes and failures of the Populist movement. For the Populists came face to face with many of the same criticial issues which now concern Americans: the nature of land ownership, the hierarchical nature of the nation's basic financial structure and the consuming threat that corporate centralization poses to our democratic heritage.

Populism is the label that has come to signify the agrarian revolt which reached its peak in America between 1892 and 1896. In the late nineteenth century, caught in the midst of a deflationary economic cycle and producing for a world market beyond their control, farmers felt that the grand old parties no longer tried to serve their best interests. Therefore, they slowly and painstakingly launched their own alternative party, program and crusade. This was especially true of the South where Populist activity was the most organized and the most sustained.

Populist protest by Southern farmers was primarily the result of exploitation and hard times. For instance, the monetary situation in the South after Reconstruction was desperate.

Massachusetts alone had five times as much national bank circulation as the entire South, while Bridgeport, Connecticut, had more than the states of Texas, Alabama, and North and South Carolina combined. The per capita figure for Rhode Island was $77.16; it was 13 cents for Arkansas. One hundred and twenty-three counties in the state of Georgia had no banking facilities of any kind.[3]

To cope with this the South became a "giant pawn shop."

Favored merchants, able to secure goods on consignment from Northern mercantile houses, "furnished" these goods to farmers, taking a "lien" on the farmer's crop as security. Across the South this merchant, with the carefully-marked ledger came to be known as "the furnishing man," or "the advancing man." To black farmers he was known as "the Man." For their services, these merchants charged interest rates which frequently ranged from 100–200 percent annually.

Once a farmer signed his first crop lien he was in bondage to his merchant until he paid up. With interest rates as high as they were, there was little chance for Southern farmers to pay up and get ahead. Further, most farmers were trapped into a single-crop economy and were not allowed to diversify. The "furnishing man," assured of some profits with cotton, would not chance extending credit to any farmer willing to experiment. Experimentation might bring a great success, but it also carried with it the possibility of complete failure.

Too much land, therefore, remained in cotton, and surplus production drove market prices down. The merchant remained secure, however, for the farmer, given depressed prices, became more and more dependent on him. In essence, the crop lien system for Southern black and white farmers was little more than slavery. Farmers were caught in a desperate cycle of "crop lien, furnish, cotton harvest, failure to pay out, and new crop lien."

In addition, American banking and corporate power struck hard against farmers. Wholesale houses, cotton buyers, grain elevator companies, railroads, land companies and livestock commission agencies lobbied for policies which were inimical to a farmer's prosperity. The powerful bankers' lobby serves as just one example of how this power worked. Due to banker pressure and orthodox financial arguments the U.S. returned to the gold standard in 1879. Though bankers marshalled a number of "moral" imperatives to support their case, there was really a more specific motive for their actions. A governmental decision to begin paying coin for its obligations would mean that, though the Civil War had been fought with fifty-cent dollars in the 1860s, the cost would be paid in one-hundred-cent dollars. The nation's taxpayers would pay the difference to the banking community holding the bonds. Farmers felt especially defrauded because this monetary policy also drove farm prices downward at the same time that interest rates climbed upward.

Because of such adverse conditions, farmers gradually organized and eventually the Populist party appeared with its chief aim to break out of this exploitative economic stranglehold. More specifically, Populists aimed to relieve their monetary burdens, and to increase the amount of credit available, especially at harvest time. Feeling no intimidation whatsoever in the face of financially orthodox arguments of "hard-money" bankers, they came up with an ingeniously dramatic and democratic alternative—the sub-treasury plan. In this plan federal warehouses were:

> to be erected in every county in the nation that annually yielded over $500,000 worth of agricultural produce. In these "sub-treasuries," farmers could store their crops to await higher prices before selling. They were to be permitted to borrow up to 80 per cent of the local market price upon storage and could sell their sub-treasury "certificates of deposit" at the prevailing market price at any time of the year. Farmers were to pay interest at the rate of 2 per cent per annum, plus small charges for grading, storage, and insurance.[3]

As the Populists expanded their crusade and aimed to create a national third party, other planks in their platform were added to attract the downtrodden throughout the nation: the creation of large-scale credit and commodity cooperatives, government ownership of the means of communication and transportation, prohibition of alien land ownership, free and unlimited coinage of silver, equitable taxation between classes, implementation of a fractional paper currency, direct election of Senators, legalization of the secret ballot, recognition of an eight-hour day for labor, and the imposition of strict frugality in the area of government spending.

This platform carried far-reaching ramifications for the whole of the American nation: agriculturally, monetarily and governmentally. But, in particular, it struck at the existing system of agricultural credit in the South and aimed to return to the crop-mortgaged farmer some direct control over the sale of his produce. It sought to alleviate the rock-bottom prices prevailing at harvest time. And it sought to replace the manipulative furnishing merchant with the Federal government. Only from the government, Populists believed, could they expect a fair deal and the prospect of real economic freedom. In many ways, the sub-treasury plan was a declaration of independence for poor black and white Southern farmers.

Nonetheless, in the end, Populists failed to achieve their third party goals. The obstacles to their success were just too extensive. First of all, there were cultural inhibitions about changing party affiliations. Ever since the Civil War, Americans voted Democratic or Republican depending on their sectional loyalties. Northerners tended to vote Republican as a sign of their continued Unionist patriotism. Southerners, in contrast, voted Democratic in defiance of what they considered to be past Republican wartime and Reconstruction injustices. It was almost insurmountable to break through this inherited cultural pattern and to vote for a third party.

Ethnic origins, language and religion were other important obstacles. Farmers and workers needed to cooperate if Populist objectives were to become triumphant. Yet, how could a Protestant agrarian organizer in the South or the Midwest relate to an Irish Catholic factory worker in Boston? Or, what, for instance, did the agrarian cooperative crusade mean to the Germans of Pennsylvania's cities?

The transcendent American tradition of white racism cast another forbidding shadow over the prospect of uniting black and white tenants, sharecroppers and small farmers into an enduring political force across the South. On the one hand, white farmers who joined the Populist party persistently attempted to rise above their prejudices by emphasizing the similar economic problems which faced all farmers, whether black or white. More often than not, however, this racial gap could not be bridged and important unity was lost. On the other hand, there were similar racial handicaps hindering the efforts of black farmers in their approach to whites. For black farmers, Populist attacks against the "vicious corporate monopoly" and against extensive economic injustice were secondary to more important concerns about racial injustice. Given the prejudice of white Southerners, from the black point of view, both the Populist party "leader" and the corporate "monopolist" were to be feared because of their common "whiteness" and their common belief that all blacks belonged to a lower caste in Southern society.

Therefore, because of these divisive problems, Populists were never able to displace either of the two major parties in voter loyalty. Yet, despite their failure to gain a national following, the Populist revolt was the most elaborate example of mass insurgency and the largest and most intense mass democratic movement in our national past. Not surprisingly, then, historians have been divided in their evaluation of the Populist legacy in American history.

Frederick Jackson Turner, famed for his argument that the American frontier was the key determinant of American character, offered the first major interpretation of the Populist movement. Predictably, Turner saw Populism as yet another progressive, liberal reform movement stimulated by America's frontier experience. For Turner, the "frontier" increased an American's faith in democracy because it offered more equality of opportunity than the more structured European societies and because it blurred traditional class and hereditary distinctions. Populism, from Turner's point of view, was just another manifestation of the effects of the frontier on American thinking.

A more critical interpretation of Populism began with the outbreak of World War II. Revisionist interpretations emerged which questioned the liberalism of the Populists and which argued that Populists were anti-democratic and also irrational. Revisionist historians saw a neo-Fascist and an authoritarian personality in the Populist makeup. Revisionists noted that Populist crusading was easily diverted into militancy in the Spanish-American War, and that Populist conspiratorial and simplistic thinking focused on the supposed banking machinations of London-based entrepreneurs, particularly Jews, as the basis of all their troubles.

The timing of this negative interpretation is understandable when one remembers that after World War II most American intellectuals had lost faith in the "common man." The common man had supposedly supported Hitler, and from the intellectual standpoint, was the main support behind Joseph McCarthy's anti-communist crusade. It was commonly believed that McCarthyism in the 1950s coincided with the old centers of Populism in the 1890s.

In actuality, the strength of Populism rested in the South, an area relatively unmoved by the McCarthyite hysteria. Recent studies have shown that the overwhelming majority of those who sent Joe McCarthy and his supporters to the Senate were economic conservatives and anti-progressive Republicans. Thus, the alleged ties between Populism and McCarthyism were unfounded.

Recent research, in sum, has brought to light previously unstudied materials and the cycle has come full circle; a more positive interpretation of Populism has returned. In fact, some historians argue that a careful study of Populism might serve as a curative to an ever-growing American phenomenon: public resignation in the face of growing corporate power.

Today, the values and sheer power of corporate America pinch in the horizons of millions of obsequious corporate employees, tower over every American legislature, determine the modes and style of mass communications and mass education, fashion American foreign policy around the globe, and shape the rules of the American political process itself.[3]

Such concerns set the Populists off on a rampage. Today they scarcely arouse a whimper. Now Americans seem more intimidated than did the Populists about questioning supposed economic orthodoxies and about asserting their rights for more democratic control of key governmental decision-making processes. Such is the current apathy that some historians believe that the twentieth century in America may come to be dubbed "the century of sophisticated deference."[3]

SELECTED BIBLIOGRAPHY

1. Argersinger, Peter H. *Populism and Politics: William Alfred Pepper and the People's Party.* Lexington, Ky.: University Press of Kentucky. 1974.
2. Brinkley, Alan. *Voices of Protest.* New York: Alfred A. Knopf. 1982. (Though Brinkley's book is a comparative biography of Huey Long and Father Charles Coughlin, with an emphasis on the years of the Great Depression, there is nonetheless much insightful commentary on how the protest of the 1930s differed from that of the Populists).
3. Goodwyn, Lawrence. *The Populist Moment.* New York: Oxford University Press. 1978.
4. Hahn, Steven. *The Roots of Southern Populism.* New York: Oxford University Press. 1983.
5. Hicks, John D. *The Populist Revolt.* Lincoln, Neb.: University of Nebraska Press. 1959.
6. Hofstadter, Richard C. *The Age of Reform.* New York: Alfred A. Knopf. 1955.
7. Nugent, Walter T. K. *The Tolerant Populists.* Chicago: University of Chicago Press. 1963.
8. Palmer, Bruce. *"Man over Money": The Southern Populist Critique of American Capitalism.* Chapel Hill: University of North Carolina Press. 1980.
9. Pollack, Norman. *The Populist Response to Industrial America.* Cambridge, Mass.: Harvard University Press. 1962.
10. Woodward, C. Vann. *Tom Watson: Agrarian Rebel.* New York: Oxford University Press. 1938.

Did Theodore Roosevelt Plot the Panama Revolution?

Public opinion in contemporary political controversies would often be substantially modified if the historical origins of the issues were more adequately known. A perfect example was the controversy and calumny surrounding the re-negotiation of the Panama Canal Treaty during President Jimmy Carter's administration. In this instance, the actions of the U.S. government, and particularly those of Theodore Roosevelt, are open to severe criticism and moral censure. Involved is the explicit accusation that Roosevelt openly plotted and instigated the Panamanian revolution after negotiations for the canal had broken down with the Colombian government. At that time Colombia controlled the territory that later became the independent state of Panama.

There is little debate about Roosevelt's attitude regarding the necessity of an interoceanic canal. He believed it to be an indispensable prerequisite for national security in a twentieth century world and an indispensable prerequisite if the U.S. were to realize its dreams of a global destiny and international greatness.

There was much debate, however, on the question of where the canal was to be built. Originally the majority of Americans who had studied the issue, including the President himself, believed that the most advantageous route was through Nicaragua. Though the overland distance at Panama was shorter and the crossing thereby faster, Nicaragua, being closer to the U.S., was the shorter and faster route when overall mileage was considered. Nicaragua had over 50 miles of navigable lake and perhaps 60 miles of navigable rivers which could be used, leaving only 50-odd miles of digging; not much different than Panama's 51.2 miles. In addition, Nicaragua was not known as a pesthole of cholera, dysentery, yellow fever, small pox and malaria as was Panama; Lake Nicaragua offered a bountiful supply of water at the summit of the canal; Nicaragua was more politically stable than Panama; and, finally, Nicaragua did not have a bankrupted French (New Panama Canal) Company whose financial interests would have to be purchased.

Thus, Panama might have been bypassed as an alternative had it not been for an incredible turn of events which remain bizarre and baffling to this day. The story begins with the lobbying efforts of two amazing adventurers: William Nelson Cromwell and Philippe Bunau-Varilla. Their aim was to prompt an American decision making Panama the preferred canal site and to unload the New Panama Canal Company's franchise on the American government.

Cromwell was a New York attorney representing both the New Panama Canal Company and American interests in the Panama Railroad line which stood along the path of the proposed

"The twentieth century looms before us big with the fate of many nations. If we stand idly by, if we seek merely swollen, slothful ease, and ignoble peace, if we shrink from the hard contests where men must win at hazard of their lives and at the risk of all they hold dear, then the bolder and stronger peoples will pass us by and will win for themselves the domination of the world. . . . Above all, let us shrink from no strife, moral or physical, within or without the nation, provided we are certain that the strife is justified; for it is only through strife, through hard and dangerous endeavor, that we shall ultimately win the goal of true national greatness." Theodore Roosevelt, Speech "In Praise of the Strenuous Life," April 10, 1899.

canal site. Through Cromwell a $60,000 contribution was made to the Republican campaign fund in 1900. This resulted in the deletion of a preferential statement for the Nicaraguan route from the Republican platform of that year. Cromwell also was responsible for persuading Republican political boss Mark Hanna and President Roosevelt to reconsider the Panamanian position.

Bunau-Varilla was a flamboyantly-imaginative French engineer, who had become involved in Panama because of his employment with Ferdinand de Lessups's original Panama Company before its bankruptcy. The intricacies of Bunau-Varilla's efforts, both in surreptitious intrigue and in speechmaking and pamphlet-writing, are too involved and complex to completely recount here. It should be noted, however, that he had access to all the key American political leaders of the time and he carried home his arguments with vigor, inspiration and conviction.

Cromwell and Bunau-Varilla were aided by two key developments. The first was the fact that technical engineering opinion swung in favor of the Panamanian route. Putting aside the problem of disease and political instability, most engineers argued on behalf of a Panamanian canal because it would be approximately 135 miles shorter, terminal to terminal; it would have fewer curves; the time in transit through the canal would be less than what Nicaragua required; fewer locks would be needed; Panama had better harbors and an already-constructed railroad; a Panama canal would cost less to run; and it posed no major engineering obstacles in its construction.

Nonetheless, a Nicaraguan canal, if undertaken, would not have been a failure either. Hence the importance of the second development—volcanic eruptions. Bunau-Varilla had earlier brought to public attention the danger of volcanoes along the Nicaraguan route. Like much of his propaganda, this was more the result of a fertile imagination than a serious concern on his part. Yet, during the Senate debate on the issue, Mount Pelée on the Caribbean island of Martinique exploded in late April 1902. On May 14, news came that Mount Momotombo in Nicaragua exploded. On May 20, Pelée exploded again, levelling the town of St. Pierre, and on the island of St. Vincent, just south of Martinique, still another volcano erupted.

Bunau-Varilla secured 90 Nicaraguan postage stamps portraying Mount Momotombo in eruption and sent one affixed to a sheet of paper to each U.S. Senator. On this sheet of paper he typed the words: "An official witness of the volcanic activity on the isthmus of Nicaragua." The Senate vote was taken on the afternoon of June 19. The vote was 42–34 in favor of Panama, i.e., the Hepburn bill and Spooner amendment.

Negotiations with Colombia now began in haste since the Hepburn bill and Spooner amendment stated that unless major progress could be made with Colombia in a "reasonable" period of time, the Nicaraguan site should again be given priority. Friction with Colombia immediately arose, however, over the question of sovereignty within the canal zone. The Hay-Herrán Treaty which the U.S. first submitted to the Colombian government for approval was rejected by the Colombian Senate because the U.S. would have perpetual control of the canal zone, because a system of mixed courts was to be instituted and because the monetary terms were not deemed satisfactory.

Colombians were further upset that French interests in the New Panama Canal Company were being sold to the U.S. without securing Colombian consent or some recognition of Colombian rights in the transfer. Therefore, the Colombian government decided to stall negotiations with the U.S. until October 1904. At that time the New Panama Canal Company's rights to build the canal would expire and the $40 million earmarked for Bunau-Varilla's and Cromwell's organization could go to Colombia.

For Roosevelt, October 1904 was too long a delay. Roosevelt had a presidential election to consider in 1904 and he was expecting the Panama achievement to be the high point in his Administration. Consequently, his reaction to the Colombian Senate's rejection of the Treaty on August 12, 1903, was vehement. Roosevelt had a number of alternatives before him. One was to improve the terms of the Treaty for the Colombians. Second, he could manipulate the Colombian-U.S. transit treaty of 1846 to American advantage. Third was the alternative of supporting a Panamanian revolution. Finally, Roosevelt had the option of turning to the Nicaraguan route. We now know that Panama's revolution and declaration of independence from Colombia resolved the issue.

The question remains: To what extent was Theodore Roosevelt involved in the plotting of this revolution? We have no direct evidence that Roosevelt was explicitly involved. But we do know that Roosevelt and Secretary of State John Hay did make it clear that the U.S. would look benignly on any revolution that might occur. Indeed, Hay had gone so far as to confide to Bunau-Varilla that American ships had been ordered "to sail towards the Pacific." Thus encouraged, Bunau-Varilla and Cromwell embarked on a series of intrigues and meetings with the Panamanian rebels that largely triggered their decision to revolt on November 3.

Helpful, too, was the arrival of the USS Nashville at the Panamanian harbor of Colón the day before the uprising began. The Nashville was under orders to "maintain free and uninterrupted transit" and to "prevent landing of any armed force." Essentially this insured against any Colombian reinforcement of its Panamanian garrison.*

After the revolution, Roosevelt hastily proclaimed *de facto* recognition of the Panamanian Republic and negotiations were promptly begun on a new canal treaty. Bunau-Varilla, as a reward for his part in the revolution, insisted that he be selected minister plenipotentiary of the Republic of Panama during the treaty negotiations. This was reluctantly agreed upon by the new Panamanian government, as Bunau-Varilla was a French citizen. In the end the treaty that Hay and Bunau-Varilla drew up was so favorable to the U.S. that the Panamanians were aghast. However, since Panama was fully dependent on U.S. aid for their independence, they could do nothing but ratify the treaty.

Perhaps embarrassed by the unabashed haste and arrogance that the U.S. displayed during the revolutionary events, in 1914, when the canal opened, President Woodrow Wilson sent to the Senate a treaty with Colombia. This treaty called for an expression of "sincere regrets" for "past actions" and an indemnity of $25 million. The treaty was defeated by angry Republicans, led by Henry Cabot Lodge, who believed that the bill was an unnecessary slur upon Roosevelt's honor. In 1921, these Republican Senators reversed their decision and agreed to pay the $25 million to Colombia, but they would not agree to include the expressed apology. The fact that oil was discovered in Colombia at this time was vigorously denied by all Senators concerned as being an influencing factor in their decision.

For us today, the question of Panama has another significance beyond the fact that U.S. actions were not above reproach. This involves the role of public opinion in foreign policy: Can public opinion ever make foreign policy or can it only support or oppose policy already made? In this regard, it should be recognized that many of the above-mentioned intrigues were made known to the public at the time by the *New York Times,* the *New York World,* and the *Washing-*

---

*I think it is worth adding at this point that Roosevelt's high-handedness was only an extreme instance of a general American attitude toward the countries of Central and South America. There were repeated examples in the late nineteenth and early twentieth centuries of U.S. military intervention and economic exploitation in Latin America, not to mention the political damage caused by the private adventurers the U.S. government sent around as "diplomats."

ton Star. All three newspapers passionately protested the Senate vote and the rejection of the Nicaraguan alternative. These newspaper reports were largely ignored by the general public, as Roosevelt sensed that they would be. Like so many influential politicians in the past, Roosevelt attained much of his political success because he served so faithfully as a medium of national hopes and aspirations.* The legacy of illwill that might be created with Colombia (or Panama) was not considered as significant to Americans of that time as their great concern about the benefits which would accrue to the U.S. due to the building of a canal. They had not learned then and many have not learned yet, that respect for the national ambitions of developing nations has about it a fuller measure of greatness than Roosevelt's "Big Stick" policies.

SELECTED BIBLIOGRAPHY

1. Chessman, G. Wallace. *Theodore Roosevelt and the Politics of Power.* Boston: Little, Brown and Company. 1969.
2. Harbaugh, William H. *The Life and Times of Theodore Roosevelt.* New York: Oxford University Press. 1975.
3. LaFeber, Walter. *The Panama Canal.* New York: Oxford University Press. 1978.
4. McCullough, David. *Mornings on Horseback.* New York: Simon and Schuster. 1981.
5. _____. *The Path Between the Seas.* New York: Simon and Schuster. 1977.
6. Morris, Edmund. *The Rise of Theodore Roosevelt.* New York: Coward, McCann and Geoghegan. 1979.
7. Mowry, George E. *Theodore Roosevelt and the Progressive Movement.* New York: Hill and Wang. 1946.
8. Pringle, Henry F. *Theodore Roosevelt: A Biography.* New York: Harcourt, Brace and Co. 1931.

*To add balance and perspective to Roosevelt's and Hay's behavior, it should be noted that Panama had a long history of intense nationalism. In fact, six times during the 53 years prior to the revolution of 1903, Panama had rebelled against Colombia. The latest revolt was in the fall of 1902 during a critical stage in the Colombian-U.S. canal negotiations. Four times–in 1861, 1862, 1885 and 1900–the Colombian government had requested American aid and intervention to restore order.

"It is always easy to make all philosophy point one particular moral and all history adorn one particular tale; but I may be forgiven the reminder that the best speculative philosophy sets forth the solidarity of the human race; that the highest moralists have taught that without the advance and improvement of the whole, no man can hope for any lasting improvement in his own moral or material individual condition; and that the subjective necessity for Social Settlements is therefore identical with that necessity, which urges us on toward social and individual salvation." Jane Addams, from the book, *Twenty Years at Hull House*, 1910.

How Progressive Were the Progressives?

The transition from one century to another is a dramatic moment. The event inspires one to contemplate what the future holds, while simultaneously evaluating what has gone before. The combination of two views, retrospective and prospective, invariably generates a unique amalgam of contrary emotions—excitement and anxiety. This was especially true of those Americans who stood at the divide of the nineteenth and twentieth centuries (1900–01).

On the one hand, there was excitement everywhere. New inventions and marvels were daily fare for the generation that grew up at this time and helped to imbue them with a sense of destiny and progress. News of the appearance of electric lights and trolleys, X-rays, wireless transmitters and automobiles, to name just a few, evoked a sense of achievement and pride. In addition, an American could look back upon a heroic age of achievement in government and economics. Bestowed by providence with the "luxuries" of isolation and rich natural resources, the American experiment seemed to fulfill the great Puritan statesman John Winthrop's prophecy that America was a "City upon a Hill" where the eyes of the world could look for leadership and guidance. For those who believed that American economic success was no accident, but rather the natural outcome of superior institutions and superior intellect, there was the "supporting" fact that the national wealth had almost doubled in the previous decade.

Nonetheless, there was also cause for concern. This generation of Americans looked with trepidation upon a developing urban-industrial colossus where, in 1900, the richest 2 percent of Americans owned 60 percent of the nation's wealth, where 1,664,000 industrial accidents went uncompensated, where an estimated ten million Americans were so poor that they were slowly starving to death, and where American industry moved toward greater consolidation and monopoly. On this last point, whereas in 1896 there were only 86 industrial combinations in America with a capitalization of less than $1.5 billion, by 1904 there were 318 "trusts" with a capitalization of over $7 billion. So encompassing was their power that it took only six such groups to control 95 percent of America's railway mileage. In the steel industry it took only one company, United States Steel, America's first billion-dollar corporation, to determine steel prices everywhere in the U.S. The power of such corporations dwarfed that of most cities and many states.

This new America belied the Jeffersonian belief that American greatness grew out of yeoman farmer virtues set in a rural and pastoral environment. Americans entering the twentieth century looked askance at the mechanization of production and distribution. They feared the new impersonality of social relations, the large corporations, and the tremendous centralization of power that this modernization brought with it. There was concern about the future strength and resilience of American character. There was fear that mass systems of communication would lead to uniformity of attitudes.

There was anxiety, too, over the future course of government. There had been significant corruption in the American political system in the recent past. American Presidents, since the Civil War, were not noted for their leadership qualities. Most had been content to administer rather than lead. Some led private lives which invited reproach.

Meanwhile, social problems accumulated as millions of new immigrants poured into America. Unplanned and disorganized, cities ballooned in size. There were sewage, health and sanitation problems crying for solution. Further, in the scramble of Americans to get ahead, little thought was given to those who could not keep up: the aged, the blind, the injured, the orphaned, the mentally and physically disabled, and the poor.

The popular response to this unique combination of optimism and pessimism was a typically American one—the Progressive movement. Ever since the 1870s, middle-class, city-dwelling Americans had worried about the forces of urbanization, industrialization, immigration and social disruption. Nothing much was done, however, until the depression of the 1890s, which brought these fears into sharper focus. By the turn of the century, with increasing prosperity, the time was ripe for reform. Middle class "progressives" banded together in a broad, diverse, reform effort and in a democratic quest to right the wrongs which plagued American society. Many progressives, however, turned to reform more out of fear that if nothing were done to remedy America's ills, perhaps more radical solutions, even "foreign ideologies," might become more attractive to discontented Americans. After all, labor union memberships had jumped from 800,000 in 1900, to over two million in 1904. The forces of socialism had grown from an estimated 21,000 voters in 1892, to almost one million in 1912.

Was corporate America, tending toward monopoly, perverting the future of U. S. democracy? If so, there must be anti-trust legislation, equitable taxation laws, and fair-practices acts to remedy the situation. Were political machines threatening national, state and local government? Then new laws (the initiative, the referendum, and the recall) aimed at returning power to the people, and thereby reinvigorating democracy, must be passed. Further, a people's mayor, governor or president must be elected to counter this oligarchic trend. Were workers and immigrants innocent victims of forces beyond their control? Then child labor laws, minimum wage acts, and accident insurance legislation must be considered.

This is the traditional story of the challenge and the response which characterized U. S. history from the end of the Spanish-American War in 1898 to America's entry into World War I in 1917. It is the story of a reform movement with a variety of goals, and a coalition of diverse groups. It is the story of a political movement of exuberance, optimism and pragmatism aimed at restoring government to the "people," abolishing special privileges, insuring economic opportunities for all, and creating a democratic and humane society based on egalitarian ideals and social compassion. The two Presidents associated with this quest for improvement and progress were Theodore Roosevelt and Woodrow Wilson. When the Progressives were finished, so the traditional account goes, America was left with the beginnings of social justice and social equity. Large industries were brought to heel and the overall governmental system was democratized by the passage of many innovative laws and the inclusion of constructive amendments to the Constitution, particularly the Sixteenth, Seventeenth and Nineteenth.

However, since World War II, historians have been challenging this traditional view of the Progressive Movement. Two schools of historical thought which are especially important for their insights and criticisms are the neo-Conservatives and the New Left. The neo-Conservatives disagree with the portrayal of these years in American history as a simple morality play between the forces of evil and the forces of good. American history at this time, they argue, is not correctly depicted when viewed as a struggle between the forces of democracy and the forces of aristocracy or as a battle between the special interests and the people. Neo-Conservatives see a basic homogeneity, a basic unity among Americans as regards the fundamentals of democracy. They insist that the debate that did occur between Americans of different political persuasions concerned means rather than ends.

As a result, the reputation of the Progressives has generally suffered in the writings of the neo-Conservatives. Progressives have been portrayed as amateurish in their actions and superficial, simplistic even, in their thinking. Neo-Conservatives have located and emphasized selfish and personal motivations behind so-called humanitarian and democratic impulses. Believing in the basic goodness of American society, neo-Conservatives do not praise the actions, the motivations, or the achievements of the Progressives.

At the opposite pole, the New Left is equally critical of Progessivism but for opposite reasons. For the historians of the New Left, Progressives were nothing more than the "handmaidens" of corporate enterprise; that is, they were sophisticated professionals who set the pattern for today's business-government relations and who were responsible for giving the current American corporate structure its form. In short, they believe that the Progressive movement was initiated by businessmen to aid businessmen and to effect federal regulation of society *for* the interests of business, rather than federal regulation *of* business on behalf of the public good. It was anything but a reform movement. It was the businessman's response to the modern threats of unstable markets, increasing competition and potentially radical and socialistic regulation by the government. Gabriel Kolko, representative of this critical approach, argues that Progressivism:

> was initially a movement for the political rationalization of business and industrial conditions, a movement that operated on the assumption that the general welfare of the community could be best served by satisfying the concrete needs of business. But the regulation itself was invariably controlled by leaders of the regulated industry, and directed toward ends they deemed acceptable or desirable. In part this came about because the regulatory movements were usually initiated by the dominant businesses to be regulated, but it also resulted from the nearly universal belief among political leaders in the basic justice of private property relationships as they essentially existed, a belief that set the ultimate limits on the leaders' possible actions.[8]

Because sharp divisions among historians still exist on the issue of Progressivism, a combination of these interpretations might be more valid, especially since Progressivism represented such a diverse coalition of interests. Progressives joined and formed a myriad of groups. They were men and women who were busy making a living and they were more than ready to lobby on behalf of their interests. In this way, especially, they were a precursor of modern America.

Some Progressives definitely fit into the neo-Conservative mold. They were amateurs who had not properly adjusted to the requisites of modern society. This group included many young, well-educated, Anglo-Saxon, old-stock New Englanders who looked backward to a bygone era. Their families had held significant local power in the past and they now faced status anxieties as they were displaced by powerful corporation lawyers, business executives, etc., in the decision - making process. They, therefore, longed to return to the cultural environment of the small, Protestant, New England community. These young men and women were uncertain, anxious and nostalgic. Reform was one way they gained meaning in their lives and one way in which they were able to strike back, in a subconscious way, against those who had displaced them. Possibly neo-Conservatives are right when they argue that these Progressives should have left things alone.

Aspects of the traditional approach are also correct. Many Progressives were motivated by humanitarian concerns and were originally disturbed by key problems in American society. These Progressives, forerunners of today's social workers, manned settlement houses to aid the poor and the disadvantaged in the ghettos. Jane Addams's Hull House in Chicago was the best example of what this group of Progressives was able to accomplish helping people in the slums of America's new sprawling metropolises.

New Left historians have a point when they see Progressives as businessmen who initiated reform for selfish purposes. There is no doubt that many reforms were supported by the wealthy and powerful in order to inhibit those who were on the rise and challenging the status quo.

Finally, there was another element of Progressivism characterized by a "new" middle class of professionals. This new middle class included public health officers, economists, engineers, statisticians, city planners, architects, corporation lawyers, and business executives. They saw the urgent need for a techno-industrial elite who could base decision-making on a scientific foundation. They saw a need for a centralized governing process and for professional administrators. Their creed called for standardization, planning, efficiency, and rationality. They were not characterized by either a fear or a hatred of corporate enterprise. These young men and women believed in themselves and in their abilities. They saw the potential of an America where big business and government worked in cooperation to eliminate destructive and senseless competition and disruptive business cycles. They saw immense possibilities in a business-government partnership where the "expert" would be granted paramount authority and where planning would serve as a substitute for haphazard development.

To conclude, the way one evaluates Progressivism is in part related to how one evaluates the current condition of America's power structure. For instance, if one believes that there is a unified power elite in America, with the mass of citizens having little input, then one is going to be critical of the Progressives. The Progressives would be held partly accountable for the growing enhancement of this power elite, and the decline of democracy. On the other hand, if one believes that there is not a single dominating elite, but rather a diversified and balanced plurality of elites or interest groups, with the mass of citizens having significant influence, then one is liable to view the Progressive movement with favor. Only with the passage of time and only with a greater perspective on the twentieth century can historians answer these questions with any type of assurance. Until then, we must be satisfied with a broad, inclusive approach to any evaluation of the essence and achievements of the Progressive movement.

SELECTED BIBLIOGRAPHY

1. Cherny, Robert W. *Populism, Progressivism and the Transformation of Nebraska Politics, 1885–1915.* Lincoln: University of Nebraska Press. 1981.
2. Ekirch, Jr., Arthur A. *Progressivism in America.* New York: Franklin Watts. 1974.
3. Goldman, Eric. *Rendezvous with Destiny.* New York: Alfred A. Knopf. 1952.
4. Gould, Lewis L. *Reform and Regulation: American Politics, 1900–1916.* New York: John Wiley and Sons. 1978.

5. Graham, Jr., Otis L. *The Great Campaigns*. Englewood Cliffs, N.J.: Prentice-Hall Inc. 1971.

6. Grantham, Dewey W. *Southern Progressivism: The Reconciliation of Progress and Tradition*. Knoxville: University of Tennessee Press. 1983.

7. Hofstadter, Richard C. *The Age of Reform*. New York: Alfred A. Knopf. 1955.

8. Kolko, Gabriel. *The Triumph of Conservatism*. New York: Macmillan Co. 1963.

9. Link, Arthur S. *Woodrow Wilson and the Progressive Era, 1910–1917*. New York: Harper and Row. 1954.

10. Mowry, George E. *The Era of Theodore Roosevelt and the Birth of Modern America, 1900–1912*. New York: Harper and Row. 1958.

11. Wiebe, Robert. *The Search for Order*. New York: Hill and Wang. 1967.

"The Great American Fraud"
A Look at Progressivism in Practice

One of the most dramatic muckraking campaigns in American history took place between October and January, 1905–06. *Collier's, The National Weekly's* attack on the notorious patent medicine racket was penned by Samuel Hopkins Adams in a four-month effort of exposure and denunciation. His title for this crusade reflected his central thesis, "The Great American Fraud." In the end, the clamor and agitation was to lead to the Food and Drug Act of 1906.

Medical quackery had been an intimate aspect of American social and intellectual history since Colonial times. Its study reveals penetrating insights about the anti-rational tendencies of the human psyche in its confrontation with disease and death, as well as revealing the problems of monitoring the buccaneering capitalist within the context of a democratic society.

Colonial America was fertile soil for the nostrum makers' wily artistry. Ancient lore in the form of Galen's simplistic theories continued to hold much sway. As Galen, the second-century Greek physician and writer on medicine, argued, there were four key bodily fluids, or "humours"—blood, phlegm, yellow bile and black bile. With these four kept in balance good health was assured.

Further, most believed that God or Nature had provided remedies for specific illnesses in the very same areas wherein the diseases flourished. As the New World was filled with exotic plants, a feverish search for remedies was bound to be rewarded.

The popular opinion also held that the worse a medicine tasted the better it was for you. Perhaps this was the rationale for three London hospitals recommending dried horses' hooves and wood lice. The Puritan divine, Cotton Mather, argued for the therapeutic properties of urine and horse dung.

One could always cover almost any ills with the popular "blunderbuss" approach—that is, a medicine with many substances. Especially prominent in this category was Venice Treacle, made up of sixty ingredients, one of which was the flesh of the viper.

Finally, the medical education of the average colonial man and woman was steeped in the premise that the answers to the puzzles of disease and death were more likely to be found in the occult and magical, rather than solved through human rationalism and intelligence. Why look to a doctor when a maiden aunt, a slave, or an old widow held the keys to the secrets of long life and good health.

The American Revolution brought about not only political independence, but medical independence. Instead of Colonial reliance on English patent medicines, Americans now began to develop their own veiled and mysterious formulas. Notable in this revolution of medical quackery was the emergence of a distinctive American genius. For at once the advertising became bolder, the naming of products more distinctive and dramatic.

The turning point of American patent medicine independence came with Dr. Elisha Perkins's small metal rods, called tractors. Each tractor was about three inches long; one was gold in color, the other was silver. Perkins's invention was the first patented medical device under the new Constitution, issued in 1796.

Perkins shrewdly catered to the new nation's mania with electricity. His tractors claimed to draw off the noxious electrical fluid that lay at the root of suffering, thereby curing local inflammations; pains in the head, face, teeth, breast, side, stomach, and back; rheumatism and other similar ailments. The retail price was $25.00. Highly exorbitant, but a bargain considering the good health that it promised!

To be fair, it must be admitted that patent medicine inventors were aided by the state of American medicine at this time. The most eminent physician in America, Dr. Benjamin Rush, offered what has been appropriately labeled as the "heroic" medication approach. Rush's solution was bleeding and tremendous doses of calomel. At times, Rush believed, it might be necessary to drain off as much as 80% of the body's blood. As for the large doses of calomel, they would often cause patients to lose their teeth, and even their jawbones.

Under these circumstances, an early nineteenth-century American might try Robertson's Infallible Worm and Destroying Lozenges. By the 1830s, the manufacturer of Robertson's Lozenges was making $25,000 a year.

As the Age of Jackson, or the Age of the Common Man, dawned in America, forces were to combine to launch the vendors of proprietary remedies toward a pinnacle of success.

First, there was the continued suspicion of too much booklearning. People took favorably to the idea that the farmer and the mechanic, the unschooled in general, had a practical wisdom that made them oftentimes more insightful, and more forthright, than the lettered elite. A New York doctor put it this way: "The people regard it among their vested interest to buy and swallow such physick as they in their sovereign will and pleasure shall determine; and in this free country, the democracy denounce all restrictions upon quackery as wicked monopolies for the benefit of physicians."[7]

Ironically, during this time of proclivity toward "nature's nobleman," and the "urbane savage," America was industrializing and urbanizing. This meant more pressure and less exercise. Indeed, there was a rise in the American mortality rate after 1815. No longer would the common man and woman be able to overcome their poor eating habits—salt-cured meats, fat-fried foods, few fresh fruits and vegetables—with a rural life characterized by clean air, sunshine, and vigorous physical labor. Besides, Americans ate too fast. One European traveler complained that our national slogan should be "gobble, gulp, and go." (Perhaps this slogan is still appropriate.)

Further, there was a great increase in the numbers of newspapers, due to the spread of education and the rise in literacy. The America of 1800 had twenty daily papers. By 1860, there were 400. More newspapers meant an expansion in the means for advertising.

When all these factors—growing population, popular belief in self-curing, wider reach in advertising, unabated disease and suffering—were added to the ludicrously laissez-faire patent and copyright policies of the time, patent medicine promoters were able to blaze a manufacturing trail, complete with psychological merchandizing techniques.

There was no more an inventive pioneer than William Swaim. According to his literature, Swaim's Panacea could cure cancer, scrofula, rheumatism, gout, hepatitis, the early stages of syphilis, and mercurial poisoning. Curious government chemists later analyzed the secret ingredients of Swaim's potion. They found sarsaparilla, oil of wintergreen and corrosive sublimate (the most rigorous medical form of mercury). And Swaim's Panacea was hailed to be an antidote to mercurial poisoning!

There was no end to the boldness of the claims of these quacks. They posed as doctors, they fabricated testimonials, they lied about ingredients, they created diseases and boasted cures. They were geniuses at frightening the unsuspecting into the medicinal habit, often creating dependencies on the alcohol or opium contained in their mixtures. Many nostrums contained poisonous ingredients.

Swaim and others like him played upon the average American's fascination with the remote (Wyncoop's Iceland Pectoral, Hart's Swedish Asthma Medicine); antiquity (Druid Ointment, Minerva Pill); religion (Jew David's Honey Coated Pills, Resurrection Pills); and the secrets of the American Indian (Modoc Oil, Seminole Cough Balsam).

Some of the results of this medical charlatanry were truly comical, as with Dr. Benjamin Brandreth and his Life–Addition Pills. Brandreth's pills were merely a laxative, but the genius lay in their promotion. In his advertising literature the first step was to glorify and elevate laxatives. The second step was to make indigestion and constipation the source of most disease. Between 1862 and 1883, Brandreth's annual average business surpassed $600,000.

The Civil War marked a final step in the rise of the patent medicine fakir. With the war came a great thirst for news from the fighting fronts. The size of daily papers grew and their circulations skyrocketed. The Sunday edition was born, as was the real beginning of magazine advertising.

Thus, the second half of the nineteenth century saw the heyday of the patent medicine mania. Advertising and promotional techniques of devilish cleverness abounded. Soon the American public was unwilling to try a new remedy unless a prolonged and strident campaign accompanied the product. In the 1880s, such a campaign cost $50,000. By 1900, it took about $250,000.

However, Henry T. Helmbold began his rise to fame and fortune simply by distributing pink-paged pamphlets in hotels and public toilets. The title was *The Patient's Guide, A Treatise on Disease of the Sexual Organs*. The opening lines of this extended essay were a model in scare–advertising. Could you perchance have caught a loathsome venereal disease due to "excesses in married life, early indiscretion, or self-abuse?"[7] The danger signals included "heaviness of the eyelids, black spots before the eyes, restlessness, great mobility, and the inability to contemplate disease without a feeling of horror."[7] Helmbold's cure—Buchu, supposedly found among the natives of South Africa—was taken by the likes of "Boss" William Tweed, Jay Gould, Jim Fisk, Commodore Vanderbilt, John Jacob Astor, and James Gordon Bennett.

But it was Doctor Hostetter's Celebrated Stomachic Bitters Tonic (4% herbal oils and vegetable bitters, 64% water, and 32% absolute alcohol) which apparently convinced Americans in the late nineteenth century that it was the perfect cure-all for the nation's maladies, for Hostetter left a fortune of $18,000,000 upon his death. Perhaps Carl Sandburg recognized the real reason for the Tonic's tremendous success: "Us kids heard that you could get drunk on one bottle of Hostetter's"[7]

Patent medicine proprietors could twist any of the scientific breakthroughs into an advantage for themselves. When the great research of Louis Pasteur and Robert Koch brought forth the germ theory of disease, William Radam was quick to capitalize with his Microbe Killer. As Radam was to put it to a gullible public: "A Microbe is a Microbe." Chemists found Radam's panacea to be 99.381% water, with the rest made up of traces of sulphuric and hydrochloric acids due to the manufacturing process. As Radam was to sheepishly admit later: "I killed nobody, and of course any man may cure another with water if he likes."[7]

The most flagrant of these patent medicine abuses were finally curtailed by the Food and Drug Act of 1906. After years of agitation by doctors and pharmacists, concerned government officials (especially Dr. Harvey Washington Wiley at the Department of Agriculture), women's groups, and muckraking journalists like Samuel Hopkins Adams, the opposition to reform was finally overcome.

Adams's role was especially significant. Though he was not the first to make an indictment of the patent medicine fraud, his crusade was the most extensive up to that time. The publicity alone, before his campaign, lasted for six months. Then in October 1905, began the hard-hitting and dedicated attack—ten articles in all.

Adams was the classic muckraker. He had a fetish for accuracy, he loved journalistic combat, and he possessed a zealous commitment toward improving the lot of humankind. As a *Collier's* colleague described Adams: "A character inherited from a line of insurgent theologians gave him firm conviction in his beliefs."[7] It is no wonder that his work was crowned with success.

Nevertheless, we can still turn on our television sets to see hosts of germs being devastated by innocuous syrups; stomach acids dissolving when confronted by a tiny tablet; actors impersonating doctors and recommending any number of remedies. The testimonial is still with us, in nauseating redundancy, as people rush forward to convince how such and such a product vanquished a fallen arch, rejuvenated a languid bust, or removed a hideous bag under the eye.

Have the patent medicine quacks just become more sophisticated? How many billions does the public spend in the nutrition game with foods and food supplements that are purportedly therapeutic in their effects? How many fake reducing remedies, cancer cures, and arthritis medicines still abound? How many medicine men still rush forward adjusting their masks in the wake of scientific breakthroughs?

One wonders, too, what values Americans possessed to allow such chicanery to go on for so long. Was it something in our national character that indulged such humbuggery? Was it our hostile attitude toward governmental intervention in social and economic issues? Was it a flaw in our national thinking, a flaw that allowed for a double standard of morality for private and for public conduct, for individuals and for corporations?

To a certain extent the answer to the last two questions is "yes." Two key factors in the Congressional opposition to food and drug legislation involved those who objected on constitutional grounds ("The Federal government was not created for the purpose of cutting your toe nails or corns," said one Georgian), and those who were personally interested in the perpetuation of the frauds (Patent medicine interests, organized under the name "The Proprietary Association of America," were a powerful lobbying force).

But perhaps the deeper reason for acquiescence in the face of medical quackery had less to do with traits peculiarly American, than with ones that were quintessentially human. Doctors have always been inherently handicapped in their competition with the quack. Doctors must often deal with complex, confusing diseases that require lengthy, expensive treatments, and that may result in much suffering and possible death. The quack is able to say that the problem is simple, the treatment speedy and cheap, and the cure painless and sure. Is it the same old story all over again?

Thanks to Samuel Hopkins Adams, and others like him, not quite!

SELECTED BIBLIOGRAPHY

1. Bailey, Thomas A. "Congressional Opposition to Pure Food Legislation, 1879–1906." *The American Journal of Sociology*. Vol. 36, No. 1 (July 1930).
2. Graham, Jr., Otis L. *The Great Campaigns*. Englewood Cliffs, N.J.: Prentice–Hall. 1971.
3. Hayes, L. T. and F. J. Ruff. "The Administration of the Federal Food and Drug Act." *Law and Contemporary Problems*. Vol. 1, No. 1 (December 1933).
4. Lamb, Ruth DeForest. *Chamber of Horrors*. New York: Farrar–Rhinehart. 1936.
5. Regier, C. C. "The Struggle for Federal Food and Drugs Legislation." *Law and Contemporary Problems, op. cit.*
6. Young, James Harvey. *The Medical Messiahs*. Princeton, N.J.: Princeton University Press. 1967.
7. _____. *The Toadstool Millionaires*. Princeton, N.J.: Princeton University Press. 1961.

"It is a fearful thing to lead this great peaceful people into war, into the most terrible and disastrous of all wars, civilization itself seeming to be in the balance. But the right is more precious than peace, and we shall fight for the things which we have always carried nearest our hearts,—for democracy, for the right of those who submit to authority to have a voice in their own Governments, for the rights and liberties of small nations, for a universal dominion of right by such a concert of free peoples as shall bring peace and safety to all nations and make the world itself at last free." Woodrow Wilson, War Message to Congress, April 2, 1917.

Was U.S. Entry into World War I a Question of Economics or National Security?

If one were to juxtapose a tally sheet of high costs versus low yields, American participation in World War I would seem to have been a grave error. On the one hand, the costs were 130,000 American lives lost in combat, 35,000 lives permanently disabled, 500,000 deaths in the winter after the War due to an influenza virus imported from the battlefield, and $46.5 billion in expenditures. Some of the results were twenty-five race riots in 1919, a stimulus to a prolonged period of private indulgence and social irresponsibility, and a decimation of the forces of reform for a decade. Was the defeat of Kaiser Wilhelm's Germany worth all of this? Americans would be considerably more sure if the same question were applied to Hitler's Germany a generation later. But as for the Germany of 1913, many scholars tend to agree with George Kennan:

> If one were offered the chance of having back again the Germany of 1913—a Germany run by conservative but relatively moderate people, no Nazis and no Communists, a vigorous Germany, united and unoccupied, full of energy and confidence, able to play a part again in the balancing-off of Russian power in Europe—well, there would be objections to it from many quarters, and it wouldn't make everybody happy; but in many ways it wouldn't sound so bad, in comparison with our problems of today. Now, think what this means. When you tally up the total score of the two wars, in terms of their ostensible objective, you find that if there has been any gain at all, it is pretty hard to discern.[5]

No wonder the passage of time has not cleared the air of controversy over whether the majority of Americans were correct in their decision to support President Woodrow Wilson's resolution to enter the war against Germany and its allies on April 6, 1917. Historians are divided into two fairly precise schools of thought on this issue. One school believes that Wilson was un-neutral in his policies from the start of the War, especially regarding economic matters, and they insist that the best interests of the U.S. were betrayed by entry into the conflict. The other major school of opinion argues that it was not merely economic interests, but a wide spectrum of factors which led America into the fight, and that foremost was Wilson's recognition that Germany was a proven threat to America's national security. As with earlier essays in this book, the aim here is to explain the opinions of both sides, thereby lending insights on an issue which still remains relevant.

The First World War broke out in August 1914 with the Central Powers (Germany, Austria-Hungary and the Ottoman Empire) aligned against the Allies (Great Britain, France, Russia and Serbia). As the armies of these antagonists began their titanic struggle upon the European continent, Great Britain simultaneously moved to blockade its enemies upon the seas. As significant American trade with Germany was impaired by Great Britain's decision, President Wilson's reaction was crucial. After some debate, Wilson decided that he would be preserving America's neutrality and national interests best by recognizing the British "quasi-blockade."

Historians who are critical of Wilson's policies argue that he was mistaken in this decision, for some of the British blockading practices were highly unorthodox. Examples were the British mining of the North Sea, as well as their practice of long-range blockading by cutting off whole segments of ocean. Indeed, the British never formally proclaimed a blockade, though, for the most part, they acted as if they did. The reason that the British did not officially proclaim a blockade was that it would have involved them in some difficult circumstances. International law specified very clearly that for a blockade to be legal, it had to be effective. That is, the blockading nation had to have enough ships stationed about the ports of its enemy so that all vessels could be kept out. This was a problem for the British for a couple of key reasons. First of all, most of the trade with Germany went through neutral ports, the closing of which would have both been a legal problem for the British and might have invited retaliation. Secondly, the British did not have enough ships to block all the possible neutral ports. Hence, instead of closing ports, the British adapted to the situation by placing their warships at sea, where they cruised about 15 to 20 miles apart, near enough so that most vessels would not be able to pass by without detection. This policy of long-range blockading was stretching the rules of international law to meet modern circumstances.

Further, the traditional rules of international law also stipulated that warships must stop and search neutral merchantmen at sea. The British violated this law, too. Since the size of modern ships prohibited a careful search at sea, the British forced neutral vessels into safe ports where more thorough searches could be conducted. The result of this policy often cost American businessmen dearly; their goods were liable to confiscation or to spoilage if they were perishable products. Besides, these shipowners were denied use of their ships for an indefinite period of time.

Wilson, his critics point out, could have and should have held the British accountable to the exact rules of international law. There were a number of opportunities as early as 1914, they argue, when Wilson had the leverage to exact from the British major concessions on their blockading practices. Further, while Wilson overlooked British infractions of technical points of international law, he denied equal latitude to the submarine blockade which the Germans subsequently proclaimed. If Wilson had been stricter with the British when they stretched the rules of blockade, so the argument goes, then the German government might have been more compromising in their later use of the submarine.

Critics are also upset with Wilson's failure to insist that American passengers be prohibited from travelling on belligerent ships going into the war zone. Wilson's outdated argument about the rights of American passenger travel did not accord with the realities of modern war, particularly as it pertained to the introduction of submarines. If Wilson had taken the opportunities available to ban passenger travel in the war zones, the national uproar over the death of Americans aboard the *Lusitania,* and other ships, would have been alleviated.

Critics are also incensed over Wilson's failure to be more discriminating in the way trade with the Allies was conducted. He should have foreseen that, without greater discrimination in America's trading policies, an economic situation would develop which was sure to entangle the U.S. with the future success of the Allies. Particularly blameworthy, critics argue, was Wilson's extension of American loans to the Allies and his acceptance of trade in munitions. The overall result of Wilson's actions was that the value of U.S. exports to the Allies increased from $825 million in 1914 to $3.2 billion in 1916. The value of munitions alone increased from $40 million to almost $1.3 billion in this same period. Further, by March 1917, American loans to the Allies totalled $2,262,827,544 while those to Germany totalled merely $27 million.

These statistics incline historians of this first school to argue that the U.S. government was drawn into the War by biased Presidential decisions based on economic considerations, and by the fact that President Wilson and most of his major advisers favored the Allies right from the beginning. They do not believe that the German government was a vital threat to American security and they argue that American interests would have been better served by full neutrality. As for the restraining influence of public opinion, they note how quickly moral consciences were silenced as burgeoning wartime trade with the Allies brought the nation out of its major recession of early 1914.

Historians who believe that Wilson was correct, even brilliant, in his pre-War diplomacy point out that the international situation was such that, regardless of what he had decided, Wilson could not have remained neutral in a technical sense. The economic entanglements which occurred because of the British blockade were inevitable. First of all, the British could claim numerous rights under international law that bound Americans to accept their position. For instance, the British could stop neutral vessels and confiscate all goods defined as contraband, items of war, going to their enemies. Further, the British could also seize what was called conditional contraband, or the goods clearly destined for the military forces of their enemies. The right to arm merchantmen had also long been recognized by international law. These rules, then, put Wilson in a corner where he was obligated to side with the British. In addition, if Wilson would have denied the British access to foreign trade and resources, he would have inadvertently biased the U.S. against a naval power's great weapon: the ability to acquire overseas assets. Germany, by virtue of having a powerful army, could gain access to equally precious resources by controlling territory in Europe.

When the Germans countered with their first submarine blockade in February 1915, they only had four submarines in service in the area surrounding the British Isles. Because four submarines could not truly be effective in an all-encompassing blockade, the blockade was considered illegal. Submarine warfare also represented a sharp departure from past practices of sea warfare and a violation of international law. Here, we have to remember the historical context of the times. Submarine attacks shocked the world in those days. The rules of warfare, to be sure, might have allowed belligerent ships to stop neutrals at sea and to confiscate any conditional or outright contraband. But belligerents had no right to destroy neutral ships, much less harm or kill the passengers aboard. Given the rules of the time, the sinking of the *Lusitania* was illegal.

It is, of course, possible to argue that international law was unrealistic because it did not take into account the way submarines operated. But if Wilson would have accepted that proposition, in effect, he would have abandoned America's neutral rights and abridged international law. Such a precedent would have simultaneously undermined America's legal right to challenge any other infractions of neutral rights. Hence, historians who empathize with Wilson's predicament argue that there was no choice but to protest the German decision about submarine warfare and to continue trade with the British. They agree that economic entanglements with the British and French did occur. However, they argue that there was no deviousness or calculation on the part of Wilson to encourage this development.

Pro-Wilson historians also are very critical of the German proclamation of unrestricted submarine warfare in January 1917. They view it as equal to a declaration of war, or as a last ultimatum. Germany, these historians argue, could have instituted a more limited policy, possibly declaring submarine warfare only on armed or belligerent ships. It was very clear that Wilson would have acquiesced to a more limited German decision.

Further, pro-Wilson historians support him because they believe that he correctly defined America's long-term national interest. It was Germany who would be the real threat to the U.S. after a victory in World War I. There had already been a troubled background of friction and misunderstanding between the U.S. and Germany dating back to at least 1898. More immediate, in 1917, was the notorious Zimmermann Telegram. In this telegram, German Foreign Secretary Arthur Zimmermann cabled instructions to the German envoy in Mexico to seek an alliance "in the event of hostilities" with the U.S. For their cooperation, the Germans were willing to aid Mexico in the recovery of Texas, New Mexico and Arizona. The German envoy also was to try to induce Japan into joining this scheme. To many Americans in 1917, Zimmermann's arrogant admittance that the message was true was as antagonizing as the telegram itself. After all, Zimmermann could have tactfully denied the note and allowed ill feelings to subside.

All these factors, coupled with the Russian Revolution of March 1917—which seemingly installed a republican form of government—added to the American belief in the validity of Wilson's actions and in the moral superiority of the Allied cause. What sense would there have been in Wilson's war policy if he had declared against the British blockade and refused aid and loans to democratic nations in favor of those who were autocratic and militaristic? No matter what Wilson would have done, he was bound to injure one side or the other. Why not favor those who were the least threatening to American national interests?

Such, then, is the dilemma facing students who look back into the story of America's entry into World War I. The question of the key causes of America's intervention remains unresolved. However, some light may be shed on a related concern. One of the most pervasive beliefs held by Americans is that democratic governments are less prone to war than dictatorships. Indeed, at the foundation of our political system is the feeling that public opinion is a positive and moderating force on both diplomatic and domestic decision-making. We should note, therefore, that public opinion was a positive, restraining factor on President Wilson's diplomacy throughout the pre-War period. Indeed, Wilson had to run on the rather uncomfortable slogan, "He kept us out of war," during the Presidential election campaign of 1916. Though critics might deride the role of public opinion in favor of the powerful influence of economic forces, nonetheless, one must admit that it took a special juxtaposition of circumstances before Wilson dared lead the nation into war—Zimmermann Telegram, Russian Revolution of March 1917, the Declaration of Unrestricted Submarine Warfare, etc. As is characteristic of successful politicians in a democracy, Wilson had to ascertain what stand was politically safe before he could frame it as morally right.

SELECTED BIBLIOGRAPHY

1. Fischer, Fritz. *Germany's Aims in the First World War*. New York: W. W. Norton and Co. 1967.
2. Graham, Jr., Otis L. *The Great Campaigns*. Englewood Cliffs, N.J.: Prentice-Hall Inc. 1971.

3. Gregory, Ross. *The Origins of American Intervention in the First World War*. New York: W. W. Norton and Co. 1971.

4. Hawley, Ellis W. *The Great War and the Search for a Modern Order*. New York: St. Martin's Press. 1979.

5. Kennan, George F. *American Diplomacy, 1900–1950*. Chicago: University of Chicago Press. 1951.

6. Levin, Jr., N. Gordon. *Woodrow Wilson and World Politics*. New York: Oxford University Press. 1968.

7. Link, Arthur S. *Wilson the Diplomatist*. Baltimore, Md.: Johns Hopkins Press. 1957.

8. May, Ernest R. *The World War and American Isolation, 1914–1917*. Cambridge, Mass.: Harvard University Press. 1959.

9. Remak, Joachim. *The Origins of World War I*. New York: Holt, Rinehart and Winston. 1967.

10. Smith Daniel M. *The Great Departure: The United States and World War I, 1914–1920*. New York: John Wiley and Sons. 1965.

"The greatness of America has grown out of a political and social system and a method of control of economic forces distinctly its own—our American system—which has carried this great experiment in human welfare further than ever before in all history. We are nearer today to the ideal of the abolition of poverty and fear from the lives of men and women than ever before in any land. And I again repeat that the departure from our American system by injecting principles destructive to it which our opponents propose will jeopardize the very liberty and freedom of our people, and will destroy equality of opportunity, not alone to ourselves but to our children." Herbert Hoover, Speech entitled "The American System of Self-Government," 1928.

The Great Depression: Could It Have Been Avoided?

It has been sixty-two years since Black Thursday, the dreariest day of the great Stock Market Crash of 1929. Sixty-two years, indeed! The current ebb and flow of economic events make its shadow ever more ominous. The situation then was catastrophic. In September 1929, industrials stood at 452; by November they had crashed to 224; on July 8, 1932, at the depths of the Great Depression, they had sunk to 58. In that same period, such blue chip stocks as General Motors fell from 73 to 8, U.S. Steel from 262 to 22 and Montgomery Ward from 138 to 4. Sixty-two years ago shanty towns of the dispossessed and hungry were called "Hoovervilles;" the newspapers which covered the impoverished who slept on park benches at night were called "Hoover blankets;" a trouser pocket turned inside out was called a "Hoover flag." In the Southwest, country singers were crooning the popular song, "Hoover Made a Soup-hound Outa Me."

All this, of course, was grossly unfair to Herbert Hoover. The causes of the Depression were not his fault. But it was natural for people to look for a scapegoat for these ills. And it was easy for them to pick Hoover. Later, others were to blame Franklin Roosevelt for his actions and his demagoguery, which they claimed made matters even worse. Whatever may be said about each man personally, we must recognize that neither knew how to solve the problems of the Depression. Who did? Now it is generally recognized that they were victimized by uncontrollable circumstances. In the end, it was World War II which brought prosperity back to this nation.

Historians, then, are not so narrow-minded as to blame one President or the other. But that is not to say that the argument is less emotional; it is just depersonalized. Nor can one say that the lines of the argument have shifted very much since the 1930s. Generally, historians today spread the blame much the same way that people did back then: liberals with one theory and conservatives another. These main schools of thought have fancier names now, however, the "structuralists" (or fiscal theorists) and the "monetarists." Their names reflect the essence of their arguments. The structuralists are indebted to the intellectual and economic writings of John Maynard Keynes. They argue that the Crash and Depression resulted from serious structural flaws in the American economy. The rival "monetary" theory has been gaining more and more converts lately, due to the writings of Milton Friedman, Clark Warburton, Phillip Cagan and Elmus Wicker. The monetarists argue that the nation required wiser monetary policy rather than structural reforms.

Let us look into these arguments more closely. Given the nature of today's economy, a historical perspective surely will not hurt that much, and might even offer some insights into our current economic problems. First, the structuralists argue that the immediate cause for the turndown of economic activity and the decline of the Stock Market in 1929 was the "inventory recession" which plagued the nation that summer. That is, production of industrial products had outrun consumer and investment demand. After that, structural weaknesses in the economy became apparent and were so extensive that they prohibited recovery.

For instance, there was a disastrous maldistribution of income. Structuralists point out that in 1929 the rich were indubitably rich and the poor lamentably poor. In that year, the top 5 percent of the population owned 33 percent of all personal income. What that added up to was that 26 million of the total 27.5 million American families earned less than $2,500 per year, which in 1929 was deemed necessary for a decent standard of living for a family of four.

Further, our nation's corporate structure was oligopolistic in some areas, monopolistic in others. How could capitalistic competition be maintained, structuralists ask, when one-tenth of 1 percent of American corporations earned nearly half of the net income and owned over half the assets of all corporations in the United States? Corporations were insulated from the public they served, and from the natural laws of supply and demand.

Financially, the Stock Exchange was a problem area. Wall Street was weakly regulated, and the vogue of buying stock "on margin" jeopardized the future of the American economy. America's banking system was equally unsound. There were few of the protective safeguards of today and the actions of many banks were, as a result, speculative and fraudulent. As one contemporary noted: "Banks provided everything for their customers but a roulette wheel."

Finally, structuralists point to the poor state of foreign trade. World War I made the U.S. a creditor nation and saddled most of Europe with tremendous war debts. Europeans, faced with the problems of debt payments and an unfavorable trade balance, eventually began to curtail purchases of American products. This especially hurt American agriculture, which was consequently burdened by surpluses and overexpansion.

To summarize, structuralists argue that the American economy was fundamentally unstable. For prosperity to return, domestic reforms were needed. A massive redistribution of income was needed to support enough purchasing power to keep the economic wheels turning fast enough. Banks needed to be regulated and individual deposits insured. Wall Street had to be more carefully monitored and forced to curtail reckless practices. More importantly, the Republican Party's policies of the 1920s—tax cuts for the highest incomes, high tariffs, etc.—had to be abandoned.

The monetarists vehemently disagree. For the monetarists, the Great Depression is just another example of how government mismanagement can damage an inherently healthy system of private enterprise. In this case, the culprit was the Federal Reserve System, whose monetary policies turned what would otherwise have been a mild recession into a major catastrophe. According to monetarists, the Stock Market Crash and the inventory recession of 1929 could not in themselves have produced a major collapse in economic activity. Indeed, for the first year after the crash, they argue, the recession showed signs of recovery. This recovery was thwarted, however, when the Federal Reserve System allowed the supply of money to decline by nearly 3 percent from August 1929 to October 1930. As a result, in November 1930 a series of major bank failures occurred. Again, instead of quickly moving to provide banks with more cash so that the public demand for liquid assets could be met, and the monetary debacle averted, the Fed did nothing.

Another great failure of the Fed was its panic when Great Britain went off the gold standard in 1931. Though the gold reserves of the U.S. were at a high point, the Fed raised the discount rate sharply to arrest our gold drain. The result was another spectacular increase in the number of bank failures. All told, from July 1929 to March 1933, one-third of America's banks went out of existence, the money supply had fallen by one-third, and an economic system, which was essentially stable, was damaged dramatically. What is particularly irksome to monetarists is that the Federal Reserve System was established, in large part, to prevent just this type of occurrence. The moral which Milton Friedman draws from this experience is: "Any system which gives so much power and so much discretion to a few men that mistakes—excusable or not—can have such far-reaching effects is a bad system."[1]

These are the two sides of the argument. It is impossible at this time to find a consensus on this issue; besides, tangling with Keynes and Friedman is beyond the abilities of most students of the Great Depression. Nonetheless, one might doubt if leaving troublesome issues to the "fate" of the market system is the answer. Crucial questions involving America's economic destiny have never been left to the strictures of laissez-faire. Men and women have always found ways to step in to make sure that those questions were resolved one way or another. When the government did not take political and economic responsibility, the maneuverings of the most opportunistic, and the most conniving were often given free reign. For better or worse, it would seem preferable to accept the limitations of intelligent management through democratically-controlled institutions.

SELECTED BIBLIOGRAPHY

1. Friedman, Milton and Anna Schwartz. *A Monetary History of the United States*. Princeton, N.J.: Princeton University Press. 1963.
2. _____. *The Great Contraction, 1929–1933*. Princeton, N.J.: Princeton University Press. 1965.
3. Galbraith, John Kenneth. *The Great Crash*. Boston: Houghton Mifflin Co. 1955.
4. Garraty, John A. *The Great Depression*. New York: Anchor Books, Doubleday. 1987.
5. Hawley, Ellis W. *The Great War and the Search for a Modern Order*. New York: St. Martin's Press. 1979.
6. McElvaine, Robert S. *The Great Depression: America 1929-1941*. New York: Times. 1984.
7. Sobel, Robert. *The Great Bull Market*. New York: W. W. Norton Co. 1968.
8. Soule, George. *Prosperity Decade*. New York: Holt, Rinehart and Winston. 1947.
9. Temin, Peter. *Did Monetary Forces Cause the Great Depression?* New York: W. W. Norton. 1976.
10. Wicker, Elmus R. *Federal Reserve Monetary Policy, 1917–1933*. New York: Random House. 1966.

"This great Nation will endure as it has endured, will revive and will prosper. So, first of all, let me assert my firm belief that the only thing we have to fear is fear itself—nameless, unreasoning, unjustified terror which paralyzes needed efforts to convert retreat into advance." Franklin Roosevelt, First Inaugural Address, March 4, 1933.

Did the New Deal Go too Far
or Not Far Enough?

Given the prevailing attitude that the federal government since the 1930s has become too powerful and bureaucratic, and that our economy has become gradually socialized, it might be wise to re-evaluate the New Deal era in American history. Specifically, how responsible was the New Deal for the bureaucratic morass that the United States faces today? And how far did Franklin Roosevelt depart from the established American economic traditions of the past?

Answers to these questions differ radically depending on the political persuasion of the respondents. But one fact is certain: for those liberals and conservatives who lived through the 1930s, there was a universal belief that the New Deal was a dramatic break from the past, a "revolutionary" turning point from what had transpired previously in American political history.

Embittered conservatives led by Herbert Hoover believed that under FDR's guidance America had suddenly departed from the path of freedom and individual enterprise. They looked upon the "planned economy" of the New Dealers as an amalgam of socialism, fascism, and free enterprise. Hoover himself argued that there can be "no middle road between any breed of collectivist economy and our American system;" that the market mechanism could not work if government bureaucrats meddled constantly in economic affairs. In fact, Hoover went so far as to accuse Roosevelt of undertaking the goal of a "planned economy" as a guise for increasing executive power. According to Hoover, Roosevelt had gone too far in his experimentation. If left alone, he believed, the economy would correct itself. By tampering with it, as Roosevelt was doing, the whole system might be permanently harmed.

Liberals in the 1930s agreed with conservatives that the New Deal was a revolutionary departure from previous economic and political policy. Liberals disagreed with conservatives, however, on the nature of Roosevelt's revolution. They believed that the New Deal was benign and beneficient. They believed that the Stock Market Crash and the ensuing Depression proved that the 1920s partnership between laissez-faire government and buccaneering capitalism was disastrous. In the nineteenth century, liberals argued, the laissez-faire approach worked because the nation was growing geographically and had large frontiers to fill and exploit. But in the twentieth century, with the demise of the family corporation and the rise of the impersonal, international conglomerate, laissez-faire practices only served to jeopardize the economic security of the majority of citizens. Liberals reasoned that intelligent planning by "rational" governmental administrators could redress these ominous trends. Liberals did not believe that federal intervention was synonymous with a loss of freedom. They instead saw the New Deal as enhancing freedom and democracy and as a needed economic expedient.

Today the argument continues along much the same lines, and the differing versions of the New Deal remain side by side to perplex students of American history. Nonetheless, there is some bit of consensus on this highly emotional subject. Historians today generally agree that the New Deal was not an effort at destroying capitalism, but rather an attempt at preserving it. The protests from the right that the New Deal was socialistic are viewed by the new consensus as unwarranted. Most historians do not believe that the fundamentals of our capitalistic system were changed, but instead a few of the marginal forms were modified.

To support their arguments, they point out that the location of money and power in this country has remained the same despite the New Deal. Before the New Deal, one-tenth of 1 percent of American corporations earned nearly half of the net income and owned over half of the assets of all corporations in the U.S. After the New Deal these percentages were not substantially changed. They call attention to the fact that the New Deal never departed from the general path of American economic ideals. For instance, New Dealers never set out to equalize wealth and income in the U.S., to eliminate monopoly or to institute a collectivistic ethic. If such practices had been followed, then the "socialist" label might be applicable. Further, the new consensus brings to notice the tremendous conservatism of the New Deal with regard to racial policies. Not one single piece of civil rights legislation was passed during the New Deal period. Though Roosevelt spoke out against lynching in the South, he hedged on advocating the passage of an anti-lynching law for fear of alienating conservative Southern Democrats whom he needed for political support. Finally, historians point to the conservative nature of most of the New Deal measures themselves. The National Industrial Recovery Act (NIRA) was only a modification of Hoover's own compulsory trade union idea and was aimed at cooperating with big business. The Agricultural Adjustment Act (AAA) benefitted wealthy farmers and landowners the most and drove sharecroppers and poorer farmers from the land. The Social Security Act was financed in a regressive rather than in a progressive way, since both the employer and the employee payroll taxes were paid by the workers in the long run.

In sum, most historians do not believe that the New Deal was a revolutionary departure from America's economic traditions. General agreement among historians ends there, however. First of all, there is a continuing debate on the question of FDR's responsibility for present-day bureaucratic entanglements. In Roosevelt's first year of office alone, approximately 100,000 jobs were created in the federal bureaucracy because of the myriad of new agencies and programs. Secondly, some historians believe that Roosevelt is greatly to blame for the "imperial" presidency which has emerged since World War II. It is claimed that the force of his personality, in combination with his diverse programs, brought an enormous and debilitating expansion of federal and presidential powers. For instance, his creation of the executive office of the president with its administrative assistants (later including the Council of Economic Advisers, the National Security Council and the Central Intelligence Agency) was but one example of a focussing of power in presidential hands.

In contrast, other historians believe that the dangers of a burgeoning bureaucracy were meager compared to the fact that the economy was experiencing an average unemployment rate of 25 percent and a gross national product (GNP) one half of 1929 levels when Roosevelt took office in 1933. Many of these historians also believe that World War II, the Cold War and the complexities of twentieth-century problems, in general, were most responsible for creating the massive federal bureaucracy and for strengthening the office of the Presidency.

Maybe the most that can be said in conclusion, given the disparity of views on these latter issues, is that here is a definite instance in history when one man seems to have made a significant difference. One can hardly imagine what the 1930s would have been like without Franklin Roosevelt. Through the force of his personality he created a rapport with a majority of Americans who were distressed and disillusioned by the pressing problems of the Depression. He personalized the state in the eyes of a majority who had grown to believe that the federal government was impersonal and callous. He offered a compromise between extremes so that the basics of our system could be preserved. This was no mean accomplishment, considering what other countries were experiencing in the 1930s under the rules of Hitler, Mussolini, Stalin and Franco. It was Eleanor Roosevelt who put her husband's accomplishment in its proper perspective when she remarked: "I never believed the federal government could solve the whole problem. It bought us time to think."

SELECTED BIBLIOGRAPHY

1. Badger, Anthony J. *The New Deal: The Depression Years, 1933–40.* New York: Farrar, Straus & Giroux. 1989.
2. Burns, James M. *Roosevelt: The Lion and the Fox.* New York: Harcourt, Brace and World, 1956.
3. _____. *Roosevelt: The Soldier of Freedom.* New York: Harcourt, Brace and World. 1970.
4. Conkin, Paul K. *The New Deal.* New York: Thomas Y. Crowell Co. 1967.
5. Freidel, Frank, *Franklin D. Roosevelt: A Rendezvous with Destiny.* Boston: Little, Brown and Co., 1990.
6. Friedman, Milton and Rose Friedman. *Free to Choose: A Personal Statement.* New York: Harcourt Brace Jovanovich. 1980.
7. Graham, Jr., Otis L. *The New Deal: The Critical Issues.* Boston: Little, Brown and Co. 1971.
8. Grahm, Jr., Otis L. and Meghan Robinson Wander. *Franklin D. Roosevelt: His Life and Times.* Boston: G. K. Hall. 1985.
9. Leuchtenburg, William E. *Franklin D. Roosevelt and the New Deal.* New York: Harper and Row. 1963.
10. _____. *In the Shadow of FDR: From Harry Truman to Ronald Reagan.* New York: Cornell University Press. 1983.
11. Romasco, Albert U. *The Politics of Recovery: Roosevelt's New Deal.* New York: Oxford University Press. 1983.
12. Schlesinger, Jr., Arthur M. *The Age of Roosevelt.* (3 volumes). Boston: Houghton Mifflin Co. 1957–1960.

America's Entry into World War II: Blunder, or for National Security?

To the historians poring through the declassified documents of World War II, these past forty-five years have been filled with many revelations and surprises. Lately, research has highlighted the importance of secret espionage in the winning of the war. A further surprise has come with the news that the Japanese, too, were working on an atomic weapon during the War, though their research and development of it stalled considerably after 1943. Despite the passage of time, however, one issue has remained much the same. The controversy over the validity of America's entry into the War is still based on the pattern set by the pre-Pearl Harbor debate between the "interventionists" and the "non-interventionists." Only the names have changed.

Those historians who today defend Franklin Roosevelt's conduct of foreign policy before Pearl Harbor are labeled "internationalists." Those who are critical and who argue that Roosevelt's actions were misguided and deceptive are labeled "revisionists." Though the majority opinion favors those who believe that American involvement in the War was warranted because vital American national interests were menaced by the Axis powers, it is nevertheless instructive to review the key aspects of this debate.

Internationalists find the causes for American involvement traceable to factors outside the control of the United States and determined by aggressive foreign powers, particularly Germany and Japan. Internationalists emphasize the extremely serious threats that Germany and Japan posed to the United States. Germany threatened to dominate the whole of the European continent, politically, strategically and economically. Japan, discontented with the *status quo* in the Far East and emboldened by German successes in Europe, equally jeopardized the Asian balance of power.

In light of these dangers, internationalists believe that it was right for Franklin Roosevelt to act as he did. In fact, most internationalists argue that Roosevelt was extremely sensitive to and cognizant of anti-interventionist feelings in his conduct of foreign policy. With regard to Germany, Roosevelt delayed taking any major steps until the shock of the sudden defeat of France dramatically changed the world political situation. Even then Roosevelt clung to the hope that Germany would be defeated without a U.S. declaration of war. Hence, this was the reasoning behind Roosevelt's call for economic aid for Great Britain, and eventually such actions as the repeal of the arms embargo, the bases-for-destroyers deal, the lend-lease legislation, the occupation of Iceland and the patrolling of the Atlantic by American ships.

Because Roosevelt believed that Germany was the gravest threat to American security, interventionists add, his actions have to be carefully interpreted vis-à-vis the Japanese in the Far East. Roosevelt, after all, did not want to become embroiled in a two-front confrontation. It is true that Roosevelt decided upon a harder line against the Japanese as a measure to halt their belligerency. This policy, however, was not aimed at provoking the Japanese into war. Rather, given the failure of "appeasement" in Europe (that is, the failure of British and French concessions to stop Hitler before 1939), Roosevelt decided upon actions which were more assertive. He, therefore, openly condemned Japanese aggression against China and even extended aid to the Chinese resistance. When the Japanese still refused to comply with international calls for military restraint, Roosevelt responded with economic sanctions. First, American scrap metal and iron shipments to Japan were halted. Then, after the Japanese continued to prove intransigent, Roosevelt added oil to the list of embargoed products and moved to freeze Japanese assets in the U.S.

For internationalists, the emphasis is on how restrained Roosevelt was and on how long he delayed before imposing economic sanctions. As for the placement of the American fleet at Pearl Harbor, internationalists see this, too, less as a provocation to Japan and more as a warning to the Japanese to be less aggressive in the Far East.

One group of internationalists, however, is critical of Roosevelt, but not because they believe that he incorrectly involved the U.S. in a mistaken war. Rather they are upset that he did not act sooner to stop German and Japanese bellicosity. Their belief is that active U.S. involvement in European and Asian political affairs immediately upon Roosevelt's accession to office might have alleviated a world war. For these internationalists, American foreign policy was "reactive," rather than "active." Roosevelt, they argue, was too passive in the face of Axis threats, with the result that responsibility for world peace was left to the whims of dictators. Indeed, one of the strongest nations in the world was abdicating an important charge and hiding behind neutrality legislation which misled the Axis leaders into believing that the U.S. was indifferent to the fate of Europe and Asia. To the very end, in fact, Roosevelt hesitated so that the decision for war was left to the indiscretions of Hitler and Tojo. Unwittingly, American hesitancy and isolationism became "the handmaiden of European appeasement." As the historian Robert A. Divine argues:

> Early and sustained American support of the existing balance of power in the world might well have helped England, France, and China contain the expansive thrust of the Axis nations and spared the globe the agony of World War II.[3]

Conversely, revisionists have as their basic premise the belief that the Axis powers did not constitute a serious threat to the vital interests of the U.S. Revisionists note that Germany had no concrete plans for attacking the U.S., that Hitler's quarrel was with Central and Eastern Europe and that the U.S. was safe here in the Western Hemisphere, protected as it was by two oceans. As for Japan, revisionists point out that the Japanese were never militarily capable of launching a serious invasion of the American mainland, and were only concerned with their security and their need for raw materials in Asia. What the revisionist argument amounts to, then, is that the search for the causes of World War II begins with the actions of the Roosevelt administration, rather than abroad.

Roosevelt, revisionists contend, followed policies that he suspected would lead to war with Germany and Japan. With regard to Germany, Roosevelt increasingly escalated aggressive activity, moving from aid to Great Britain, to a "shoot-on-sight" policy at German ships. At the same time, in Asia, Roosevelt provoked the Japanese by rejecting their main overture for peace, a proposal that President Roosevelt and Prime Minister Fumimaro Konoye meet personally to resolve the problems besetting Japanese-American relations. Roosevelt's rebuff, in fact, led to the ouster of Konoye from power, and to the ascendancy of the more militaristic wing of the Japanese Cabinet, headed by the extremist general, Hideki Tojo.

Further, it is argued that Roosevelt abandoned a realistic policy in the Far East when he moved from the more attainable aims of splitting the Tripartite Pact and halting Japanese expansion, to the more demanding objective of the liberation of China. Bogged down in a difficult war on the Chinese mainland, revisionists argue, the U.S. should have understood that the Japanese needed more time to extricate themselves honorably from the Chinese imbroglio. Instead, Roosevelt demanded that a halt to the Japanese war in China serve as a prerequisite for agreement on any other matter. With this as a background, it was not surprising that Japan decided on war with the U.S. once Roosevelt also applied economic pressures.

In addition, revisionists argue that Roosevelt compounded his foreign policy mistakes by purposely deceiving the American people into believing that he was really working for peace. Revisionists note Roosevelt's deceit during the *Kearny* and *Greer* crises. During these episodes Roosevelt stirred American public opinion by blatantly accusing the Nazis of unwarranted attacks on the U.S. ships *Kearny* and *Greer*. In reality, it was the U.S. which instigated the German attacks in the first place. And in the Far East, because U.S. Intelligence had cracked the Japanese code, Roosevelt was well aware that his policies were driving the Japanese to consider more and more militant alternatives. Yet he persisted in allowing the American people to believe that peace was still at hand.

Finally, revisionists argue that because the U.S. became involved in World War II, much more serious threats were neglected—the rise of the Soviet Union and Communist China to world power. For, when utter destruction was wrought on Germany and Japan, a political and geographical vacuum was created in Eastern Europe and Eastern Asia which the Soviets and the Chinese quickly moved to fill. After the war, in sum, the U.S. was in a much more dangerous position than ever before. Facing Americans now were truly dangerous enemies, which, in turn, has led us to a dependence upon a military-industrial complex and a state of war-like readiness unparalleled in our history.

Revisionists recognize that, in particular, the evils of Hitler's Germany were to be castigated. And they agree that it was a natural inclination for Americans to believe that such "immoral" forces boded ill for any future world peace. But revisionists quickly add that most of the information on the wickedness of Hitler's rule only appeared after the war, and was not readily available in the early years when Roosevelt was making his decisions. Hence, an *ex post facto* moral argument is not valid as a cause for instigating a war with Germany. Furthermore, revisionists cannot see much difference between Hitler's Germany and Stalin's Russia.

But, most emphatically, revisionists warn that U.S. government deceit in leading the nation into World War II set a precedent which made it easier for later Presidents to become involved in Korea and Vietnam. Roosevelt's policies set a trend whereby U.S. governments became negligent in seeking proper Congressional and constitutional approval for foreign intervention. Nor were later American Presidents careful to distinguish between areas of vital national interest to the U.S. and areas of minimal significance.

One should not close an account of revisionist historiography on World War II without mentioning the arguments of the New Left. The opinions of the New Left perhaps appear at their best in the pioneering work of William Appleman Williams. For Williams, twentieth cen-

145

tury U.S. foreign policy was an extension and elaboration of Secretary of State John Hay's famous Open Door Notes of 1899 and 1900. In those Notes, Hay made clear the American opinion that the Western European practice of separating off "spheres of influence" in underdeveloped areas of the world should be prohibited in the case of China. Hay argued that China's territorial integrity should be respected, and that all Great Powers should be able to trade freely throughout that nation. Behind Hay's announcement was not a concern for the people of China. Rather key business, intellectual and political leaders in the U.S. saw in the Open Door Policy an opportunity for the U.S., because of its growing economic power, to become the predominant force in the affairs of developing nations. These men believed that a healthy domestic economic situation was predicated on the existence of a healthy program of overseas trade.

For these key businessmen, intellectuals and politicians the main cause of the economic depression which plagued America in the 1890s was the "closing" of the American frontier. The frontier in American history, they had been taught, had always been a beneficial and wholesome influence on both America's democratic and economic institutions. Overseas economic activity, therefore, was to be the "new frontier."

The Open Door Policy, argues Williams, was not a military strategy nor a traditional "balance of power" strategy. Instead it was a practical, hard-headed approach to modern foreign policy which avoided the stigma of traditional colonialism. "It was conceived and designed to win the victories without the wars."[9] It was a system of informal empire which "would cast the economy and the politics of the poorer, weaker, underdeveloped countries in a pro-American mold."[9] The assumption here, of course, was that American ways and institutions were superior and worthy of emulation.

Unfortunately, argues Williams, the strategy of the Open Door Policy contained the seeds of war. Our policy-makers did not want violence. But with a "frontier-expansionist" conception of history, war was a possibility whenever a foreign power intruded into an area of the world which the U.S. deemed important to its economic welfare.

> The inherent imperialism of the system increasingly defined American foreign policy in terms of war. Given the assumption that American welfare depended upon a world marketplace system open to American economic power—and to the enlightened reformist outlook of the U.S.—the rise of militant alternatives (i.e. Germany and Japan) led naturally to military action to preserve the Open Door Policy.[9]

Friction with Japan was almost inevitable as America's economic influence in Asia grew extensively in the 1920s and 1930s. By 1937, 51.5 percent of all raw and crude materials imported into the U.S. came from Asia. Between 1931 and 1937, Asian nations received the following percentages of American exports: iron and steel, 33 percent; copper, 26 percent; industrial machinery, 15 percent; and paper products, 40 percent.

Therefore, argues Williams, Japanese moves into China just before World War II vitally affected America's whole underlying "world view." Historians miss the point, adds Williams, when they see American entry into World War II as the result of conspiratorial actions by evil political leaders. At issue was the whole scope of American foreign policy. But the real tragedy of American foreign policy was the great failure on the part of American statesmen to consider:

> how the Open Door Policy looked from the other end of empire. [American statesmen] did not raise the fundamental question as to whether the frontier-expansionist conception of history did in fact produce democracy and prosperity.[9]

146

To conclude, these are the main historical arguments which still surround America's entry into World War II. Yet, of all the historical controversies thus far discussed, perhaps it is this one which is the easiest to resolve. Given the Fascist belligerence of those times, it is almost inconceivable to expect that a great power of America's stature would renege on its responsibility for the world's future to the designs of dictators. It is even more difficult to expect that an isolationist policy would have attained a more fortunate outcome. The U.S. emerged from World War II as the greatest power in the world, with virtually no military devastation of mainland soil, and with a relatively small number of casualties in comparison with most belligerents. It was indeed one of America's "finest hours." Though historians today might depict scenarios with more favorable outcomes, one can more easily imagine the disasters that might have occurred.

SELECTED BIBLIOGRAPHY

1. Collier, Richard. *The Road to Pearl Harbor*. New York: Atheneum Publishers. 1981.
2. Dallek, Robert. *Franklin D. Roosevelt and American Foreign Policy, 1932–1945*. New York: Oxford University Press. 1979.
3. Divine, Robert A. *The Reluctant Belligerent: American Entry into World War II*. New York: John Wiley and Sons. 1979.
4. Feis, Herbert. *The Road to Pearl Harbor*. Princeton, N.J.: Princeton University Press. 1962.
5. Heinrichs, Waldo. *Threshold of War: Franklin D. Roosevelt and American Entry into World War II*. New York and Oxford: Oxford University Press. 1988.
6. MacDonald, C. A. *The United States, Britain & Appeasement*. New York: St. Martin's Press. 1981.
7. Schroeder, Paul W. *The Axis Alliance and Japanese-American Relations, 1941*. Ithaca, N.Y.: Cornell University Press. 1958.
8. Williams, William Appleman. *The Contours of American History*. Chicago: Quadrangle Books. 1966.
9. _____. *The Tragedy of American Diplomacy*. New York: Dell Publishing Co. 1962.

"*I am proud that I am an American citizen of Japanese ancestry, for my very background makes me appreciate more fully the wonderful advantages of this nation. I believe in her institutions, ideals and traditions; I glory in her heritage; I boast of her history; I trust in her future. She has granted me liberties and opportunities such as no individual enjoys in this world today. She has given me an education befitting kings. . . . She has permitted me to build a home, to earn a livelihood, to worship, think, speak and act as I please—as a free man equal to every other man.*" Statement of Faith, Japanese American Citizens League (JACL), 1940.

Was the "Relocation" of Japanese-Americans Defensible?

One of the most lamentable episodes in America's past has been the treatment accorded Japanese-Americans during World War II. There is hardly an American historian today who does not believe that the actions taken against Japanese-Americans during the harried days after Pearl Harbor were unconstitutional and motivated by unwarranted hysteria. Newly-opened historical archives make this story clearer now than ever before. So, in light of recent documents, this essay aims to present the background and reasons which prompted the decision to evacuate, relocate and detain Japanese-Americans.

Of approximately 127,000 persons of Japanese ancestry residing in the continental United States, more than 112,000 were imprisoned, including almost all of those residing in the West Coast states. This is a story which too few Americans know, despite recent publicity. In fact, an informal survey of leading college textbooks revealed that, on the average, less than a quarter of one page was devoted to this tragedy, if it was mentioned at all.

The first point to recognize is that the story does not begin at Pearl Harbor, but goes back to the 1870s when Japanese immigrants first came to this country. It was then that the Japanese were first exposed to the anti-Oriental prejudice which already was raging against the Chinese. As with all prejudice, at the heart of the matter were misperceptions, misunderstandings, fears, unwarranted stereotyping and jealous hatred. Organized labor feared that the Japanese would displace native Americans in key jobs. School officials and parents worried that the integration of Japanese children into the schools would be a pernicious influence on white youths. Business and farming interests worried that Japanese competition and expertise would decrease profits. Space does not allow for the use of the facts and statistics to prove these contentions wrong, but other more degraded fears can be easily disposed of—that the Japanese were intellectually inferior, that Japanese men were a menace to white women, and that the Japanese were unassimilable into America's traditions.

Basic prejudices were further heightened by international events, especially the Russo-Japanese War of 1904–05. Here the Japanese fought the Russians to a stalemate, the first time that white military supremacy had been challenged by a non-white people in modern history. Such events not only worsened official diplomatic and commercial relations between the U.S. and Japanese governments, but they intensified prejudice at home. For instance, California's Alien Land Law of 1913 and Congress's Quota Immigration Law of 1924 were passed with the

Japanese specifically in mind. Later foreign events—the invasion of Manchuria in 1931, the "accidental" Japanese attack on the American gunboat *Panay*, and the outbreak of the Sino-Japanese War in 1937—proved even more dramatic in their effects. But the surprise attack at Pearl Harbor was the catalyst which set this chemically-explosive mixture boiling. The popular hysteria after Pearl Harbor seemed to know no bounds. There was inordinate fear of a Japanese invasion of the Pacific Coast and the feeling that Japanese-Americans would abet the enemy in an invasion of this sort.

Many newspapers played upon the stirred and angry emotions. A sampling of the headlines after Pearl Harbor from the hitherto moderate *Los Angeles Times* gives an idea of the proportions of these fears: "Enemy Planes Sighted Over California Coast;" "Caps on Japanese Tomato Plants Point to Air Base;" "Japanese Here Sent Vital Data to Tokyo." While American newspapers attributed the belligerent actions of Germany to the deeds of evil leaders, the tendency was to attribute the actions of the Japanese government to the deeds of an evil race.

Soon important political and civic leaders succumbed to the popular hysteria. Noted examples included California's liberal governor, Culbert L. Olson; California's attorney general, Earl Warren; and columnist Walter Lippmann. Before long, Congressional representatives from California, Oregon, and Washington met to plan and to pressure for drastic actions.

At the source of a growing movement for relocation were key West Coast military officials stationed at the Presidio in San Francisco, particularly General John L. DeWitt, General Allen W. Gullion and Colonel Karl R. Bendetsen. It was these prominent Army officers who were responsible for leaking to the newspapers false information about supposed Japanese-American espionage units working in the Pacific Coast states and supposed enemy attacks at various locations along the western coast.

We know now that these reports were completely incorrect, and that anti-Japanese prejudice, short-sightedness and incompetence were the determining factors behind the actions of the Presidio team. Records of phone conversations and daily decision-making documents are available now and the indictments against these men can be made on a personal basis. The documents emphasize how influential a handful of misinformed and misguided bureaucrats can be as they set about creating a more important role for themselves in the governmental and military structure. On their behalf, one must recognize that the fallacious Roberts Report had just been published by the U.S. government, indicting certain Japanese residents in Hawaii for collaborating with the Pearl Harbor attackers. Hence, these Presidio officers feared being disgraced by inadequate precautions, such as happened to Lieutenant General Walter C. Short, who was in charge of the defense of Hawaii before the air invasion of December 7. However, in their zealousness, they over-reacted. This fact, in combination with their prejudices, incompetence and ambitions, caused them to misread the whole situation. Note the fantastic line of reasoning in DeWitt's official report, "Final Recommendation . . . to the Secretary of War . . . Subject: Evacuation of Japanese and other Subversive Persons from the Pacific Coast": "The Japanese race is an enemy race . . . along the vital Pacific Coast over 112,000 potential enemies, of Japanese extraction, are at large today. There are indications that these are organized and ready for concerted action at a favorable opportunity. *The very fact that no sabotage has taken place to date is a disturbing and confirming indication that such action will be taken.*" [The italics are inserted.]

The influence of a competent commander who could recognize the true realities of the military situation should not be underestimated. For example, in Hawaii, where the Japanese population made up over 37 percent of the total, General Delos C. Emmons staunchly refused to go along with relocation plans. He argued that such policies would have more negative repercussions logistically than positive, and he believed that the danger of espionage was exaggerated. Hence, relocation plans were scuttled and, as Emmons predicted, no significant disloyalty resulted. If West Coast officials had shown equal military foresight, the same could have occurred on the mainland. This is borne out by the fact that, to the end, Army Chief of Staff George C. Marshall and FBI Director J. Edgar Hoover argued that the mass relocation of the whole Japanese-American community was unnecessary. Finally, but reluctantly, they conceded to West Coast pressure.

Of course, no such unconstitutional and prejudiced decisions could have been implemented against Japanese-Americans if public opinion in the continental U.S. itself had been more balanced. Decisions made by key politicians and military officials were fearlessly executed because they knew that they would be popular with the general public. In fact, President Franklin Roosevelt's final acquiescence was because of popular opinion and his own anti-Japanese prejudices. He believed that the decision for relocation would receive bipartisan support and would help to promote national solidarity behind the war effort. On February 19, 1942, Roosevelt signed the lamentable Executive Order 9066, authorizing the secretary of war "whenever he or any designated Commander deems such action necessary or desirable, to prescribe military areas . . . from which any or all persons may be excluded."

Another factor in the relocation issue was the performance of the federal judiciary. The U.S. Supreme Court constitutionally validated the actions of the federal executive by refusing to inhibit the president's broad war and police powers. In the key court cases of *Hirabayashi v. U.S., Korematsu v. U.S.* and *Ex parte Endo,* the court accepted the premise of "collective ancestral guilt." For whites, cases of treason were to be decided on an individual basis during the war; for the Japanese, guilt was decided collectively. So, in the end, the Supreme Court offered Japanese-Americans no legal protection.

Even more damning is the new evidence uncovered by Peter Irons in an example of historical detective work at its best.[6] Irons combined the meticulous examination of internal justice department documents with a careful interviewing of the surviving lawyers who participated in the legal battles over relocation and incarceration. The result was a magnificent contribution to both the historical record and to the reversal of the 1942 conviction of Fred Korematsu in federal district court in November 1983. From his efforts, Irons discovered that the justice department allowed the government briefs to the Supreme Court to misstate the facts, even though the department knew that major aspects of the army's case against Japanese-Americans were simply fabricated.

Finally, and sadly, Japanese-Americans filled the need for a national scapegoat. The first six months after Pearl Harbor were months of unmitigated military disaster for American fighting units, particularly in the Pacific. As defeat piled upon defeat, hatreds at home were whetted and it was no accident that the process of relocation coincided almost exactly with America's greatest military disasters.

For these reasons, then, relocation plans were *implemented without regard for the human costs and economic losses involved. A conservative estimate shows that the economic losses of Japanese-Americans because of the relocation process were in the neighborhood of $400 million. The total claims finally paid to Japanese-Americans by the U.S. government totalled merely $38 million. Furthermore, claims were made on the basis of 1942 prices and payment was made in inflated postwar dollars.

In the long run, of course, all Americans were the losers. For a precedent was set, both legally and historically, for the evacuation, relocation and detention procedure. Both a state of emergency and an "acceptable" target group would have to exist. But those requirements being met, the whole process could occur at the mere issuance of a presidential executive order.

SELECTED BIBLIOGRAPHY

1. Bosworth, Allan R. *America's Concentration Camps.* New York: W. W. Norton Company. 1967.
2. Daniels, Roger. *The Decision to Relocate the Japanese Americans.* New York: J. B. Lippincott Company. 1975.
3. Girdner, Audrie and Anne Loftis. *The Great Betrayal.* New York: Macmillan and Company. 1969.
4. Grodzins, Morton. *Americans Betrayed: Politics and the Japanese Evacuation.* Chicago: University of Chicago Press. 1949.
5. Hosokawa, Bill, *Nisei: The Quiet Americans.* New York: W. Morrow Company. 1969.
6. Irons, Peter. *Justice at War: The Inside Story of Japanese-American Internment.* New York: Oxford University Press. 1983.
7. Kitano, Harry H. L. *Japanese Americans: The Evolution of a Subculture.* Englewood Cliffs, N.J.: Prentice-Hall Co. 1969.
8. ten Broek, Jacobus, Edward N. Barnhart, and Floyd W. Matson. *Prejudice, War, and the Constitution.* Berkeley and Los Angeles: University of California Press. 1954.

On August 10, 1988, President Reagan signed into law the Civil Liberties Act of 1988 (PL 100-383) which offered an apology and $1.25 billion in reparations to the estimated 65,000 Japanese-Americans who were still alive. This law was not meant to remedy the financial injustice suffered during the war years, but rather to add real meaning and significance to the U.S. Government's official apology. The Civil Liberties Act also provided $21.4 million in compensation to the eligible Aleuts who suffered removal, too, during the war.

The Teheran Conference: Was It the "Second" Most Important Event of World War II?

November 1988 marked the forty-fifty anniversary of the Teheran Conference, the first meeting of the Big Three (Churchill, Roosevelt and Stalin) during the critical years of World War II. Unlike other crucial aspects of World War II hardly a word of commemoration marked this anniversary date, for few fully recognized the import of this great turning point in history. The Teheran Conference is one of those historical episodes whose significance gains with the passage of time.

Far more well-known of the World War II meetings is the Yalta Conference. Yalta's juxtaposition in time to Soviet aggressions in Eastern Europe led an unsuspecting American public to draw a proximate line of cause and effect between the two events. Further, the fact that Roosevelt was ill at Yalta and died soon thereafter, and the fact that Alger Hiss was a U.S. delegate at Yalta made for convenient scapegoating by a frustrated American public, surprised and angered by the notorious developments in postwar Eastern Europe.*

Nonetheless, historians have recognized for a number of years that the Teheran Conference (November 28–December 1, 1943) was the crucial strategy meeting of World War II, and that it marked the critical juncture in the subsequent events which took place in Eastern Europe. One historian, Robert Beitzell, has gone so far as to state: "Except for the development of the atomic bomb, the Teheran Conference was probably the most important event in the Second World War. By acts of commission and omission, it has shaped nearly three (sic) decades of postwar history. . . . Not Yalta, not Potsdam, but here was the seat and center of decision."[1]

Despite the shift in recognition from Yalta to Teheran, one aspect of historical debate has remained the same: arguments still rage over the correctness of American diplomacy. The belief still persists that the United States could have done more to save Eastern Europe from Soviet control. Arguments are still heard that Franklin Roosevelt exhibited grave weaknesses in his negotiations with the Russians; that he exhibited political naïveté by focussing too exclusively on the military problems of fighting the Germans and the Japanese; and that he failed to heed Clausewitz's dictum that war is simply an instrument of policy and should not overshadow more crucial political concerns. Roosevelt himself once admitted his confusion in dealing with Stalin: "I don't know a good Russian from a bad Russian. I can tell a good Frenchman from a bad

*Alger Hiss was later to be convicted of perjury and revealed as a member of the pre-World War II communist apparatus in America.

Frenchman. I can tell a good Italian, I know a good Greek when I see one. But I don't understand the Russians."

From the vantage point of almost fifty years, let us review the two sides of the argument in light of the latest historical materials and private documents. This very first gathering of the leaders of the emergent superpowers might lend insight into whether face-to-face meetings of the leaders of great powers actually do lessen suspicions and improve relations.

Critics of Roosevelt's strategic policies as exemplified at Teheran begin their argument with FDR's decision in favor of Operation OVERLORD, the plan for the Normandy invasion of France. Critics believe that Winston Churchill's idea of an invasion of the Balkans was more appropriate not only for fighting the Germans, but also for containing the Russians in the postwar period. The strongest American advocate for this idea was William C. Bullitt, former Ambassador to the Soviet Union. In top secret memoranda to Roosevelt in mid-1943, Bullitt argued that Stalin's war aims were not those of the West. Those diplomats who believed that the war against the Fascist powers had purged Stalin of his autocratic and expansionist tendencies, Bullitt continued, were sadly mistaken. A Soviet-dominated Europe was as dangerous as one dominated by the Nazis. The solution to the problem, Bullitt concluded, was an attack by American forces in the Balkans and Eastern Europe to counter Soviet plans for postwar domination. "War is an attempt to achieve political objectives by fighting," Bullitt concluded, "and political objectives must be kept in mind in planning operations."

Bullitt's advice was ignored by Roosevelt, and the decision for OVERLORD, argue critics, assured that the Russians would be the conquerors and liberators of Eastern Europe and assured that the Russians would dominate over one-half of the European continent. American political naïveté, and a militarily impatient "let's get it over with" attitude ignored a threat which was as ominous as that of Hitler's.

A second area of criticism at Teheran involves Roosevelt's great reliance on the "personal touch" in his dealings with the Russians. Roosevelt hoped that a sign of generosity and warmth toward Stalin would ease the tensions that had emerged between the Russians and the Americans in the summer of 1943. Stalin had been particularly upset with the postponement of a major Anglo-American invasion of Europe. Roosevelt had first promised such an invasion in 1942, and now Stalin was being told that it would be delayed until 1944. Stalin was further upset at the delays in Lend-Lease shipments which had occurred just when the German pressure on the Soviet Union was at its height. Such was Stalin's dismay that he removed Ambassador Ivan Maisky from Great Britain and Ambassador Maxim Litvinov from the U.S. Further, he sent a personal message to both Roosevelt and Churchill in which he virtually accused his Western allies of purposely watching Germany and Russia cripple themselves, while the West preserved its resources with the aim of being the sole arbiters of an exhausted Europe after the war. The last paragraph of Stalin's message read as follows:

> You say that you 'quite understand' my disappointment. I must tell you that the point here is not just the disappointment of the Soviet Government, but the preservation of its confidence in its allies, a confidence which is being subjected to severe stress. One should not forget that it is a question of saving millions of lives in the occupied areas of Western Europe and Russia and of reducing the enormous sacrifices of the Soviet armies, compared with which the sacrifices of the Anglo–American armies are insignificant.

154

To ease these tensions, Roosevelt set out to use his charm on Stalin at Teheran. He hoped that a display of candidness might ease the dictator's fears. He also made it a point to avoid conveying the impression that he and Churchill were out to "gang up" on Stalin.

The outcome of this candidness, critics argue, was that Stalin was given too much leeway with regard to Eastern Europe. Indeed, Stalin was given the impression that his designs on Eastern Europe would not be opposed. Even Churchill was to show a lightheartedness in his remarks on Eastern Europe. In contrast, Stalin was cautious and shrewd. Indeed, Stalin, who had expected to have some difficulties with the implementation of his designs for Eastern Europe, found that the West conceded his fondest dreams with hardly an argument. Roosevelt, in his blanket approach to the issues and stakes in Eastern Europe, failed to carefully ascertain beforehand which Eastern European nations were fated to be dominated by the Soviets, and which had a very good chance to gain their aspirations for national self-determination and the holding of free elections. Critics cite the example of the negotiations over the future of Finland. Here both Roosevelt and Churchill hoisted a warning signal, and Stalin eventually backed down.

In sum, the principles of the Atlantic Charter were scrapped without a real fight. National self-determination and boundary-territorial changes, contrary to the wishes of the people immediately concerned, were forfeited by Roosevelt without the caution which the circumstances warranted. Equally disastrous was Roosevelt's failure to reveal to the American people what had transpired at Teheran and his failure to prepare the American people for the day when the Soviet people would emerge as a superpower in the postwar world. Finally, Roosevelt failed to understand the essence of the Soviet system. As the historian Adam Ulam has written, Roosevelt failed to perceive that, whatever the Russian dictator's feelings for the West, "Stalin could not in the long run withstand the logic of his position as the ruler of a totalitarian society and as the supreme head of a movement that seeks security through constant expansion."

The other side of this controversy finds much to laud in the decision-making at Teheran. First of all, a careful examination of both the published and the unpublished documents reveals that the U.S. did indeed consider both political and military factors in the decision for OVERLORD. The danger of Soviet expansion into Europe was carefully weighed against the military necessities of the time.

In the summer of 1943, as mentioned, the West was faced with a deterioration in Soviet-American relations. Further, the Russian victory at Stalingrad in the winter of 1942–1943 was emerging as the turning point in the war against Germany. In addition, the Russians had just scored key victories around Kursk, Orel and Kharkov.

In light of these political and military problems, Roosevelt, Army Chief of Staff George C. Marshall, and the Joint Chiefs of Staff rejected the Balkans approach as inadequate for American concerns and needs. Churchill's interest in a Mediterranean invasion fit perfectly with British goals. It was a piecemeal, slow-paced invasion which would not only husband their slender manpower resources but would be focussed in an area of the world, the Eastern Mediterranean, which was geopolitically significant for the preservation of the British Empire.

For the U.S., however, the dangers of a Mediterranean invasion were greater than the rewards. Extended supply lines in the mountains and inhospitable regions of the Balkans might bog down the American effort. The U.S. would then be in the position of "holding the leg for Stalin to skin the deer."* While an Anglo-American invasion made slow headway in the Balkans, the Soviet advance would possibly end up somewhere in western Germany or along the

*Secretary of War Henry Stimson's characterization.

155

Rhine frontier itself. Besides, if relations with the Russians were to deteriorate in the future, Western Europe would be the best place for American troops to be based. A landing in the Balkans could not be easily held if a determined Russian attack were to take place.

Furthermore, an invasion of the Balkans might lead to a complete disruption of just those ties with the Russians which Roosevelt was aiming to preserve. Since July 1941, Stalin had made clear his attitudes about Russian boundaries in Eastern Europe, and an invasion in the Balkans might threaten the Russians at exactly the time that the Red Army was needed for victory. Roosevelt was still concerned about the possibility of another Nazi-Soviet Pact. He wanted to keep the Russians in the war in order to minimize American casualties and in order to maintain his view of the American role as the "arsenal of democracy."

One must remember too that the Far East outlook was not so very rosy in 1943. Victory still seemed a long way off, as Chiang Kai-Shek's forces were proving to be a disappointment in the fighting against Japan. The recent Russian promise to enter the war against Japan after the defeat of Germany was a promise that Roosevelt sought to preserve and reinforce in his negotiations at Teheran. The atomic bomb at this time remained in the purely hypothetical stages of its development and was still known to only a few key scientific and military leaders.

Finally, domestically, Roosevelt needed progress in the West against Germany; otherwise American public opinion might grow restive with the Administration's "Germany first" strategy and call for even more of an effort against Japan.

For all these reasons, then, the decision was made for the Anglo–American invasion to take place in France. In fact, the American military had a backup plan both to quickly occupy Western Europe in the case of an unforeseen German collapse and to block Russian attempts at undue expansion. That plan was code-named RANKIN. RANKIN was the American response to the danger that the Soviets might attempt to take advantage of the fact that the West had not yet made substantial inroads against Germany on the European continent.

Supporters of Roosevelt's diplomacy also find much to praise in his reliance on the personal touch in his approach to the Russians. His aim to charm Stalin appears not so naïve on closer inspection. Roosevelt knew that in totalitarian regimes progress with the leader at the top affects relations with the whole of the nation. It is worth noting that in the past few decades progress with the Soviets has occurred at just those times when relations between the two key leaders have been the most cordial: Eisenhower and Khrushchev after the 1955 summit meeting, Kennedy and Khrushchev after the Cuban Missile Crisis in 1962, Nixon and Brezhnev in the early 1970s and Reagan and Gorbachev in the late 1980s. Charming Stalin and lessening his suspicions may have been impossible, but given the great uncertainties which lie ahead in 1943, Roosevelt's attempt must be respected.

Roosevelt was aiming at a type of containment of the Russians that might be characterized as containment by integration. Roosevelt hoped that lessening the distrust of the Soviets, bringing them back into the center of world diplomacy, and respecting their new emergence as one of the two superpowers might diminish their feeling of insecurity.

Finally, supporters of Roosevelt find that much of the criticism of the way events turned out in Eastern Europe is tinged with a large dose of unrealism. Critics have inferred that American leaders were duped diplomatically and militarily by the Russians. Supporters retort that it is more correct to say that the critics have deluded themselves. Critics of Roosevelt seem to have expected the Russians to defeat the Germans in the most destructive war in all history, and then to voluntarily concede the fruits of that triumph. The Soviets, because of their predominant contribution against the Germans, held all the trumps in the negotiations at Teheran. The Red Army had turned the tide of the war against the Germans by the summer of 1943. By January 1944 they were to cross into the prewar boundaries of Poland. And the Americans and the British had still to launch OVERLORD. There was simply no way to prevent Soviet domination of Eastern Europe if Hitler were to be beaten. From the American point of view the key treasures in the balance of power lie in the West, especially the Ruhr basin in Germany. Rather than recognizing the great advantages that the Americans did gain after the war, critics have mistakenly emphasized the geopolitical significance of the Balkans. As the historian Mark Stoler argued at a 1983 meeting of the American Historical Association: "Roosevelt's policies succeeded in keeping an unlikely alliance together to defeat a feared enemy. Stalin gained no more than Tsar Nicholas II would have gained had he been around in 1918."

What conclusions might one draw after reading the discussion that surrounds the meeting of the Big Three at Teheran? One is that Churchill's and Bullitt's ideas have few champions today; most agree that a Balkan invasion would have been a political gamble with the future of Western Europe and, given the difficulties of terrain, a military gamble to boot. Second, after the decisions made at Teheran, the ability to easily resist a Soviet sphere of influence in Eastern Europe probably ended. Third, Teheran marked a subtle shift in the balance of power, with Great Britain on the wane and the Soviet Union on the rise. At Teheran we see the Soviet Union first asserting itself as an equal in the Grand Alliance. Teheran was a turning point not only in Eastern Europe, then, but on a global level. Finally, from our current perspective, the West's and Eastern Europe's loss was only temporarily the Soviet Union's gain. In the long run, Soviet security was not truly enhanced as result of the settlement in Eastern Europe.

SELECTED BIBLIOGRAPHY

1. Beitzell, Robert. *The Uneasy Alliance.* New York: Alfred A. Knopf. 1972.
2. Feis, Herbert. *Churchill, Roosevelt, and Stalin: The War They Waged and the Peace They Sought.* Princeton, N.J.: Princeton University Press. 1957.
3. Mark, Eduard. "American Policy toward Eastern Europe and the Origins of the Cold War." *Journal of American History.* Vol. 68, No. 2 (September 1981).
4. Mastny, Vojtech. *Russia's Road to the Cold War.* New York: Columbia University Press. 1979.
5. _____. "Soviet War Aims at the Moscow and Teheran Conferences of 1943." *Journal of Modern History.* Vol. 47, No. 3 (September 1975).
6. Neumann, William L. *After Victory: Churchill, Roosevelt, Stalin, and the Making of the Peace.* New York: Harper and Row. 1967.
7. Nicholls, Anthony and John W. Wheeler–Bennett. *The Semblance of Peace.* New York: St. Martin's. 1972.
8. Sainsbury, Keith. *The Turning Point. Roosevelt, Stalin, Churchill, and Chiang Kai–Shek, 1943: The Moscow, Cairo, and Teheran Conferences.* New York: Oxford University Press. 1985.
9. Smith, Gaddis. *American Diplomacy during the Second World War.* New York: Wiley. 1965.
10. Stoler, Mark A. "The 'Pacific–First' Alternative." *The International Historical Review.* Vol. 2, No. 3 (July 1980).
11. _____. "The 'Second Front' and American Fear of Soviet Expansion, 1941–1943." *Military Affairs.* Vol. 39, No. 3 (October 1975).

Was It Really Necessary
to Use the Atomic Bomb?

Ever since revisionist historians ingeniously speculated that the atomic bombs used against Japan in 1945 were dropped mainly as a demonstration against Soviet Russia, scholars and laymen have developed a new interest in the old but perennially debatable questions. Why were the atomic bombs dropped on Japan? Could less drastic alternatives have been implemented? Did the dropping of the bomb contribute to the Cold War? Particularly thought-provoking are the five alternatives that have frequently been put forward as more humane, yet equally efficient substitutes to the military use of the bomb: 1) awaiting Soviet entry and/or declaration of war against Japan; 2) supplying a noncombat demonstration of the weapon; 3) modifying the terms of unconditional surrender so that the Japanese could retain their imperial institution; 4) pursuing alleged Japanese peace feelers; or 5) utilizing conventional warfare for a longer period. The question that concerns us is the current status of this argument. More specifically, what insights do the new documents and the latest scholarly literature have to offer on these perplexing questions and challenging alternatives?

Historians now approach the issue by pointing out that Harry Truman acted largely on the basis of assumptions which the Franklin Roosevelt administration bequeathed to him. Roosevelt initially set the foundation for Truman's later decision by assuming that the bomb was a legitimate weapon to use in wartime, by deciding to build the bomb in partnership with the British, by opting to keep the Soviets officially uninformed (the Soviets had gained some information through their espionage network), and by blocking any effort, in the initial stages, at international control of atomic energy.

When Truman became President on April 12, 1945, he was incompletely informed on many of Roosevelt's most secret policy decisions. As Vice-President, he was not briefed on the exact nature of the Manhattan Project and was not fully aware that it was aimed toward the creation of an atomic bomb. Though Truman was legally free to revise Roosevelt's policies, consider the tremendous personal and political obstacles inhibiting him. The fact that Roosevelt had been such a magnetic and popular President deterred Truman from any rash re-evaluation. Further, he most probably contemplated the electoral catastrophe which potentially awaited him if the American public ever learned that he had unilaterally reversed Roosevelt's policies and shared with the Soviets a secret which had cost the U.S. $2 billion in research and development monies. For Truman, the question was never one of challenging Roosevelt's assumptions and commitments. On the contrary, he was solely concerned with how these policies might be implemented.

By the time of the Potsdam Conference in July 1945, Truman was faced with his first key decision and the following dilemma. According to earlier requests made by the U.S. at Teheran and Yalta, the Soviet Union had agreed to enter the Pacific war on August 8. However, since April 1945 Japan no longer posed as serious a threat. Japan's navy had been swept from the seas, and they could not now shift their Manchurian army to the Japanese homelands to meet an American invasion. Soviet entry was not needed under the new circumstances. More than that, Soviet promises to the U.S. were now an obstacle. Could the U.S. keep the Soviet Union out of the Pacific war? Was this the goal of Truman at Potsdam? Evidence suggests that Soviet exclusion from significant penetration into the Pacific theatre was indeed the aim at Potsdam. Given the difficulties in stopping Soviet advances in Eastern Europe, plus the problems encountered during negotiations with the Soviets over the Polish and German questions, it is doubtful that Truman relished a repeat of this type of confrontation with Stalin in the Far East. The easiest way to avoid this dreaded possibility was to use the atomic bomb to get the war over with as quickly as possible, before the real weight of Soviet influence could be felt.

An additional bonus to this approach was offered by the fact that Truman and his advisers believed that a combat demonstration of the bomb would "impress" the Soviets and make them more amenable to American wishes in the future. Hence, the reasoning behind Truman's failure to invite Stalin to sign the Potsdam Proclamation of July 26 calling for Japan's unconditional surrender, and his very casual statement to Stalin at Potsdam that the U.S. had developed "a new weapon of unusual destructive force" for use against Japan, without explicitly informing Stalin that it was an atomic weapon.

Some historians have suggested that the real reason for Truman's actions with regard to the Potsdam Proclamation and the casual announcement actually reflected a clever strategy: these scholars maintain that Truman wanted to use the bomb and feared that Stalin's signature to a declaration of war, or his knowledge of extensive American progress on the atomic bomb would prompt him to hasten Soviet intervention; thus, catapulting Japan to surrender and thereby making a nuclear attack unnecessary, even impossible. In other words, they argue that Truman was working to delay Japan's surrender specifically to guarantee use of the new weapon. The major difficulty with this revisionist hypothesis is that it exaggerates and claims too much. More explicitly, Truman wanted to avoid requesting any more favors from the Soviets and, further, he was adamantly against discussing atomic energy with Stalin.

In conclusion, let us apply these new insights to the alternatives listed above. We can now understand why Truman's administration did not await Soviet entry and/or a declaration of war, why a noncombat demonstration of the weapon was not provided and why conventional warfare was not relied upon for a longer period of time. Contrary to all these alternatives, Truman was aiming to minimize the effects of Soviet entry and considered the bomb a legitimate and efficient way both to end the war rapidly and impress the Russians. Truman believed that the bomb would make a significant diplomatic and military impression on the Japanese and Soviet governments only if it had also been shown to have demonstrated military worth on the field of battle.

Further, as to the question of the pursuance of alleged peace feelers, the fact is that the Japanese never approached the U.S. directly to negotiate a peace settlement, but rather these peace feelers were a series of messages from their foreign minister to their ambassador in Moscow asking him to research the possibility of having the Soviets serve as intermediaries in future U.S.-Japanese peace negotiations. Since American intelligence had cracked the Japanese ambassadorial code even before the Pearl Harbor attack, these messages, once intercepted, were quickly decoded and analyzed. As these Japanese proposals included the demand that the Emperor be retained, they were never seriously considered as adequately fulfilling American expectations.

Finally, what about the alternative of redefining unconditional surrender to guarantee Japan's imperial institutions? The evidence suggests that Truman believed that any concession to the Japanese might be interpreted as a sign of appeasement on the part of the American public; even worse it might be considered a grave mistake given the experience with Germany after the First World War. It is here that Truman and his advisers most tragically erred. For neither bomb need have been necessary if the words "unconditional surrender" were removed from the U.S. peace demands. It is now clear that from July 13 onward, the only obstacle in the way of a Japanese decision to surrender was the requirement that it be "unconditional." The importance of this issue to the Japanese can best be measured when one remembers that even after the dropping of the two bombs on Hiroshima and Nagasaki, and after the Soviet declaration of war, the Japanese government still held to their demand that the Emperor and the dynasty be retained. In the end, the U.S. compromised on this issue by implicitly recognizing the Emperor, but requiring him to subject his power to the orders of the Allied supreme commander.

Today, then, the real lament is not what the revisionist historians have suggested in their accusation—that the U.S. used the bomb solely to influence the Russians. Rather, the agony lies in the fact that the Truman administration devoted most of its thought to *how* the bombs would be used, rather than to the moral question of *whether* they should be used. Almost totally neglected by these policymakers was the contaminated fallout which would accompany a nuclear explosion. Practically no one foresaw that war was moving from the deliberate killing and maiming of men and women in the present to the killing and maiming of future generations.

SELECTED BIBLIOGRAPHY

1. Alperovitz, Gar. *Atomic Diplomacy.* New York: Simon and Schuster. 1965.
2. Baker, Paul R., ed. *The Atomic Bomb: The Great Decision.* Hinsdale, Ill.: The Dryden Press. 1968.
3. Bernstein, Barton J., ed. *The Atomic Bomb: The Critical Issues.* Boston: Little, Brown and Co. 1976.
4. Feis, Herbert. *The Atomic Bomb and the End of World War II.* Princeton, N.J.: Princeton University Press. 1966.
5. Ferrell, Robert H., ed. "Truman at Potsdam," *American Heritage,* Vol. 31, No. 4 (June/July 1980), pp. 36–47.
6. Groueff, Stephane. *Manhattan Project: The Untold Story of the Making of the Atomic Bomb.* Boston: Little, Brown and Co. 1967.
7. Herken, Gregg F. *The Winning Weapon: The Atomic Bomb in the Cold War.* New York: Alfred A. Knopf. 1981.
8. Lifton, Robert J. *Death in Life.* New York: Random House. 1968.
9. Mandelbaum, Michael. *The Nuclear Question: The United States and Nuclear Weapons, 1946–1976.* New York: Cambridge University Press. 1979.
10. _____. *The Nuclear Revolution: International Politics before and after Hiroshima.* New York: Cambridge University Press. 1981.
11. Sherwin, Martin J. *A World Destroyed.* New York: Alfred A. Knopf. 1975.

"The strongest reason for giving woman all the opportunities for higher education, for the full development of her faculties, her forces of mind and body; for giving her the most enlarged freedom of thought and action; a complete emancipation from all forms of bondage, of custom, dependence, superstition; from all the crippling influences of fear—is the solitude and personal responsibility of her own individual life. The strongest reason why we ask for woman a voice in the government under which she lives; in the religion she is asked to believe; equality in social life, where she is the chief factor; a place in the trades and professions, where she may earn her bread, is because of her birthright to self-sovereignty; because, as an individual, she must rely on herself." Elizabeth Cady Stanton, Speech, "The Solitude of Self," 1892.

31

The Home Front During World War II: A Victory Over the Great Depression

One of the least studied facets of the American World War II experience is the Home Front and the triumph that took place there: the Victory over the Great Depression. If two words had to be chosen to characterize the American experience at home during World War II, they would be size and abundance. The domestic reality was ebullient prosperity and the mood was expectant buoyancy. This reality also carried important policy implications, conceivably as significant as those of the war itself. The newly prosperous, naturally, attributed their great wealth and progress to the blessings of free private enterprise. It would have been un-American to do otherwise. But more correctly, America had triumphed over its traditions and its history, and had created for itself a genuine middle-class democracy.

At first, it seemed as if the domestic experience of World War II might ominously repeat the experience of World War I, where American business prospered mightily, but the economic gains and sacrifices for the rest of society were unequally and unfairly distributed. For once again, government caved in to the pressures of America's corporate elite.

Government promised to bear the brunt of the cost of business expansion, guaranteed that military contracts would be profitable with the cost-plus-a-fixed-fee contract, and suspended its antitrust laws as they related to war production. At the same time, the many New Deal agencies which had been created to protect the poor were disbanded.

When, in the winter of 1942–43, Franklin Roosevelt moved to remedy some of the incipient inequities by introducing a more rigorous tax bill aimed to trim war profits, Congress immediately slapped it down and passed, over FDR's veto, a version of its own. A curious tax bill it was. Taxes were lowered on incomes in the $6000 to $12,000 a year range—Congressmen earned $10,000 a year—and taxes were increased on those making less than $1200 a year. In the end, the Congressional tax bill raised extra monies, mainly from the poor, whereas Roosevelt's bill would have raised the monies chiefly from the well-to-do.

Between Congressional and executive policies, then, big business was assured that the production miracle of World War II would also be a cornucopia of profits. Corporate profits, after taxes, climbed from $6.4 billion in 1940 to $10.8 billion in 1944. Corporate assets rose from $54 billion in 1939 to nearly $100 billion in 1945.

But, unlike World War I, this growth of corporate wealth did not occur at the expense of any one group, rather the total economic pie was expanded by unprecedented deficit spending.

The result was that all classes gained significantly. Indeed, the war brought about an unexpected redistribution of incomes.

Before the war, income distribution had not been much improved by the New Deal programs; in fact, a look at income apportionment in the years between World War I and World War II shows that, as a whole, income was more fairly apportioned in 1918 than it was twenty years later. (See Chart I: Shares of National Income). America might be said to be a reincarnation of Disraeli's England, a nation of two worlds, "those with decent work and those without it."

Keynesian spending and the requisites of war were to change all this. Specifically, to meet the challenges of war, the government provided the key element needed for a massive reduction of economic inequalities: money. By July 1940, U.S. defense spending was at a rate of $165,000,000 a month. Six months later it had quintupled to $900,000,000 a month. By December 1941, it increased twelve-fold, to nearly $2 billion a month. At its peak in November 1943, U.S. defense spending was $6 billion a month. On the one hand, the national debt jumped from $40 billion to $260 billion. On the other hand, full employment returned and, as with the profits of big business, wages, salaries, and other elements of personal income soared.

At the time of Pearl Harbor, the liquid assets of individuals came to $50 billion; by the end of 1944 that figure had reached a record $140 billion. Personal income rose from $72.6 billion in 1939 to $172 billion in 1945; even allowing for inflation, the real growth was 68% in just six years. The effects of this economic revolution can be seen in the following charts. (See Charts II, III, and IV).

This positive transformation in the lifestyle of Americans was also the result of the government not letting its veterans down, but rather treating them with the dignity and respect that they had earned. Indeed, veterans and their dependents, calculated by 1950 to be one-third of the nation, were transformed into a privileged group. That one-third of the population was to receive educational, medical, and material benefits unequaled in American, or any other nation's World War II history. As one author has remarked, it was "social welfare without Socialism," or "Social Welfare the American Way."[7]

CHART I

Shares of National Income	1918	1929	1937
Lowest Fifth	6.8	5.4	3.6
Second Fifth	12.6	10.1	10.4
Third Fifth	14.6	14.4	15.7
Fourth Fifth	18.3	17.9	21.8
Highest Fifth	47.4	51.3	48.5

CHART II
Distribution of Family Incomes
1935–1936

Incomes of less than $1000 per annum 43.5%
Incomes of $1000–1999 per annum 34.2%
Incomes of $2000–2999 per annum 13.1%
Incomes of $3000–3999 per annum 4.4%
Incomes of $4000–4999 per annum 1.7%
Incomes of $5000 and more per annum 3.1%

CHART III
Distribution of Family Incomes
1945–1946

Incomes of less than $1000 per annum 8.8%
Incomes of $1000–1999 per annum 17.6%
Incomes of $2000–2999 per annum 20.3%
Incomes of $3000–3999 per annum 19.8%
Incomes of $4000–4999 per annum 12.4%
Incomes of $5000 and more per annum 21.1%

CHART IV
Family Incomes Increase
1941–1945

Incomes Level	Increase
Lowest Fifth	+68%
Second Fifth	+59%
Third Fifth	+36%
Fourth Fifth	+30%
Top Fifth	+20%

As with incomes, the war brought about a transformation in the way health and medical benefits were distributed in the nation. The distressful nature of health before the war can be perceived by the yardstick which conscription provided. The Army had purposely pegged its minimum requirements low, because of the pressures for manpower and because of the anticipated weaknesses of a nation coming off a decade of depression. A draftee had merely to be five feet tall, weigh 105 pounds, have correctable vision, have half his teeth, no flat feet, no hernias, and no venereal diseases. Army officials had expected a rejection rate of 20 percent. The startling reality was that rejections averaged 50 percent. The main reason was the malnutrition from the many years of poverty.

With the onset of the war, the nation found that its medical resources had to be as effectively mobilized as its defense industries. The Federal government moved in to build hospitals and clinics, and to aid young medical and dental students in their schooling. Experiments in new pre–paid medical plans were made, and eventually came to be commonplace. Concerns for nutrition and balanced meals at war plants were encouraged by government agencies. Further, 16,000,000 men in the services, and many of their dependents, were, in effect, under a program of socialized medicine. Finally, the wartime prosperity allowed people to provide health care for themselves.

The results were stunning. Twice as many doctors and dentists graduated in 1944 as any depression year. There was a drop in the death rate and a clear–cut improvement in the infant mortality rate—indeed, the lowest in the country's history. As wartime casualties represented less than five percent of all American deaths between December 1941 and August 1945, life expectancy, which had hardly improved between 1932 and 1939, increased three years between 1939 and 1945. For blacks, the increase was five years. Death rates for infants under one year of age was cut by more than a third.

To be sure, the Home Front was not without its share of anxieties and problems. The war was tough, for a number of reasons, on families. Housing was always inadequate. Rationing was often a problem. For all Japanese-Americans, most blacks, and some American Jews, Italian-Americans, German-Americans, and Mexican-Americans, there were infringements on civil rights and varying periods of circumscribed liberties. Further, the injury rates in the war industries were quite disturbing, in fact, more than twice as high as they were in the military. (Remember that only one serviceman in ten was ever exposed to combat).

Nonetheless, a look at the prosperity of the Home Front in World War II and the manner in which it was achieved is instructive to Americans. Granted, a key reason for America's good fortune was geographical—our nation was isolated from any real threat of attack.

Still, at a time when the Federal government's leadership, Keynesian economics, and social welfare programs are the bane of informed thinking, it is sobering to reflect on the World War II experience. The then-government leadership, deficit spending, and a sense of purpose and teamwork allowed for national leaders in the private and public sectors to effect unprecedented progress for almost all social groups. It was more than a victory over our enemies, it was also a victory over our own traditions and our history.

SELECTED BIBLIOGRAPHY

1. Blum, John Morton. *V Was For Victory*. New York and London: Harcourt Brace Jovanovich. 1976.
2. Honey, Maureen. *Creating Roșie the Riveter*. Amherst: University of Massachusetts Press. 1984.
3. Kolko, Gabriel. *Wealth and Power in America*. New York: Praeger. 1962.
4. Lampman, Robert J. *The Share of Top Wealthholders in National Wealth, 1922–56*. Princeton, N.J.: Princeton University Press. 1962.
5. Lichtenstein, Nelson. *Labor's War at Home*. New York: Cambridge University Press. 1982.
6. Nash, Gerald D. *The American West Transformed: The Impact of the Second World War*. Bloomington, Ind.: Indiana University Press. 1985.
7. Perrett, Geoffrey. *Days of Sadness, Years of Triumph*. New York: Coward, McCann and Geoghegan. 1973.
8. Polenberg, Richard. *War and Society*. Philadelphia and New York: J.B. Lippincott. 1972.
9. Vatter, Harold G. *The U.S. Economy in World War II*. New York: Columbia University Press. 1985.

Who Started the Cold War?

The Cold War is generally defined as the period of intense political, economic, military and ideological rivalry which has characterized the relationship between the U.S. and the Soviet Union since the defeat of Germany in 1945. In a way, the Cold War—a term meant to symbolize an "armed truce" and the avoidance of military confrontation—is a misnomer, for Americans and other peoples have shed much blood in this rivalry, particularly during the U.S. interventions in Korea and Vietnam. Nonetheless, the name has stuck and historians have adopted it in their research and writings.

A key question which has preoccupied historians is the question of who was "to blame" for initiating this rivalry. As expected, there is intense disagreement on the answer to this involved question. Basically, the disagreement focuses on two schools of thought: the Orthodox and the Revisionist.

The Orthodox view places the main blame and responsibility on the Soviet Union. Harry Truman, because of his memoirs and speeches, can be considered the first Orthodox spokesman. Their argument emphasizes that after World War II the U.S. was anxiously trying to demobilize, that it had no territorial ambitions, that Americans wanted a peaceful world, and that we were trying to get back to the "normalcy" of the pre-war years. But the Soviet Union, in the grip of a militant ideology, hostile to capitalism in all its forms and internally a totalitarian state, launched a challenge to the free world by its callous actions in Eastern Europe. Given these developments, Orthodox historians argue, there was no choice for the U.S. but to react to the challenge and take up the charge.

Revisionist historians disagree and are more inclined to see the U.S. as primarily responsible for the beginning of the Cold War. Revisionists believe that since the U.S. was the most powerful nation in the world after World War II, Americans should have been the least insecure, and the most able to compromise. Instead, argue the Revisionists, the U.S. mistakenly perceived the Soviet Union as an imminent threat and began an aggressive foreign policy which pushed into areas of Europe and Asia where no vital national interests were involved.

One segment of Revisionism sees a major source for error in the American tendency to approach foreign policy in a moralistic and ethnocentric manner. As a result, the U.S. thought that it knew what was best for other nations and was blinded to the special needs and particular circumstances of other countries. Another segment of Revisionism sees a major source for U.S. error in the structures and imperatives of American capitalism. According to this view, American economic elites aggressively promote business interests abroad, a practice which in turn carries inevitable military and political ramifications.

As is usual in this series of essays on prominent controversies in American historiography, it is very difficult to resolve such differences of approach and opinion in the span of a few pages. Not surprisingly, my personal opinion follows a middle path. Both nations, I believe, were responsible for starting the Cold War. The Soviet Union's Marxist-Leninist ideology and totalitarian political structure were bound to create fears and insecurities in American minds. And the American ideals of national self-determination and liberal capitalism were bound to create suspicions in a Soviet mind already determined to avoid a repetition of the German invasions of World War I and World War II. Further, I believe that the emotional postwar situation in 1945, with its 54 million dead, with the shocking appearance of atomic weapons, etc., was especially conducive to mutual fear and mistrust. It was natural, then, under these circumstances, for most Americans to accept the assumption that since Russia's tsarist tradition had been expansionist and aggressive, the Soviet Union, now Marxist and totalitarian, would be a doubly dangerous threat.

At this point the Revisionist challenge intrudes. It may have been an understandable assumption for Americans to make, but was it a correct one? Let us look at the issue more closely, beginning first with a look at Russia's imperial tsarist tradition. It was indeed an expanionist tradition, but with varied motives. It was not correct to assess Russian expansionism in tsarist times as aiming at world domination. Messianic universalism was not really the inspiration for their expansion. Rather, growth was defensive, and motivated by fear as much as by a desire for glory or profit. This fear is easy to understand when one considers the repeated invasions of Russia. There were 160 foreign invasions during the period of Western Europe's Renaissance; 10 great wars with Sweden and Poland during the Age of Enlightenment; Napoleon's invasion, the Crimean War and the Russo-Turkish War in the nineteenth century; the Russo-Japanese War, World War I and World War II in the twentieth century. To simply label Russian aims during these five centuries as a reflection of inherent expansionism and aggressivism misses the key point. The threat of invasion and the experience of war were ever-present.

What about the expansionism and aggressivism inherent in Soviet Marxism? Was it correct for Americans to assume that the Soviets' Communist ideology and totalitarian domestic system would necessarily entail a subversive and expansionistic foreign policy? In this regard it is important to note that by the time of Stalin's accession to power, Marxist ideological rhetoric had most significantly been utilized in the domestic arena rather than in foreign affairs. Foreign policy in the hands of Stalin had repeatedly been shown to be based on pragmatic interests, not on ideological sentiments. In fact, Soviet foreign policy had been moderated to such a large degree that socialist concerns were essentially subordinated to the concerns of Soviet patriotism. The lack of Soviet support for Mao, Soviet anger with Yugoslavia over Trieste, and the Soviet Union's restrained actions in Finland, Austria and Iran after World War II are examples which seem to support the conclusion that the Soviet Union was acting primarily with defensive rather than with Marxist ideological concerns in mind.

Further, it should have come as no surprise to the U.S. that the Soviet Union would be intransigent over the future of Poland, where the German invasions had been launched; and that they would be equally stubborn over Czechoslovakia, the strategic key to control over Eastern Europe. After all, Eastern Europe was not vital to American security, particularly from the Soviet point of view. For the U.S. the real prizes were West Germany and Japan, and U.S. hegemony over those areas was never compromised. Nor can it be said that the U.S. fared so badly after World War II. It is not an overstatement to say that the U.S., because of World War II, emerged as the greatest industrial and economic power in the world.

Once again, it was too much for the American public or the U.S. government, with the emotions of the time, to evaluate the situation objectively. But today objectivity and rationality are mandatory. It is for this reason that I believe that the Revisionist view of the origins of the Cold War is most important. It forces Americans to stop, to rethink and to be self-critical at a time when crucial decisions are often too quickly made, especially in the realm of the U.S.'s growing role as the world's policeman and "guardian" of international morality.

It appears that not enough public review in terms of manpower and resources and dollars has been given to the network of institutions which has sprung up in our nation dealing with the Cold War—a network rightly labeled the military-industrial complex. By 1967 the Senate Foreign Relations Committee figured that the U.S. had spent $1 trillion on the Cold War. By 1972 that estimate was up to $1.4 trillion. In this same vein, by 1970 the Department of Defense had greater assets than America's 75 largest industrial corporations and employed nearly as many people as the top 30 firms. In 1981, the Reagan Administration embarked on the nation's largest peacetime military buildup, one totaling some $1.5 trillion over the first five years.

Today there is no steadfast voice in the political spectrum which speaks out in opposition to the armaments industry. Ever since the paranoia of the 1950s, championed by Senator Joe McCarthy, an alternative policy to escalating defense budgets has been lost, for neither political party dares to expose itself to the accusation that it is or has been an "appeaser." At a time when every international event is emotionally scrutinized in terms of America's "national security" and when U.S. smugness and self-righteousness is at a highpoint, the Revisionist point of view seems a necessary bit of intellectual reading in order to have a balanced view of the Cold War and its origins.

SELECTED BIBLIOGRAPHY

1. Brown, Seyom. *The Faces of Power: Constancy and Change in United States Foreign Policy from Truman to Johnson.* New York: Columbia University Press. 1969.
2. Gaddis, John Lewis. *Strategies of Containment.* New York: Oxford University Press. 1982.
3. _____. *The United States and the Origins of the Cold War.* New York: Columbia University Press. 1972.
4. Gardner, Lloyd C. *Architects of Illusion.* Chicago: Quadrangle Books. 1970.
5. Iriye, Akira. *The Cold War in Asia: A Historical Introduction.* Englewood Cliffs, N.J.: Prentice-Hall. 1974.
6. Kuniholm, Bruce R. *The Origins of the Cold War in the Near East.* Princeton, N.J.: Princeton University Press. 1980.
7. LaFeber, Walter. *America, Russia, and the Cold War.* New York: John Wiley and Sons. 1967.
8. Paterson, Thomas G. and Robert J. McMahon. eds. *The Origins of the Cold War.* Lexington, Mass. and Toronto: D.C. Heath and Co. Third Edition. 1991.
9. Yergin, Daniel. *Shattered Peace: The Origins of the Cold War and the National Security State.* Boston: Houghton Mifflin Company. 1978.

"Since the end of [World War II], the United States has invested its substance and its energy in a great constructive effort to restore peace, stability, and freedom in the world. We have sought no territory and we have imposed our will on none. We have asked for no privileges we would not extend to others. We have constantly and vigorously supported the United Nations. . . . We have consistently advocated and relied upon peaceful settlement of disputes among nations." Harry S. Truman, Inaugural Address, January 20, 1949.

33

Was Truman a "Great" or "Near-Great" President?

There is a soft spot in American hearts today for Harry S Truman. In the midst of present-day political difficulties, "Give'em Hell Harry" offers a reassuring image. He was a plain, direct, impeccably honest man, deeply reverent of the office that he held. He showed that the grandeur of the Presidency need not lead to a lordly lifestyle while in office, nor a great accumulation of personal wealth and riches for the years after office. He further demonstrated that the immense powers of the Presidency need not lead to corruption. But perhaps Americans retain a feeling of special affection for Harry Truman because we sympathize with his predicament: he was the first to grapple with the immense post-World War II problems associated with the Cold War; he was the first to preside over the horrors associated with a nuclear age.

How warranted is this nostalgia for the Truman Presidency? Does close historical scrutiny of Truman's legacy substantiate the popular image? The record is conflicting. A look at both sides of the Truman controversy will reveal the dilemmas of professing an assured verdict.

Critics find crucial mistakes in both foreign and domestic affairs, mistakes that mark a watershed in American history. At a time when a great leader might have risen above the mundane and led the international community into a grander age, the most powerful nation in the world was shackled, according to these critics, to the narrow-minded views of a "courthouse" politician. For instance, critics hold Truman responsible for a large share of the Cold War and the beginning of an arms race with the Soviet Union. Three key oversights on the part of the Truman Administration, they argue, were particularly disastrous in this regard.

First of all, Truman was callous to Soviet feelings of insecurity over the postwar fate of Eastern Europe. According to critics, there were many examples in 1946 and 1947 when the Soviets displayed flexibility in their decisions and actions in Eastern Europe. It was only after Truman's intransigence that the Soviets finally decided to drop the "Iron Curtain" and proclaim the whole of Eastern Europe as their sphere of influence. Secondly, Truman unnecessarily poisoned relations between the two superpowers by abruptly ending Lend-Lease to the Russians and also, equally abruptly, refusing them a promised postwar loan. Finally, Truman's suspicious and uninformed attitudes sabotaged viable plans for the international control of atomic energy, it is argued, and thereby contributed to the subsequently debilitating nuclear arms race. Ignoring the pleas of many scientists, the Russians were kept uninformed during the war about the development of the atomic bomb. Truman compounded this sign of distrust in the postwar period by

171

refusing the Russians access to our atomic "secrets" unless they allowed the United Nations to inspect their defense capabilities. Such an approach on Truman's part killed all chances for progress or compromise on the atomic energy issue.

In sum, the general belief of critics on these key issues is that Truman acted too hastily, and did not give diplomacy a full chance. He did not sympathize with the very real fears the Soviets held, and in the end misjudged their intentions and their potential to threaten the U.S. Later, in 1950, Truman compounded these mistakes by hurriedly and rashly adopting a National Security Council document known as NSC-68. NSC-68 was the result of a review that the National Security Council had undertaken of America's strategic position in the world. The basic assumptions about the Soviet Union which underpinned the document were exceedingly pessimistic, and the alternatives of action presented to President Truman were exceedingly narrow. The drafters of NSC-68 especially encouraged Truman to engage in a "bold and massive program of rebuilding the West's defensive potential to surpass that of the Soviet world." Truman was urged to abandon the $15 billion ceiling which was then set on defense spending, and to prepare the American people for defense spending of up to 20 percent of the gross national product, on the scale of $50 billion annually. Despite its debatable premises and options, Truman initialed this startling document without hesitation and referred to it as "my five-year plan for peace." As a result, critics argue, the U.S. over-reacted under Truman's guidance and committed itself prematurely to an expensive policy of global containment and to the buildup of a military-industrial complex of menacing proportions.

In another important area of controversy, the Korean War, critics believe that Truman was mistaken when he decided to go beyond the 38th parallel in September 1950, and when he allowed peace negotiations to bog down on negligible matters later in 1951 and 1952. Especially unfortunate, say critics, was Truman's failure to call for a Congressional vote or resolution on the Administration's conduct of the war.

Domestically, critics find the list of errors equally long. First of all, Truman's failure to get Congress to pass his reform package, the Fair Deal, is attributed to a lack of caution and restraint. As the domestic political situation was very delicate, they argue that Truman might have been more successful had he not attempted to push through his entire program all at once.

Secondly, critics argue that Truman exhibited a short-sighted impetuousness when he seized the country's steel mills in 1952. Though the threatened steel strike of that year seemed likely to disrupt production of an essential commodity needed in the Korean War and elsewhere, Truman had an alternative that was not "above the law"—use of the injunction provision of the Taft-Hartley Act. But Truman, believing that a strong President was necessary for successful government, disliking the injunction provision of the Taft-Hartley Act, and worrying about maintaining essential supplies of steel for U.N. troops in Korea, incautiously seized the steel mills. The result was a major defeat for Truman as the Supreme Court in *Youngstown Sheet & Tube Company v. Sawyer* (1952) ruled that his actions were unconstitutional.

Thirdly, Truman is blamed for a share of the responsibility for the rise of McCarthyism. Truman was the one who first used the "communist in government" ploy to smear Progressive Party presidential candidate Henry Wallace. Also, he played up the "communist conspiracy abroad" idea to secure approval for his Truman Doctrine, and he set a dangerous precedent when he launched a loyalty program that disregarded important personal civil liberties.

Fourthly, Truman is criticized for the general mediocrity of his political appointments to the Cabinet, to the White House Staff and to the Supreme Court. As Truman himself was not a charismatic leader, it was of utmost importance that his appointees be dynamic, intelligent and honest. Instead, with some notable exceptions such as George C. Marshall as Secretary of State, most were ill-prepared for the important appointments they received. Not surprisingly, many of his cronies later became involved in corrupt practices. Truman compounded this problem by first proving reluctant to believe the accusations, and then allowing excessive loyalty to his friends to inhibit him from imposing strict and swift punishments. I.F. Stone best captured this failure when he wrote: "The Truman era was the era of the moocher. The place was full of Wimpys who could be had for a hamburger."

Truman was hurt, too, by his tendency to involve himself in political bickering and personal squabbling of the most mundane sort. The most notorious example was Truman's vehement attack on music critic Paul Hume, who had just reviewed Margaret Truman's concert at Constitution Hall:

> I have just read your lousy review buried in the back pages. You sound like a frustrated man that never made a success, an eight-ulcer man on a four-ulcer job, and all four ulcers working. I never met you, but if I do you'll need a new nose and plenty of beefsteak and perhaps a supporter below. Westbrook Pegler, a guttersnipe, is a gentleman compared to you. You can take that as more of an insult than a reflection on your ancestry.

This type of demeaning language and behavior cost Truman dearly in public esteem.

There is much to criticize in the Truman Presidency. But, on the other hand, many of these same judgments can be softened if taken from another perspective. As regards the Cold War, criticism of Truman may be measurably lessened when one recognizes that seldom in history have wartime alliances lasted after the threat of the common enemy disappeared. Invariably, members of victorious wartime alliances have grown to fear each other before much time has elapsed. One thinks readily of the great European coalition which was formed to defeat Napoleon—England, Austria, Prussia and Russia. Once the signs were clear that Napoleon was going to be defeated, the Austrian foreign minister Klemens von Metternich began to plot against the growing power of Russia. At the peace conference itself, war almost broke out as England, France and Austria aligned on one side, and Prussia and Russia on the other, in a dispute involving the future of Poland and Saxony. Examples such as this might be found throughout the history of humankind, going back to ancient times. From this perspective, then, one might see the Cold War as inevitable, especially given the nature of the Soviet political system. Historians do not require a special vision to recognize that Stalin, far more than Truman, was a believer in the theory that struggle and force were the key determinants of successful diplomacy. Under such circumstances, it is quite ethnocentric to claim that the Soviet Union always acted in response to American actions, without their own independent sources of conduct and behavior, and that they only "reacted" to American policies during the Cold War.

It is also illusory not to recognize the role of public and Congressional opinion at this crucial time. For instance, Congress was against continued Lend-Lease to the Russians, and many Congressmen were equally hostile to both the loan issue and to the sharing of our atomic secrets with the rest of the world. Even one of Truman's great achievements, the Marshall Plan, was threatened by the suspicious and isolationist attitudes of many Congressmen.

It is true that mistakes were made in Korea, but from another perspective one might be thankful that Truman brought the U.S. through that war without using nuclear weapons, and without allowing it to escalate into an even wider international conflict. Similarly, a hypothesis might be made that Truman exhibited greatness in refusing to become involved in a potentially unwinnable situation in the Chinese Civil War. While critics in 1949 lambasted Truman for "losing" China, Truman held his ground and most likely saved the U.S. from a disastrous involvement.

Domestically, the Truman record may be adjudged in an equally positive manner. Though it is true that the key bills of the Fair Deal were not passed—examples included Aid to Education, the Fair Employment Practices Act, Civil Rights legislation, and National Health Insurance—a host of other important bills were passed. In fact, the New Deal was both consolidated and expanded by Truman. After all, the public mood after the war was not geared toward continued sacrifice for further reforms. The nation was anxious to get back to normalcy and to a free economy with fewer governmental restrictions and guidelines. Americans had been through a Depression and a World War in succession and they were expecting to indulge in the materialistic lifestyle that they thought their due now that victory was achieved.

If public opinion, then, did not favor the Fair Deal, neither did other political realities. The Constitution of the U.S. may give a President important powers in the area of foreign affairs, but in domestic matters he is effectively stymied by hallowed checks and balances. Even Franklin Roosevelt, with all his charisma and public support, found Congress responsive for only a short time. Reform for Truman was made more difficult by the fact that he never did have "safe" working majorities in his Congresses. *De facto* Congressional control was held by a coalition of conservatives from the South and the Midwest. And, because of the difficult foreign policy situation, with the exception of the Israeli question, Truman could never sacrifice an important foreign policy position in exchange for a domestic concession. Under these circumstances, it is amazing, say some historians, that Truman passed any significant legislation at all.

As for McCarthyism, it was a problem that transcended the Presidency. Forces deep in the American psyche, and changes in the postwar world too rapid for the average American to comprehend were most responsible for this phenomenon. Specifically, the "surprise" of Truman's victory in the Election of 1948 ended bipartisanship in foreign affairs. Republicans now turned to more extreme measures and strategies in their attacks on Democrats. Further, the "fall of China" in 1949, followed by the shocks of Alger Hiss's perjury and the successful explosion of an atomic bomb by the Russians created a groundswell of discontent and frustration upon which Joseph McCarthy worked his demagogic magic.

Finally, Truman should be credited with guiding the U.S. through a difficult postwar economic reconversion without an ensuing Depression, and with keeping inflation reasonable during his years in office. Through it all, despite periods of unpopularity, Truman was able to convey his concern for the welfare of the average American.

Returning to our major theme: Was Truman a near-great President? The issue of what constitutes "presidential greatness" is in itself a thorny question. Is it the publicly-announced purpose of policy, or the privately-decided reasons behind policy? Is it the effects and consequences of policy judged in terms of success or failure in advancing national survival and the public interest? Or is it some combination of all of the above?

In a recent survey of 49 historians and political scientists conducted for the *Chicago Tribune Magazine,* the 10 best and 10 worst American presidents were selected and rated. Presidents were judged on their leadership qualities, their accomplishments and crisis management abilities, their political skill, their appointments, and their character. Respondents seemed to agree that the best Presidents were men with "a vision." As Robert V. Remini, history professor at the University of Illinois, argued:

The best presidents have been strong political leaders with a vision, if not a complete program, of where they think the country should go to preserve, protect and sometimes advance the liberty and rights of all people. The worst presidents have usually lacked this vision. They simply drifted or were so inept in their relations with the people and Congress as to frustrate any effort toward achieving their goals.

Using Remini's comments as a standard of evaluation, and with the pro's and con's of Truman's administration presented, one can judge with fairly reasonable accuracy that Truman was not a great President. As an unknown who unexpectedly became President at Roosevelt's death, he proved to be more competent and able than many forecast. Possibly, as Dean Acheson remarked, "He was the greatest little man" that America had known.

But there were too many mistakes and oversights to be accorded the mantle of greatness given to a Lincoln, to a Washington or to a Franklin Roosevelt. For all his feistiness and his hard work, Truman was not a man who placed the stamp of his personality on an age; he was not a man who was able to impose his vision on the American people; he was not a man whose force of will shaped the national course. Had he been such a leader, then he would properly be judged great.

Nonetheless, if he was not of heroic proportions, he lived during very difficult times when continents could be hurled into turbulence by a mere short-sighted or stubborn decision. With all his faults, Truman was careful to make no decision which could threaten a Third World War. In fact, he rejected repeated arguments for a "preventive war" against the Soviet Union which some advisers believed would redress the world balance of power in one stroke. Given the horrors that might have accompanied such a course of action, America would consider itself lucky if it were always governed by men and women of the calibre and ability of a Harry Truman. As the historians in the recently-conducted survey concluded, Truman was ranked as the eighth-best among America's Presidents.

SELECTED BIBLIOGRAPHY

1. Bernstein, Barton J., ed. *Politics and Policies of the Truman Administration*. Chicago: Quadrangle Books. 1970.
2. Cochran, Bert. *Harry Truman and the Crisis Presidency*. New York: Funk and Wagnalls. 1973.
3. Ferrell, Robert H. *Harry S. Truman and the Modern American Presidency*. Boston: Little, Brown and Co. 1983.
4. Gosnell, Harold F. *Truman's Crises: A Political Biography of Harry S. Truman*. Westport, Conn.: Greenwood Press. 1980.
5. Hamby, Alonzo L. *Beyond the New Deal: Harry S. Truman and American Liberalism*. New York: Columbia University Press. 1973.
6. Kirkendall, Richard S., ed. *The Truman Period as a Research Field*. Columbia: University of Missouri Press. 1974.
7. McCoy, Donald R. *The Presidency of Harry S. Truman*. Lawrence: University of Kansas Press. 1984.
8. Marcus, Maeva. *Truman and the Steel Seizure Case: The Limits of Presidential Power*. New York: Columbia University Press. 1977.
9. Theoharis, Athan. *Seeds of Repression: Harry S. Truman and the Origins of McCarthyism*. Chicago: Quadrangle Books. 1971.

The Korean War:
What Were the Crucial Issues?

Any occasion where 34,000 U.S. soldiers died would be a somber one for Americans to note, but the memory of the Korean War remains particularly poignant given the domestic turmoil of recent years in South Korea. In fact, the repeated resurgence of political protest and the questionable methods of the South Korean military government remind one of the dilemmas which faced the U.S. in 1950. Perhaps the best way to add perspective to the Korean situation of today is to ponder anew the crucial questions which surrounded America's involvement in Korea more than 40 years ago. Specifically, who was primarily responsible for the outbreak of the Korean War? How much were the Russians involved in the immediate events, and what were their ultimate intentions? Was the Allied invasion north of the 38th parallel a mistake? What have been the recognizable effects and lessons of the war? Finally, do any of these events offer insights into recent developments in Korea?

Before directly discussing these issues, some background information is essential. The division of Korea along the 38th parallel goes back to 1945 when, according to a Soviet-American agreement, the defeated Japanese armies in Korea were disarmed north of the 38th parallel by the Soviet Union and south of that line by the U.S. Lengthy conferences after World War II failed to unify the Korean nation, for neither the Soviets nor the Americans wanted to risk the possibility that a unified Korea would move into the opposing camp. Hence, satellite regimes were set up by the Soviets and Americans in their respective zones.

Regarding the beginnings of the Korean War itself, what may surprise many Americans, instilled with the widely-held belief of blatant North Korean aggression, is the fact that the responsibility for the outbreak of the war is still disputed. For instance, a few years ago, an Indian scholar, Karunakar Gupta, claimed to have discovered evidence that South Korea had actually struck the first blow in the confused events of June 25, 1950. Still another school of revisionist thought recognizes that the North Koreans were responsible for the initial attack, but they excuse this aggression by arguing that threatening behavior on the part of the South Koreans provoked the North to do so. The vast majority of historians, however, accept the traditional interpretation that the war was caused by the direct invasion of South Korea by communist forces from the North.

To what extent were the Russians involved in the immediate events that led to war? As the Russian historical archives are tightly closed, this second area of questioning is impossible to resolve with any degree of certainty. However, it is doubtful that the North Korean leader Kim Il Sung would have acted independently of Soviet approval. Soviet occupation forces were not only nearby in Manchuria, but the Soviets carefully monitored events in North Korea. Further, the build-up of North Korean forces along the 38th parallel well before the invasion of June 25 must have been obvious to the Soviets.

What might have been Soviet intentions in encouraging a North Korean build-up and eventual invasion? Again, given the paucity of Soviet documents there is no assured answer. Still, the best guess is that the North Korean attack was to serve as a "probe by proxy" into an area which the Truman administration had announced as not immediately vital to American national security. Specifically, General Douglas MacArthur had told a *New York Times* correspondent in Tokyo on March 1, 1949, that, strategically, the U.S. could live with hostile forces controlling Formosa or the Korean peninsula. This point was repeated by Secretary of State Dean Acheson in a speech before the National Press Club of Washington on January 12, 1950, when he stated that America's "defense perimeter" did not include either Korea or Formosa. In addition to these statements, the Soviets might have surmised that if the U.S. government had acquiesced in the victory of the communists in China, why would they act decisively in Korea? Further, a North Korean victory would recoup much of the lost prestige which the Soviets suffered from the failure of the Berlin blockade a year earlier. Finally, a North Korean victory might serve as a psychological thrust against Japan. If the U.S. did nothing, Japan might have believed it necessary to better accommodate itself to the surge of communist influence in Asia. Or conversely, if the U.S. over-reacted in Korea, the Russians might find the opportunity to expand their sphere of influence in Europe.

Whoever was the most to blame for initiating the war, and whatever the intentions of the communists, the U.S. reaction was decisive and immediate for several important reasons. First of all, the attack across the 38th parallel represented a direct challenge to a trustee nation of the United Nations, reminding everyone that acquiescence to unrestrained attacks on the League of Nations in the 1930s foreshadowed World War II. Secondly, the failure of "appeasement" to deter Germany in the 1930s was similarly fresh in everyone's mind. Finally, many U.S. foreign policy experts had warned that the Soviet strategy for expansion in the atomic age would most likely utilize a series of limited, piecemeal aggressions.

In the end, these factors provided the rationale for both U.S. and U.N. involvement. A peace resolution was passed through the U.N. Security Council, and troops under a United Nations Command, headed by General MacArthur, were committed to halting the North Korean invasion. In essence, the U.S. gained international sanction for a check on Soviet actions. The Soviet Union was unable to exercise its veto over U.N. involvement. At the time their representative was boycotting the Security Council because of its refusal to replace the Nationalist Chinese delegate with a representative of Red China.

At first, the war went badly for the U.N. armies. Then came General MacArthur's brilliant invasion behind communist lines at Inchon, and the rout of the North Koreans began. In the excitement of impending victory, however, U.N. forces were authorized to extend their invasion north of the 38th parallel. The farther north MacArthur's armies went, the clearer became the Chinese warnings that they would not view with indifference the elimination of North Korean sovereignty, nor would they ignore the threat that rapidly-advancing U.N. forces posed to their own newly-won autonomy.

Was this northward invasion a key mistake, given the limited objectives of the war?* This question was at the heart of the Truman-MacArthur controversy. First of all, MacArthur ignored the Chinese warnings, and his own intelligence studies, which indicated that the Chinese were not bluffing in their threats of entering the war. Later, after the Chinese invasion, MacArthur publicly advocated a policy of all-out war for an unqualified victory, including the blockading and atomic bombing of China as a part of this overall plan. Truman, on the other hand, argued for the continuation of a limited war, fought for moderate objectives. He feared that bombing Chinese bases beyond the Yalu River would provoke a full-scale war with China, and possibly with Russia, with the result that the U.S. would become embroiled, to use General Omar Bradley's words, "in the wrong war, at the wrong place, at the wrong time and with the wrong enemy."

Congress tensely listened to both sides of this debate and gave grudging support to Truman. For the most part, the initiative passed to the communists and the war dragged on until, in 1953, it finally ended with a disheartening compromise, as far as the majority of Americans were then concerned.

What have been the more long-range effects and lessons of the Korean War? Were the Americans of that time warranted in their disillusionment? The lessons are mixed. On the one hand, the Korean War created a pattern of response to communist aggression that was to characterize the U.S. government for the next three decades. The U.S. vastly increased defense expenditures and began to commit itself even more heavily to anti-communist factions throughout the world. The Korean experience seemed to prove to top American officials that a world-wide conspiracy of communism existed and had to be stopped.

More positively, after 1953, general peace ensued in Northeast Asia and this respite allowed for the economic resurgence of both South Korea and Japan. No one needs to be reminded of the economic miracles of the Japanese. But not so readily known is the fact that South Korea is the thirteenth largest trading partner with the U.S., and one of a very few nations in the world that buys over $1 billion worth of farm products from the U.S. each year.

In conclusion, what insights might all of this offer into the domestic unrest of present-day South Korea? To begin, there is a distinct parallel between the arbitrary methods now being employed in South Korea and those of Syngman Rhee, first President of South Korea, in the years after World War II. The U.S. is still, over thirty years later, in the uncomfortable position of supporting an ally whose conduct of internal affairs leaves much to be desired. Secondly, there remains the strategic dilemma of South Korea with regard to U.S. security needs. Again, after all these years, Korea still is considered of peripheral significance, as our first line of defense lies in a line running from the Aleutian Islands off Alaska, to Japan, to Okinawa south of Japan, and on to the Philippines. Finally, one notices that the whole of the Korean question suffers from an inherent ambiguity. This stems from the fact that after World War II the Cold War rivalry between the Soviets and the Americans inhibited the natural course of Korean development. The division of Korea is in no sense the immediate cause of the recent turmoil in the South. But as an underlying factor it continues to affect all major political decision-making. Until a unified Korea is one day allowed to decide its own future, there is bound to be that sense of emptiness and confusion which besets any divided nation.

---

*Four-fifths of all American casualties in the war occurred after U.N. forces crossed the 38th parallel.

SELECTED BIBLIOGRAPHY

1. Caridi, Ronald J. *The Korean War and American Politics.* Philadelphia: University of Pennsylvania Press. 1969.
2. Cumings, Bruce. *The Origins of the Korean War.* Princeton: Princeton University Press. 1981.
3. Dobbs, Charles M. *The Unwanted Symbol: American Foreign Policy, the Cold War, and Korea, 1945–1950.* Kent, Ohio: Kent State University Press. 1981.
4. Goulden, Joseph C. *Korea: The Untold Story of the War.* New York: McGraw-Hill. 1982.
5. Hastings, Max. *The Korean War.* New York: Simon and Schuster. 1987.
6. Paige, Glen D. *The Korean Decision, June 24–30, 1950.* New York: Free Press. 1968.
7. Rees, David. *Korea: The Limited War.* New York: St. Martin's Press. 1964.
8. Stone, I.F. *The Hidden History of the Korean War.* New York: Monthly Review Press. 1969.
9. Stueck, Jr., William Whitney. *The Road to Confrontation: American Policy Toward China and Korea, 1947–1950.* Chapel Hill: University of North Carolina Press. 1981.
10. Whiting, Allen S. *China Crosses the Yalu.* New York: Macmillan Co. 1960.

Was Eisenhower a Do-Nothing President?

Until very recently, the 1950s have not been a favorite focus for scholarly inquiry. Despite the general public's interest in the 1950s and the nostalgia boom that this has evoked, for most historians and political scientists the times were best forgotten. This evaluation by the noted historian Eric Goldman was typical of many:

> Goodbye to the Fifties—and good riddance. (The era was one wherein) we've grown unbelievably prosperous and we maunder along in a stupor of fat. . . . We live in a heavy, humorless, sanctimonious, stultifying atmosphere, singularly lacking in the self-mockery that is self-criticism. Probably the climate of the late 50's was the dullest and dreariest in all our history.[7]

Equally critical was the opinion of *New York Post* editorialist William V. Shannon:

> The Eisenhower years have been years of flabbiness and self-satisfaction and gross materialism. . . . The loudest sound in the land has been the oink-and-grunt of private hoggishness. . . . It has been the age of the slob.[13]

Correspondingly, Dwight D. Eisenhower was seen as a President perfectly matched for such times. He was an aging hero who lacked the energy, vitality, education, and motivation to provide creative leadership. He reigned, more than ruled. He relied on a great popularity secured by a renowned war record and on a reputation for rectitude, openness, and geniality. But he never cashed in on this great fund of goodwill to lead the nation out of its complacency. It was an age of "great postponement," some said. Others believed that Eisenhower was merely a "caretaker President." Lastly, Ike, the common man writ large, was criticized for middle-brow intellectual capabilities and political inexperience. Journalists deemed him too dependent on bad advisors and too uninformed to handle complex domestic and foreign affairs.

This interpretation has now dramatically changed, however. Completely overturned is the traditional view of Eisenhower as a passive and unskilled politician. Newly-opened archives at the Dwight D. Eisenhower Library in Abilene, Kansas, reveal a man who was politically astute, highly informed on most of the crucial issues facing his administration, and actively engaged in providing vital and decisive leadership behind the scenes.

Eisenhower's tendency to hold so many meetings "off the record" gave an impression of inactivity to journalists and political scientists at the time, but Ike preferred this mode of maneuver for a number of reasons. First of all, it accorded with his view of the Presidency as an institution which should be "above the fray." Public knowledge of behind-the-scenes maneuver-

"In the councils of government, we must guard against the acquisition of unwarranted influence, whether sought or unsought, by the military-industrial complex. The potential for the disastrous rise of misplaced power exists and will persist. We must never let the weight of this combination endanger our liberties or democratic processes. We should take nothing for granted. Only an alert and knowledgeable citizenry can compel the proper meshing of the huge industrial and military machinery of defense with our peaceful methods and goals, so that security and liberty may prosper together." Dwight D. Eisenhower, Farewell Address, January 17, 1961.

ings would destroy the dignity which he believed the Presidency as an institution should always convey. Further, an image of political activism, he judged, would interfere with the bipartisan approach to Congress which he always tried to maintain. Finally, he feared awareness of his backroom compromising and "middle-of-the-road" politicking would alienate the right wing of his party.

An anecdote related by Presidential Secretary James Hagerty is insightful in this regard:

> President Eisenhower would say, "Do it this way." I would say, "If I go to that press conference and say what you want me to say, I would get hell." With that, he would smile, get up and walk around the desk, pat me on the back and say, "My boy, better you than me."

New information has also dispelled the myth that Eisenhower delegated real authority and power to his subordinates and/or Cabinet officials. Particularly relevant here are the traditional beliefs that Chief Presidential Assistant Sherman Adams was the real power in domestic affairs and Secretary of State John Foster Dulles in international relations. It is now clear that neither Adams nor Dulles was a prime policy mover. Rather, they explicated the policies that Eisenhower helped to formulate. For example, newly-released telephone transcripts show that Dulles was in daily contact with Eisenhower on all aspects of State Department decision-making. Dulles's hard-line rhetoric and sloganizing—"agonizing reappraisal," "brinkmanship," "liberation," "massive retaliation"—were carefully calculated to keep the hawks in Congress happy, to offer an emotional release for millions of frustrated Americans, and to confuse the Russians as to real American intentions. Always Eisenhower followed a basically conciliatory approach in the daily negotiations of international diplomacy.

The idea that Eisenhower was a fuzzy-headed thinker and a mediocre intellectual has also been jettisoned. Private papers and communications which are now available reveal a high intelligence and a skilled and sophisticated ability on Eisenhower's part to manipulate the English language. It has now been argued that the mangled syntax of public speeches and the feigned ignorance at press conferences were carefully planned for political and diplomatic purposes. Many remember only Eisenhower's supposed mistakes at these news conferences. Forgotten is the fact that such was his confidence that he met with the press on 193 different occasions, far more than any other president in history.

One of the best examples of Eisenhower's masterly use of vagueness and ambiguity to serve multiple purposes at a press conference was during the Matsu and Quemoy Crisis of 1955. Joseph Harsch of the *Christian Science Monitor* asked whether or not atomic weapons might be used in defending those islands. Eisenhower replied:

> Well, Mr. Harsch, I must confess I cannot answer that question in advance. The only thing I know about war are two things: the most unpredictable factor in war is human nature in its day-by-day manifestation; but the only unchanging factor in war is human nature. And the next thing is that every war is going to astonish you in the way it occurred, and in the way it is carried out. So that for a man to predict, particularly if he has the responsibility for making the decision, to predict what he is going to use, how he is going to do it, would I think exhibit his ignorance of war; that is what I believe. So I think you just have to wait; and that is the kind of prayerful decision that may some day face a president.

There was a little something for everyone in this response: for the potentially divisive right wing "China Firster" Republicans, for the People's Republic of China, and for the American public.

The image of the genial old hero has also been revised. Instead, historians are now witness to a man who was a political natural. Eisenhower was a man of drive, ambition and, at times, ruthlessness. He did not earn his stars or the Presidency through luck or through charm. Eisenhower had an enormous self-discipline which he harnessed in order to control a very hot temper and to achieve his goals. Indeed, at times, he even sounds downright prescient, as in this letter to Secretary of Defense Charles E. Wilson: "Any person who doesn't clearly understand that national security and national solvency are mutually dependent . . . should not be entrusted with any kind of responsibility in our country." Or again in "The Chance for Peace" speech of April 16, 1953:

> Every gun that is made, every warship launched, every rocket fired, signifies, in the final sense, a theft from those who hunger and are not fed, those who are cold and are not clothed. . . . This world in arms is not spending money alone. It is spending the sweat of its laborers, the genius of its scientists, the hopes of its children. . . . This is not a way of life at all, in any true sense. Under the cloud of threatening war, it is humanity hanging from a cross of iron.

The passage of time has set in even bolder relief many of Eisenhower's noted achievements. For example, the fact that he ended a difficult Asian war and entered no new wars seems these days to be an act of Presidential wizardry. Equally amazing, given the history of more recent years, is the fact that Eisenhower was able to keep military spending down while American military superiority over the Russians was maintained. Domestically, spending in the public sector was carefully limited, warding off another of today's problems: inflation. And new information shows that Eisenhower was more active than hitherto supposed in striking down an equal nemesis: Joseph McCarthy.

From the perspective of the 1990's and the recent assault on civil rights from the Reagan administration, Eisenhower even looks like a far-sighted humanitarian: he did not defy the Supreme Court in the Brown decision; he sent federal troops to Little Rock, Arkansas, in 1957 to support integration; he signed the first Civil Rights Act since the Era of Reconstruction; he supported the creation of the Civil Rights Division in the Department of Justice; and he set up the U.S. Commission on Civil Rights.

In sum, historians have discovered a new Eisenhower: intelligent, active, ambitious, and inspiring. The question which now seems logical, given the fast-paced reinterpretations of American history, is: How long will this new perspective on Eisenhower last? Or, in other words, what aspects of Eisenhower's record will be most susceptible to future revisions?

Vietnam will most likely remain one blemish in the Eisenhower record. Though Eisenhower's innate caution and his excellent competence in military matters imply that he would not have made the mistakes in Vietnam that his successors did, the issue is still debatable. It was Eisenhower and Dulles who actively worked to shore up the fortunes of the unpopular Ngo Dinh Diem, President of South Vietnam, ignoring provisions which America had implicitly agreed to in the Geneva Accords. In the process they disregarded, or failed to perceive, key Vietnamese social, political, and economic problems. Because of Eisenhower's decisions, the U.S. can be given a major share of the blame for the destruction of the Geneva agreements of 1954.

Another stumbling block in the way of a clean Eisenhower reputation was his "creative" use of the CIA in foreign policy. In contrast to Harry Truman, Eisenhower expanded the scope of the CIA's covert activities. Key examples were the decisions to overthrow legal governments in Guatemala and Iran. Also Eisenhower condoned CIA interference in Cuba, the Congo, and

Indonesia. This could be the area of Eisenhower's greatest failure. Instead of utilizing administrative, political, and economic creativity in refashioning an outdated approach to the Third World, the Administration's ingenuity was channeled into many heavy-handed and brutal policies.

These criticisms will probably be the focal point of much historical controversy in the upcoming years. Two observations might be related here. First of all, it is easy to see why Eisenhower's historical fortunes are currently running at high tide. The areas wherein he was most successful are those most troublesome for Americans today, whereas his failures, given the mood of our times, hardly matter. For instance, regarding Vietnam and Iran, Americans are either tired of assessing responsibility for the origins of those conflicts or are in the process of convincing themselves that U.S. actions there were, in actuality, honorable. Further, the tough-mindedness which characterizes recent American official opinion does not lend itself to criticizing the efforts of the CIA. On the other hand, Eisenhower was most successful in those areas about which Americans are currently most worried: peace, inflation, and decisive leadership.

Secondly, who would have guessed in the 1950s that the popular myths about Eisenhower would be so completely dispelled within a mere twenty years? And who would have guessed that in the future Eisenhower would be judged on events rarely revealed to the general public of that time? Such is the value of both historical perspective and the opening of official archives for careful investigation.

In the end, whatever one's opinion about the future evaluation of Eisenhower's reputation, present-day historians are correct to recognize that Ike was a "Cold War Warrior" with a difference; that difference being maturity, depth and astuteness. Hence, aspiring young leaders can learn significant lessons from Eisenhower's style of leadership and from aspects of his personality. As the British General Bernard Montgomery said of Eisenhower: "He has the power of drawing the hearts of men towards him as a magnet attracts the bits of metal. He merely has to smile at you, and you trust him at once."

As a human being, Eisenhower's was an appealing personality. He cherished his family. He was prosperous in his vocation. He prided himself on his objectivity and fairness in dealing with others. In fact, he actively disliked few people. If someone betrayed him, offended him, or insulted him, he tried to put that person out of his mind. If he had to work with someone on a daily basis whom he disliked (Montgomery during the war is the perfect example), he disciplined himself to control his feelings so that their work together could be productive.

Eisenhower (unlike his Vice-President) understood that true leadership meant avoiding self-pity and resentment; for those tendencies work like toxic substances upon one's character and one's productivity. Eisenhower understood that most people are not for you or against you, but mostly just preoccupied with themselves. And Eisenhower understood that the trick for the great leader is to break out of comfortable imprisonments to become a truly sharing and caring individual.

As a man of strong character, Eisenhower shunned the path of least resistance in his relations with opposing politicians. He tried never to publicly denounce opponents, to publicly question their motives, even when he believed them to be selfish, unprincipled, or merely stupid. He tried to co-opt or incorporate people of talent into his sphere of leadership, regardless of personal feelings about them individually. It is instructive to note that, with one exception, Eisenhower did not choose one friend for his White House Staff or Cabinet. His concern when selecting his Cabinet and Staff was to find people who had a record of administrative success, who had a record of thinking and doing big things.

185

George C. Marshall recognized Eisenhower's ability to build up those he worked with when he chose him to be the Supreme Commander of the Allied Forces in Europe. He knew that Eisenhower could get a Patton, a Montgomery, and a Bradley to productively work together—while also keeping his own ego in check.

It takes great strength to remain on speaking terms with your fiercest opponents, or with those whom you intensely dislike. It also offers useful information, and sometimes just plain unnerves your opposition. Perhaps this is why Lyndon Johnson once remarked: "Hug your friends tight, but your enemies tighter—hug 'em so tight they can't wiggle." Eisenhower understood that what the brilliant British statesman, George Canning, said about great nations also applies to great leaders: "No eternal friendships; certainly no eternal enmities; only eternal interests."

Finally, Eisenhower liked making decisions. His self-confidence was such that he believed himself to be the most qualified American of that time to be president. His mind was quick and agile. He was intelligent, with a gifted memory. He could shift from one concern to another with ease. He could recall pertinent facts on dozens of subjects, facts learned months or even years earlier.

To reiterate, the aim of this conclusion is not to argue that Eisenhower was without important mistakes. Rather my aim is to argue that Eisenhower's personal qualities offer significant insights into why he got to where he did in our political system and, when at the top, why his performance was so effective.

Eisenhower's career may even serve as a standard by which to evaluate our current leaders, President Bush and Vice-President Quayle.

As human beings, are George Bush and Daniel Quayle appealing? Do they pride themselves on being objective and fair? Are self-pity and resentment characteristics of their personalities? Are they agile, quick, and gifted mentally?

Do they work easily with opposing politicians, or are they more comfortable with reliable cronies? Do they have the ability to bring out the best in their staffs?

Do they enjoy decision-making, and do they have the confidence to stick with the hard choices? Did they get to the top by repeated success in their careers, where their mettle was tested all along the way?

For the historian who prefers to wait for key documents, the answers to these questions do not come easily. Alas, if Ralph Waldo Emerson is correct, we all may have to wait awhile: "The measure of a master is his success in bringing all men round to his opinion twenty years later."

That, indeed, was the case with Eisenhower!

SELECTED BIBLIOGRAPHY

1. Alexander, Charles C. *Holding the Line: The Eisenhower Era, 1952–1961*. Bloomington, Ind.: Indiana University Press. 1975.
2. Ambrose, Stephen E. *Eisenhower*. 2 volumes. New York: Simon and Schuster. 1983–84.
3. Cook, Blanche Wiesen. *The Declassified Eisenhower: A Divided Legacy*. Garden City, N. Y.: Doubleday. 1981.
4. Divine, Robert A. *Eisenhower and the Cold War*. New York: Oxford University Press. 1981.
5. Donovan, Robert J. *Eisenhower: The Inside Story*. New York: Harper and Brothers. 1956.

6. Ewald, Jr., William Bragg. *Eisenhower the President: Crucial Days, 1951–1960*. Englewood Cliffs, N. J.: Prentice Hall. 1981.

7. Goldman, Eric F. "Good-By to the Fifties—and Good Riddance," *Harper's Magazine*, Vol. 220, No. 1316 (January 1960).

8. Greenstein, Fred I. *The Hidden-Hand Presidency: Eisenhower As Leader*. New York: Basic Books. 1982.

9. Larson, Arthur. *The President Nobody Knew*. New York: Charles Scribner's Sons. 1968.

10. Lyon, Peter. *Eisenhower: Portrait of the Hero*. Boston: Little, Brown and Company. 1974.

11. Richardson, Elmo. *The Presidency of Dwight D. Eisenhower*. Lawrence, Kan.: The Regents Press of Kansas. 1979.

12. Rovere, Richard H. "Eisenhower Over the Shoulder," *The American Scholar*, Vol. 31, No. 2 (Spring 1962).

We shall overcome,
We shall overcome,
We shall overcome,
Someday.
Oh, deep in my heart,
I do believe, that
We shall overcome
Someday.

Stanza, *We Shall Overcome,* **Anthem of the Civil Rights Movement**

Brown v. Board of Education: Has It Left a Mixed Legacy?

1991 marks the thirty-seventh anniversary of the Supreme Court's famous desegregation decision of *Brown v. Board of Education* (1954). In that decision the Supreme Court unanimously ruled that racial segregation in the nation's schools was unconstitutional. Before that, America's public school system had been based on the separate-but-equal principle established in the court case of *Plessy v. Ferguson* (1896). But with the Brown decision a dramatic turning point in race relations had been effected. No longer did American blacks have to rely solely on moral arguments to secure the removal of discriminatory legislation. Now such discrimination was judged to be illegal. The Warren Court concluded that continued segregation would have disastrous results on the social health of American society and would serve to obstruct, forever, the goals of social equity which Americans had set for themselves in the Declaration of Independence. Earl Warren's exact words were: "To separate (Negro children) from others of similar age and qualifications solely because of their race generates a feeling of inferiority as to their status in the community that may affect their hearts and minds in a way never to be undone." It was a Court decision which reached into the daily lives of all Americans. It was a decision which tackled a problem that had been a part of American life ever since the freeing of the slaves during the Civil War. In fact, it was a decision which culminated almost 100 years of agitation for civil rights, beginning with the end of the Civil War.

From a historian's point of view, this whole issue evokes penetrating historical parallels between the struggle for black freedom and the abolition of slavery in the nineteenth century, and the struggle for black equality in the twentieth century. For instance, let us compare the 1850s and the 1950s. Both decades were characterized by public agitation and concerted efforts on the part of a minority to educate and awaken the consciences of a majority. In the 1850s it was the abolitionist movement which aroused consciences and warned against a moral apathy with regard to slavery. Abolitionists actively fought for the reversal of a disreputable Supreme Court decision—the Dred Scott decision which opened up the American West to the expansion of slavery and which emphasized that slaves were merely chattel property. Also, abolitionists were active in manning the fabled "underground" railroad that provided sanctuary for thousands of slaves fleeing the South. The melodramatic highlight of this moral crusade was the publication of *Uncle Tom's Cabin* in 1852. The South in the 1850s reacted predictably to this moral attack. Southerners became ever more sophisticated in their rationalizations that slavery was a "positive good," and they extensively armed themselves just in case their intellectual arguments did not persuade Northern doubters.

Note the parallels with the 1950s. Again, a vigorous minority was responsible for stirring consciences and awakening moral concern. Again, court case was the object of much protest—the aforementioned Plessy v. Ferguson. The active civil rights minority in the 1950s was led by the NAACP and due to their efforts a landmark civil rights report was published and the Plessy decision was overturned. Later, Martin Luther King, Jr., helped stage the Montgomery Bus Boycott of 1955–56, a nonviolent challenge to segregation practices on the South's public transportation system. Meanwhile, the South fought hard to preserve all aspects of white supremacy. Little Rock, Arkansas became a storm center in 1957 as Governor Orval Faubus led the fight against public school integration in that state. The Ku Klux Klan resorted to vigilante violence, and "Impeach Earl Warren" billboards sprung up throughout the South.

In sum, despite the passing of a century, one readily sees the similarities between the 1850s and the 1950s: both decades were a time of civil rights agitation, a time of increased moral concern and a time of Southern "reaction." Yet, all in all, both decades set the stage for later, more important achievements.

The decade of the 'Sixties proved to be the highpoint of the civil rights movement in both centuries. In 1861 the Civil War began, largely to settle once and for all the future of slavery in the U.S. In 1863 Lincoln delivered his Emancipation Proclamation freeing the slaves in the rebellious Southern states. In 1866 Congress passed an epic Civil Rights Act and, in 1867, passed important postwar "reconstruction" legislation. Finally, in 1868, the Fourteenth amendment was added to the Constitution to protect black citizenship and voting rights. Similarly, the 1960s were the apogee of the twentieth century. The Civil Rights Act of 1964 which Lyndon Johnson guided through Congress was a major achievement, as was the Voting Rights Act of 1965. These acts finally assured full political participation for blacks in the Southern states. There were even more dramatic gains nationwide in black income and employment.

Few historians have bothered to continue with this exercise of drawing parallels into the decade of the 'Seventies. For the 1870s were an ignoble time of back-tracking and regression in the area of black rights. In the 1870s Northern liberals finally tired of their vigilance of reconstruction procedures in the South. Further, in the notorious Compromise of 1877, Northern Congressmen offered white Southerners the opportunity to regain their prominent political position over black people in the South, if these Southern Congressmen would support the Northern Republican candidate for President, Rutherford B. Hayes, in the disputed election of 1876. White Southerners gladly abandoned the Democratic candidate Samuel J. Tilden and the bargain was sealed. Southerners received full control over their own domestic affairs, and the last Northern troops were removed from the South. In return, Northern Republicans secured the election of Hayes as President.

Surely the 1970s had no comparable instances of regression! In many ways this assumption is correct. Blacks have made significant gains in our nation's economic and political arenas as of late. Yet, if the reader will grant me certain premises, perhaps a parallel can be made. Will you accept the premise that the integration of our public schools in the last 30 years has been a significant accomplishment? Will you accede to the same conclusion as regards gains in black income and employment? If so, then recent setbacks in these areas may prove insightful.

First, let us take California as an instance of a growing national phenomenon: the white exodus from integrated public schools. In Los Angeles, alone, when busing was still being implemented to integrate public schools, more than 100,000 white students left those schools in six years and enrolled in private schools. As a result, the Los Angeles public school population slipped to less than 33 percent Anglo-Caucasian in 1979, as compared to 45 percent in 1970–71. Pasadena offered a similar example. Pasadena's public schools lost half their white students at the same time that their private schools were flourishing. Statewide the tendency was equally dramatic. In 1979, less than 1 out of 10 students attended private schools. But, if busing had been continued, educators estimated that in 30 years the number of white students in private schools would have outnumbered those in public schools.

It should be noted that similar shifts are occurring, or have occurred, nationwide. California is not the exception. Between 1972 and 1975, some 40,000 white students left Atlanta's public schools, so that black students now make up nearly 90 percent of the student public school population, up from 56 percent in 1972. Public schools in Baltimore, Detroit, Newark, New Orleans, St. Louis, Chicago and Philadelphia are 70 to 85 percent nonwhite. In 1954, only Washington, D.C., among the nation's largest cities, had a white minority in its public schools; today, whites are a minority in the schools of 18 of the country's 20 largest cities.

When we turn to statistics dealing with black family income and employment, similar trends are noted. The median income of black families, expressed as a percentage of median white income, increased between 1950 and 1970, but it never reached higher than 61 percent that of white incomes. Between 1970 and 1977, it declined to about 57 percent. From 1950 to the mid-1960s, the black unemployment rate always averaged slightly more than *twice* the rate for whites. Then it began to improve until in the early 1970s it reached a low of 1.8 to 1. Again, however, the positive trend ebbed, until in the last quarter of 1977 a historic postwar high of 2.3 to 1 was recorded.

In some ways, then, the parallels are remarkable between the 1870s and the 1970s. In both eras black rights slipped somewhat after earlier gains, and in both eras liberals tired of the moral activism which had characterized them in earlier decades. Sadly, the 1870s witnessed the emergence of the Ku Klux Klan and the 1970s witnessed its resurgence.

Remarkably, the parallels can be extended between the 1880s and the 1980s. The 1880s were a type of transition period in the South between the Reconstruction era when blacks had full suffrage and the 1890s when state laws were implemented to disfranchise them. With full legal segregation a secondary concern of upper-class Southerners in the 1880s, primary consideration was instead aimed toward full control in the economic realm. Indeed, it was in the economic arena where blacks were particulary exploited—through the sharecropping and the convict-lease systems.

Significantly, the paternalistic attitudes and economic machinations of the "New South's" leaders worked to the detriment, not only of blacks, but of whites. Whereas large numbers of independent landowning whites in the ante-bellum South were poor, they still retained their independence. In the 1880s, however, more and more of these white farmers were directly exploited by Southern economic elites and were pushed to a status of direct dependence.

The 1880s were also noted nationwide for business "boosterism" and for the special glorification of the Protestant ethic of self-help and individual self-reliance. An unquestioning faith in liberal capitalism, transmogrified by the simultaneous popularity of Social Darwinism, made it easy for secure middle-class Americans to believe that no one owed anyone anything, and that those who were not willing to work had no right to live. Blacks, in particular, were urged to look to themselves for success, and to reject political/governmental solutions to their problems. White philanthropists were cautioned that it was actually more dangerous to help blacks too much, than too little. Therefore, instead of protection from financial insecurity or from starvation

191

or from racial discrimination, blacks received moral advice, and some economic aid in the areas of vocational and industrial education. An apt example of white moralizing was the first volume of Joel Chandler Harris's *Uncle Remus: His Songs and His Sayings*, published to great national acclaim in 1880. At one point, Uncle Remus argues that: "Hit's agin de mor'l law fer niggers fer ter eat when dy don't wuk;" later, he adds, "You slap de law onter a nigger a time or two, an' larn 'im dat he's got fer to look atter his own rashuns an' keep out'n udder foke's chick'n coops, an' sorter coax 'im ter feed 'is own chilluns, an' I be blessed ef you ain't got 'm on risin' ground!"

There are few who will dispute that the 1980s witnessed another cycle of popular glorification of our liberal-capitalist productive power. Again, the Protestant ethic of self-help, hard work and frugality was consistently invoked by key American leaders, led fervently by an enthusiastic President Reagan. And, once more, the companion argument appeared that government aid and welfare were doing more to harm blacks than help them. One hundred years after Joel Chandler Harris's *Uncle Remus*, Milton and Rose Friedman's *Free to Choose* was published, to similar national acclaim (*Free to Choose* eventually appeared as a television series on PBS):*

> What produced this [U.S. economic] miracle? . . . The millions of immigrants from all over the world were free to work for themselves, as independent farmers or businessmen, or to work for others, at terms mutually agreed. They were free to experiment with new techniques—at their risk if the experiment failed, and to their profit if it succeeded. They got little assistance from government. Even more important, they encountered little interference from government. . . .

Whatever one's ideological position regarding the free market system, the fact is that there were similar problems for blacks (and poor whites) in both the 1880s and in the 1980s. Available statistics seem to confirm that the quality of life for black Americans continued in the 1980s the decline that had begun in the 1970s. The National Urban League's annual *State of Black America* report of January 1990 contained, among many findings, the following for 1988: 1) The median income of black families was $19,329 while white families' median income was $33,915; 2) Black Americans were 2.5 times as likely as whites to be jobless and more likely to be jobless for more than five weeks; 3) One of every eleven blacks surveyed said they went without health care because it was unaffordable (compared with one of every twenty whites), and 50 percent of all black Americans surveyed said they received no dental care (compared with 36 percent of whites); and 4) Roughly one-half of the black children under the age of eighteen lived below the poverty line, and the vast majority of these children had only a mother to come home to. As mentioned, for whites, too, the 1980s were difficult. Homelessness became a more common occurrence, to the point of national disgrace, and numerous economic surveys concluded that the Reagan years, with its attendant tax "reforms," had in truth created a situation where the rich did grow richer while the poor became poorer.

In conclusion, as we move through the 1990s, the legacy of the 1954 Supreme Court decision is mixed. On the one hand, few can deny that tremendous progress has been made and that enormous opportunities have been opened to black Americans as our nation has valiantly attempted to live up to its noble ideals. Yet, certain trends remain ominous and prompt us to rethink just how much of that hard-won progress has been tarnished by recent developments.

---

*I do not mean to infer that either the 1880s' racism or Social Darwinism are beliefs of the Friedmans. Rather, I am citing the popularity of *Free to Choose* as an example of the resurgent faith in the capitalist system which marked the 1980s.

SELECTED BIBLIOGRAPHY

1. Branch, Taylor. *Parting the Waters: America in the King Years, 1954–63.* New York: Simon and Schuster. 1988.
2. Carson, Clayborne. *In Struggle: SNCC and the Black Awakening of the 1960s.* Cambridge, Mass.: Harvard University Press. 1981.
3. Franklin, John Hope. *From Slavery to Freedom: A History of Negro Americans.* New York: Alfred A. Knopf. 1967.
4. Friedman, Milton and Rose Friedman. *Free to Choose: A Personal Statement.* New York: Harcourt Brace Jovanovich. 1980.
5. Harding, Vincent. *There Is a River.* New York: Harcourt Brace Jovanovich. 1981.
6. Muse, Benjamin. *Ten Years of Prelude.* New York: Viking Press. 1964.
7. _____. *The American Negro Revolution.* Bloomington, Ind.: Indiana University Press. 1968.
8. Polenberg, Richard. *One Nation Divisible: Class, Race, and Ethnicity in the United States Since 1938.* New York: Viking Press. 1980.
9. Silberman, Charles E. *Crisis in Black and White.* New York: Random House. 1964.
10. Sitkoff, Harvard. *The Struggle for Black Equality, 1954–1980.* New York: Hill and Wang. 1981.
11. Wilkinson, J. Harvie. *From Brown to Bakke.* New York: Oxford University Press. 1979.
12. Williamson, Joel. *The Crucible of Race: Black-White Relations in the American South since Emancipation.* New York: Oxford University Press. 1984.
13. Woodward, C. Vann. *The Strange Career of Jim Crow.* New York: Oxford University Press. 1974.

The Kennedy Legacy: Will It Endure?

John Kennedy's Presidency is still one that is approached with much emotion. Whatever their view there are few scholars who are not touched by the flair and verve of the man and his administration. There are some who argue that Kennedy's "public relations bridged the gap between promise and performance" and who lament that "Kennedy's dazzling style obscured the thin substance of his government."[5] This is partly true. But it is also beside the point for "the President's style created its own reality, his dash its own momentum."[5]

How long will the Kennedy mystique continue to interest both admirers and critics? After all, Kennedy was President for such a short time. Which of our Presidents now judged great would be so considered if they had been killed in the third year of their first term? It is this question which sets the theme for this essay. What will be the place of John Fitzgerald Kennedy in history? In the history books of the future, will Kennedy be relegated to the scholarly indifference that most Americans currently give to the other Presidents who died in their first term: William Henry Harrison, Zachary Taylor, James Garfield, and Warren Harding? Or will something positive remain to make the Kennedy legacy a vibrant one?

The first evaluations of the Kennedy Presidency were overwhelmingly positive. The assassination with its mix of mean villany and heroic tragedy created an atmosphere where the first heart-rending accounts from Administration insiders sealed the "Camelot" image as the dominant one in the popular mind. The dramatic contrast between the grass-roots and folksy Lyndon Johnson and the urbane and sophisticated John Kennedy added to this first inclination. The Camelot image of Kennedy implied a leader who was progressive and creative, who was endowed with an abundance of personal attractiveness and charisma. As Camelot, Kennedy exhibited a keen analytical intellect which was skeptical, objective, cool and candid. Like a robust, popular prince he radiated youthful energy, zest for life, articulate and moving rhetoric, and a saving sense of humor.

The knights of Kennedy's Round Table came in for their fair share of praise, too. Indeed, they were evaluated as the most competent, dedicated and brilliant of Presidential "Brain Trusts" in American history. In choosing these men, it was said, Kennedy paid little attention to party qualifications; rather ability, drive and imagination were the requisites for selection.

As far as specific programs and accomplishments, admirers saw Kennedy leading the nation in new directions in three key areas of American policy. First, in the field of economics, Kennedy aimed to instruct the American public about various economic myths which characterized their thinking. For Kennedy the persistence of economic "mythology" was the main obstacle impeding implementation of the sophisticated solutions mandatory for economic success in the 1960s. His most important effort in this regard was a Commencement Speech given at Yale University on June 11, 1962. The political scientist Bruce Miroff succinctly summarized the focal points of Kennedy's discussion in that speech:

> First was the myth of oversized government. Kennedy contended that the growth of the federal government had to be understood in relative terms; he pointed out that, leaving aside defense and space expenditures, the federal government since the Second World War had expanded less rapidly than any other sector of the economy. A second myth concerned fiscal policy and budget. The record of the postwar years, Kennedy remarked, demolished the notion that budget surpluses kept prices stable while budget deficits produced inflation. The same record also undermined the popular myth of a skyrocketing federal debt; the federal debt was, in fact, climbing far more slowly than either private debt or the debts of state and local governments. Finally, Kennedy assaulted the claim that each and every setback to the economy derived from business's lack of confidence in the national administration.[4]

At the end of the speech Kennedy returned to the key economic themes of his administration: that a business-government alliance was needed to solve modern problems, and that specific economic "ideologies" had to be abandoned in favor of improved managerial expertise.

> What is at stake is not some grand warfare of rival ideologies which will sweep the country with passion, but the practical management of a modern economy. What we need is not labels and clichés but more basic discussion of the sophisticated and technical questions involved in keeping a great economic machinery moving ahead.

Secondly, admirers saw Kennedy broaching an equally new era in international relations as exemplified in yet another speech, this time at American University on June 10, 1963. In this speech, Kennedy rose above the tired old clichés of the Cold War and put forward a new basis for peace and compromise in a nuclear age. He specifically sought to break the logjam that had developed in the negotiations with the Soviets on atmospheric nuclear testing. Hence, Kennedy announced his decision to send a high-level negotiating team to Moscow to bargain with Nikita Khrushchev. He also urged Americans to reexamine their attitudes toward Russia. "For in the final analysis, our most common link is that we all inhabit this small planet. We all breathe the same air. We all cherish our children's future. And we are all mortal." Khrushchev called this speech "the greatest speech by an American President since Roosevelt." It was reprinted in its entirety in the Soviet newspaper *Pravda*. Such was its impact that, by July 25, a treaty prohibiting nuclear testing in the atmosphere, in space, and under water was initialed in Moscow by the U.S., Great Britain and the U.S.S.R. The limited test ban treaty has often been called "Kennedy's finest legacy to the world."

Lastly, Kennedy's Civil Rights speech of June 11, 1963 marked a new beginning in domestic affairs. An American President finally and unequivocally placed the federal government against the studied intransigence of an anachronistic system of Southern segregation policies. Kennedy had foreshadowed such a speech when he sent federal troops and deputies to the University of Mississippi in 1962 to enforce the court-ordered enrollment of James Meredith. He followed this speech with a forceful message to Congress eight days later, and a legislative package which finally became known as the Civil Rights Act of 1964.

In sum, early admirers saw Kennedy as a President whose keen intelligence in an age of political mediocrity, whose inspiration of hope in an age of uncertainty, and whose appeal to social ethics in an age of materialism, made especially tragic the promise which the assassination shattered. Lately, however, the Kennedy historical literature has been characterized more by criticism than by praise. Critics concur with admirers that Kennedy brought a sense of movement to the Presidency, but they disagree that this sense of movement was always positive.

In foreign affairs, for instance, critics argue that Kennedy's impatience, his proclivity for action, and his lack of caution did much to make the early 1960s dangerous years. Due to Kennedy's tendency to view politics in dramatic terms, characterized by tests of personal will, he too easily convinced himself that his Presidency would mark a watershed in the face of a massive Soviet world offensive. With this attitude, it is no wonder, critics remark, that Kennedy's Presidency was distinguished by crisis: the Bay of Pigs, the Cuban Missile Confrontation, the Berlin Scares, and the Fallout Shelter hysteria.

Regarding relations with the Third World, critics find Kennedy as obtuse and uncomprehending as John Foster Dulles, Eisenhower's Secretary of State, often was. Kennedy exhibited a typically American, narrow-minded morality, exemplified by alternating beliefs in the efficacy of overt or covert military threats to insure American supremacy in Third World affairs. The most notorious example here was CIA involvement in the Ngo Dinh Diem coup of November 1963. When Diem became expendable (i.e. not in the U.S. interest consistent with its containment policy) the Kennedy Administration did not really reexamine old attitudes and myths, but instead sought another leader whose regime could be used to contain Ho Chi Minh by counter-insurgency. To summarize, critics see Kennedy as basically a "Cold Warrior" in foreign policy, whose actions, possibly more than Soviet intentions, were responsible for heating up the Cold War. Kennedy seemed blind to the fact that our contradictory wayward world often does not fit into ideological formulations. JFK also had the tendency to interpret freedom solely in Western terms—with elected parliaments, party systems and uncensored journalism as criteria for evaluation. He neglected to note that for many Third World peoples there was another set of more important priorities: freedom from hunger, disease and illiteracy.

On domestic matters, critics argue that Kennedy had nothing new to offer; indeed, that he was the prisoner of the most fundamental of American biases. Some historians see Kennedy as an enlightened conservative, at best. For example, Kennedy consistently dashed liberal hopes and expectations by being excessively cautious in his approach to Congress and catering too extensively to Southern conservatives in his program planning. The narrowness of Kennedy's defeat on Medicare, on Aid to Education and on his original tax reform program, critics believe, demonstrated how successful he might have been if he had been more aggressive and more principled. Further, for critics, the fact that Kennedy acquiesced so easily in a tax cut without tax reform attested to the conventionality of his economic beliefs. In 1962, Kennedy proposed a budget deficit through tax reduction; this was put into effect in 1964, after his death and out of tribute to him, when Congress implemented a tax cut of more than $10 billion. In 1962, Kennedy signed a large depreciation allowance for business and in 1963 he reduced corporate income taxes by 20 percent. A pet idea of Kennedy's was to withhold taxes on interest and dividend income—a piece of legislation that had to wait until the Ronald Reagan administration advocated it in 1982, though it was repealed in 1983. At the time, Michael Harrington, the political economist and sociologist, referred to Kennedy's economic policies as "reactionary Keynesianism." That, of course, was before the 1980s, when just about every group but the poor was aided or favored by economic legislation that truly epitomized reactionary Keynesianism. Kennedy's speech to the American Federation of Labor just before his death is indicative, to critics, of how much in the mainstream his economic attitudes were: "No one gains by being admitted to a lunch counter if he has no money to spend. No one gains from attending a better school if he doesn't have a job after graduation." There is no moral outrage here with the despicable segregationist policies of that time.

Regarding Civil Rights, critics argue that Kennedy was too deeply rooted in elite political values and assumptions to fully come to terms with the black political concern for more democratic representation. They point to Kennedy's attempts to blunt or to channel much of the black protest into areas which he deemed appropriate, rather than encouraging or accepting a black politics of mass participation.

Sadly, many are now aware of Kennedy's sexual indiscretions. Though salacious rumors and unreliable sources have distorted much of the truth—especially surrounding actress Marilyn Monroe—nonetheless, Kennedy was promiscuous. And this becomes a problem when the person involved is President of the United States. It meant that Kennedy was vulnerable to blackmail. J. Edgar Hoover is a central character here, for he had information dating from World War II about Kennedy's affair with the beautiful Inga Arvad, eventually revealed to be a Nazi spy. Hoover also knew that one of Kennedy's liaisons had been Judith Campbell, one-time "friend" of underworld figures Sam Giancana and John Rosselli. Armed with such information, critics contend, Hoover often got his way against Kennedy's real wishes: the wire-tapping of Martin Luther King, Jr., significant obstruction in integration cases and slip-shod screening of federal judges. Kennedy's decision to place his brother Robert at the Justice department, it has been suggested, might have been influenced by his desire to keep a close eye on Hoover. Who else would be more reliable in protecting the Kennedy name in the face of possible FBI smear tactics? Kennedy's sexual episodes even adversely affected a sound investigation of his very own murder. Both Robert Kennedy and J. Edgar Hoover were obstructionists here. Hoover obstructed the investigation because he was afraid the Warren Commission's investigation would contradict the FBI's report (which stated that there was no conspiracy, but rather a lone assassin, Lee Harvey Oswald). Robert obstructed because he feared knowledge of CIA attempts to assassinate Castro might come to light, attempts which included an approach to Giancana and Rosselli.[6, 7, 9, 12]

Critics, then, basically evaluate Kennedy as "a relatively conventional American politician longing to be an unconventional hero."[4] As for Kennedy's "knights," though there was no denying their overall brilliance, there was still little guarantee that even the "best and the brightest" would deliver wise or successful policy. As it turned out, a goodly portion of the brain-trust of advisers recruited by the Kennedy Administration brought with them intellectual baggage that contained a set of policy assumptions that was distinctly "cold-war" in character and questionable in value.

In fact, with the perspective of time, Garry Wills argues that what we remember to be the dynamic liberalism of the early 1960s might be better associated with someone else—i.e., Martin Luther King, Jr.[12] There was no purpose more noble than King's—the imploring white Americans to include in their creed brothers and sisters of a different color. King was only asking for his followers what most Americans already had—equality of opportunity. To attain this goal, he utilized two methods: civil disobedience and nonviolence. This was so "un-American" as to seem positively revolutionary. For most Americans claimed to obey the law, while rarely turning the other cheek in the face of violence.

King's results speak for themselves. Whose work has done more to change the way present-day Americans live their daily lives? Whose speeches now arouse the most emotion and are memorized the most frequently? Who now mimics the clever antitheses and alliterations of the

Kennedy speeches? King's oratory still lives, and will probably live as long as the English language is spoken. While the "best and the brightest" were leading the way into Vietnam, King was arousing a far more inspiring march toward the front of the bus.

With this historiographical debate as a background, how then might we assess the Kennedy legacy? One key factor which both critics and admirers tend to minimize is the great continuity which characterized the Kennedy and Johnson Presidencies. Kennedy laid the foundation for Johnson's legislative successes. Kennedy cultivated and stimulated a proper political mood and moral concern without which social legislation cannot be passed. More specifically, Kennedy's tax cut program and his Civil Rights package were well on their way toward enactment. Medicare and Aid to Education were formulated and appropriate strategies plotted. All in all, the embryo of Johnson's great "War on Poverty" was in place. In fact, both Johnson and Kennedy fit into the post-World War II New Deal Tradition. When Johnson took over the essentials of Kennedy's stalled domestic program, there was a culmination taking place of not only the New Frontier but of the New and Fair Deals.

In conclusion, the Kennedy Presidency will always be difficult to assess because of the unique problems which are associated with it: its brevity, the gap between expectations and performance, and the fact that the assassination evokes sympathy and pathos. Nonetheless, unlike America's other Presidents who failed to finish their first term, Kennedy was a man who had begun a reshaping of American society. He sensed a shift in the public mood and touched a responsive chord. Above all else, behind the promises Kennedy held a vision, a political prescience, and an ability to move people. He injected idealism into American politics. These factors will not warrant Kennedy a place among America's great Presidents, but they will insure him a special niche more inspired and hallowed than that occupied by William Henry Harrison, Zachary Taylor, James Garfield, and Warren Harding.

SELECTED BIBLIOGRAPHY

1. Brauer, Carl M. *John F. Kennedy and the Second Reconstruction.* New York: Columbia University Press. 1977.
2. Burner, David. *John F. Kennedy and a New Generation.* Glenview, Ill. and Boston: Scott, Foresman and Co. 1988.
3. Fairlie, Henry. *The Kennedy Promise.* Garden City, N.Y.: Doubleday Inc. 1973.
4. Miroff, Bruce. *Pragmatic Illusions.* New York: David McKay Company. 1976.
5. O'Neill, William. *Coming Apart: An Informal History of America in the 1960's.* New York: Quadrangle Books, Inc. 1971.
6. Parmet, Herbert. *Jack: The Struggles of John F. Kennedy.* New York: The Dial Press. 1980.
7. _____. *JFK: The Presidency of John F. Kennedy.* New York: The Dial Press. 1983.
8. Schlesinger, Jr., Arthur M. *A Thousand Days.* Boston: Houghton Mifflin Company. 1965.
9. Snyder, J. Richard. ed. *John F. Kennedy: Person, Policy, Presidency.* Wilmington, Del.: Scholarly Resources Inc. 1988.
10. Sorensen, Theodore C. *Kennedy.* New York: Harper and Row. 1965.
11. Walton, Richard J. *Cold War and Counter-Revolution: The Foreign Policy of John F. Kennedy.* New York: Viking Press. 1972.
12. Wills, Garry. *The Kennedy Imprisonment.* Boston: Little, Brown and Co. 1982.

"*Let the word go forth from this time and place, to friend and foe alike, that the torch has been passed to a new generation of Americans—born in this century, tempered by war, disciplined by a hard and bitter peace, proud of our ancient heritage—and unwilling to witness or permit the slow undoing of those human rights to which this nation has always been committed, and to which we are committed today at home and around the world. Let every nation know, whether it wishes us well or ill, that we shall pay any price, bear any burden, meet any hardship, support any friend, oppose any foe to assure the survival and the success of liberty.*" John F. Kennedy, Inaugural Address, January 20, 1961.

Did Kennedy Precipitate the Nuclear Confrontation over Cuba?

Ever since those dramatic October days in 1962, the Cuban Missile Crisis has been a subject of heated academic debate. For one group of historians, the crisis was John Kennedy's finest hour. During it he skillfully juxtaposed seven days of careful deliberations and detailed planning with six days of crisis-management of the shrewdest sort. Particularly praiseworthy, these academics argue, was Kennedy's choice of a blockade, or "quarantine," as the initial response to the Soviet incursion. The quarantine, which blocked delivery of additional missiles to Cuba, was a perceptive middle course of action, an act aggressive enough to communicate firmness, but not so passive as to imply lassitude. Further, the decision for a quarantine allowed Nikita Khrushchev sufficient time to reconsider his decisions and to engineer a retreat with the minimum of humiliation.

For a more critical group of historians, the opposite conclusion seems nearer the truth. They believe that the crisis was both unnecessary and dangerously mishandled. They argue that the decision for a blockade amounted to an act of war against Cuba according to International Law, and could have led to disastrous consequences. Others even contend that the Soviet missiles were not a significant military hazard to American security in the first place, and that Kennedy over-reacted. Indeed, these critics point out, during the confrontation weaknesses in Kennedy's personality were evident: his habit of investing ordinary events with "decisive global significance," his faulty dramatic instinct, and his flawed tendency of personalizing issues, thereby converting them into tests of will.

As is immediately seen, the Cuban Missile controversy has many different facets: Was the Soviet deployment of missiles in Cuba a real military hazard to American security? Was the choice of a blockade a dangerous military move constituting an act of war against Cuba? Was it a character weakness on Kennedy's part to force a confrontation in public rather than in secret, thereby endangering the prestige on both sides?

Recently-opened archives focus the heart of the debate on still another key facet of the crisis—Kennedy's refusal to accept a Turkish-Cuban missile exchange. This refusal is said by critics to have left Khrushchev with the stark choice of either outright submission or a resort to nuclear war. In fact, of all the charges leveled at Kennedy's conduct of the crisis, it is this last criticism which I believe is the most valid.

At issue here is a series of events that occurred between Friday, October 26, and Saturday, October 27. On Friday, Kennedy received an emotional and highly revealing letter from Khrushchev. By then the blockade had already been in effect for four days. In this letter, Khrushchev agreed to remove the missiles from Cuba in exchange for a U.S. pledge not to invade the island in the future. Kennedy and members of the Executive Committee (ExCom) specially organized to deal with the Cuban missile challenge breathed a sigh of relief. It seemed as if the crisis were over. It would not be a major problem for the U.S. to accept Khrushchev's non-invasion proposal, since no future invasion was seriously planned.

Then came a second note on Saturday morning, which looked as if it had the more intransigent hand of the Soviet military elite imprinted upon it. This second letter agreed to a removal of Soviet missiles, echoing the first note, but insisted that the U.S. also agree to remove its Jupiter missiles from Turkey. Arriving at the same time as the Soviet second note was ominous news from Cuba: Soviet-installed surface-to-air missiles (SAMs) had just downed a U.S. U-2 reconnaisance plane in flight over the island.

No one on ExCom believed that the second note was acceptable. Hence, preparations were advanced for war. But, simultaneously, an ingenious suggestion by Robert Kennedy was also implemented: that the U.S. respond to the first note and agree to its provisions, while simply ignoring the second request. In the end, this ploy worked! The Russians accepted negotiations on the basis of the first note!

Despite the favorable outcome, many historians argue that Kennedy was pushing brinkmanship too far by refusing the second letter. They point out that the Jupiter missiles in Turkey were obsolete liquid-fueled intermediate-range ballistic missiles (IRBMs). Not only were these missiles quite inaccurate, but they took hours to ready before firing. Further, they were so vulnerable that a sniper's bullet could puncture the Jupiter's thin skin, thereby rendering it inoperable.

Kennedy's response to this criticism was that a Turkish-Cuban missile exchange could not be considered, under such Soviet pressure, without destroying U.S. credibility with NATO. Nonetheless, critics counter that the U.S. could have reaped even more credibility and goodwill by demonstrating discretion and a willingness to compromise. After all, the world was on the verge of a nuclear holocaust. Besides, critics continue, the U.S. was beginning to deploy the more advanced Polaris submarines in the Mediterranean anyway. In addition, the U.S. would still have its land-based missiles in both Italy and Great Britain, since the second Soviet note did not mention these weapons. In sum, for many historians it was the Soviet Union's restraint during this crisis which was the key to averting war.

Historians who are sympathetic to Kennedy's decision-making believe very strongly that the Soviet military build-up in Cuba was a significant threat to the U.S. After all, the 72 missiles to be placed in Cuba would have doubled the Soviet Union's first-strike capabilities. (And what guarantee was there that the Soviets would stop with just 72?) Further, as the missiles were only 90 miles from U.S. shores, accuracy would be improved and with it each missile's fire power on its target would be enhanced. In addition, the proximity of these missiles drastically shortened America's warning-time in case of attack, from 20 minutes to merely 2 or 3. When one considers that most of America's Strategic Air Command (SAC) bomber bases were located in the Southern U.S., on fifteen-minute alert, the import of this development is obvious. Finally, because these missiles were stationed on America's southern periphery, they outflanked the U.S.'s Ballistic Missile Early Warning System (BMEWS).

As for the crucial weekend of October 26–27, this second group of historians argues that even on this issue Kennedy demonstrated restraint. For example, on that Saturday morning, Kennedy accepted the loss of an American U-2 and of the life of its pilot rather than stopping negotiations. In fact, he overturned a previous ExCom decision which would have initiated an attack on the SAM bases responsible. Further, as a sign to the Soviets that the Turkish missiles would not be used during the crisis, Kennedy ordered them defused, to the great anger of the Joint Chiefs of Staff. Finally, Kennedy arranged a private deal, a meeting between Robert Kennedy and Soviet Ambassador Anatoly Dobrynin, in which the Turkish missiles were sacrificed secretly.

It can also be argued that Kennedy's acceptance of a non-invasion pledge was in itself a major concession that would protect Khrushchev from humiliation. After all, Khrushchev did get everything that he wanted, even when the second note is considered: the blockade was ended, the American missiles in Turkey were removed, and Cuban security from an American invasion was implicitly guaranteed. It is true that the Soviets had to agree to remove their missiles from Cuba as a preliminary for U.S. concessions; but there were no missiles there in the first place! In a way, Khrushchev got something for nothing!

Important, too, in understanding Kennedy's brinkmanship is the fact that he had information that at no stage during the crisis did the Soviets go on a military alert equivalent to that of the U.S. Nevertheless, the dilemma remains: What would Kennedy have done if Khrushchev had not retreated? The information available still leaves this central issue unresolved.

But one aspect of this controversy, I believe, is particularly clear. While it may be difficult to fault Kennedy's actions once the missiles were discovered in Cuba and the crisis was fully underway, Kennedy does deserve strong criticism for precipitating an event that could have easily been avoided. Kennedy's failure lies in a policy toward Cuba which was based on premises and fears that were exaggerated, superficial, and mistaken. Kennedy did not appreciate the depth of Cuban nationalism. Nor did he understand how much the Cubans despised the many years of blatant American imperialism, or the degree of animosity that was felt for the American-supported dictator Fulgencio Batista. Furthermore, Kennedy, along with most Americans, did not grasp the motivations behind Castro's embrace of socialism. Socialism, from the Cuban point of view, was an ideology which promised them full independence. It was an ideology which would serve as a means of national self-assertion against Americans who, before Castro's accession, owned 35 percent of Cuba's sugar industry, 90 percent of Cuba's public utilities, and, with Royal/Dutch Shell, all of Cuba's oil refineries.

Ignoring the Cuban peoples' emotional needs and misunderstanding their leader, Kennedy, upon taking office, embarked upon a number of questionable steps: he authorized the Bay of Pigs invasion; he increased aid through the CIA for rebels in Miami; he condoned preparations for another invasion plan, coded "Operation Mongoose;" he worked to oust Cuba from the OAS; he tightened the economic blockade around Cuba; he refused to open diplomatic relations with Havana; he pressed other Latin American nations to break diplomatic relations with Castro; he energized anti-Cuban propaganda efforts through the USIA; and finally, it appears that he tolerated assassination plans aimed at Castro. Then, when Kennedy discovered that Soviet forces were constructing missile sites in Cuba, he blockaded the island, called on the Russians to remove any missiles and dismantle the sites, and escalated the crisis to the level of a nuclear confrontation.

Of course, Khrushchev, too, deserves criticism for bringing on an unnecessary crisis. Though it might be technically argued on the basis of international law that Khrushchev was justified in sending Soviet missiles to Cuba, a more important maxim should have prevailed in his thinking—common sense. He should have known that no American President could have acquiesced. American-Cuban relations were at their nadir, hardly a propitious time for Khrushchev to make a move involving vast military and political repercussions. Further, Khrushchev could have protected Cuba, if that was his concern, with less extreme measures. For instance, he could have sent a contingent of Soviet troups to serve as a "trip-wire," as Americans have done in Western Europe. Lastly, Khrushchev's strategy for a number of years of using intimidation and nuclear "sabre-rattling" was highly questionable.

Nonetheless, Kennedy's responsibility in precipitating the eventual crisis is significant. Historians who focus solely on the thirteen days of that tense October may miss the important seeds of catastrophe which were planted earlier by the Kennedy administration, and before him by the Eisenhower administration.

In conclusion, whatever one's final judgment of Kennedy's handling of this crisis, his legacy and importance will remain simply because he was the first President to experience a direct nuclear confrontation with the Soviet Union. In any future confrontation of equal significance, American Presidents will gauge their choices, measure their actions, and evaluate their outcomes on the basis of Kennedy's harrowing precedent.

SELECTED BIBLIOGRAPHY

1. Abel, Elie. *The Missile Crisis*. Philadelphia: J. P. Lippincott Co. 1966.
2. Allison, Graham T. *Essence of Decision*. Boston: Little, Brown and Co. 1971.
3. Bernstein, Barton J. "The Cuban Missile Crisis: Trading the Jupiters in Turkey?," *Political Science Quarterly*, Vol. 95, No. 1 (Spring 1980), pp. 97–125.
4. Blight, James G. and David A. Welch. eds. *On the Brink: Americans and Soviets Reexamine the Cuban Missile Crisis*. New York: Hill and Wang. 1989.
5. Dinerstein, Herbert S. *The Making of a Missile Crisis: October 1962*. Baltimore: John Hopkins Press. 1976.
6. Garthoff, Raymond L. *Reflections on the Cuban Missile Crisis*. Washington, D.C.: The Brookings Institution. 1987.
7. Hinckle, Warren and William Turner. *The Fish Is Red: The Story of the Secret War Against Castro*. New York: Harper and Row. 1981.
8. Kennedy, Robert F. *Thirteen Days*. New York: W. W. Norton Co. 1969.
9. Paterson, Thomas G. *Kennedy's Quest for Victory: American Foreign Policy, 1961–1963*. New York and Oxford: Oxford University Press. 1989.
10. Wyden, Peter. *Bay of Pigs: The Untold Story*. New York: Simon and Schuster. 1979.

Was Lyndon Johnson a Failure as President?

It would seem that as the divisive memories surrounding the Vietnam War recede, Lyndon Johnson's star would correspondingly be on the rise. Such has not thus far been the case, however. In general, Johnson is judged as a poor President by the present generation of American historians, and the outlook for the near future does not suggest much of a change.

At first glance, this predominance of negative appraisal is rather surprising. Johnson's talents as a man and as a politician are rarely disputed. He brought to the Presidency keen analytical abilities, a knack for asking the right questions when confronted with perplexing issues, a "superhuman" energy, and a dedication to the job that rivaled any President in our history. Further given his twenty-three years in Congress, plus his three years as understudy to John Kennedy, Johnson was probably better prepared than any Vice-President in our history to become President. During his days as Senate Majority Leader, he utilized his talents of persuasion, his masterful sense of timing, and his keen intuition, to dominate the Senate as few had done before.

Even as President, Johnson's virtues quickly became recognizable, for he offered strength and dignity during the difficult period of transition after President Kennedy's assassination. At a moment when America was in intense emotional disarray, he conducted national affairs with skill and surety. Even these assets, however, were quickly overshadowed by another more impressive feat: Johnson took over Kennedy's stalled legislative program, and with adroit management, guided it through an often reluctant Congress. In fact, eighty-nine important bills were passed by Johnson's Congresses, ranging from Medicare, Aid to Education, and aid to the poor, to consumer protection and highway beautification. Like a seasoned field commander, he employed strategy and carefully-timed maneuvers to carry the legislative day. To his credit, during his Presidency the ranks of the impoverished were actually reduced by 12.5 million. Further, no Chief Executive in American history was more committed to Civil Rights than Lyndon Johnson. As a tribute to John Kennedy, he guided the Civil Rights Bill of 1964 through Congress. Then, after the November 1964 election, his 89th Congress added the important Voting Rights Act of 1965, and his 90th Congress the Open Housing Act of 1968.

Why, then, all the criticism? If most historians concede LBJ's great humanitarianism, where are the areas of weakness? For most historians Johnson's incredible vanity and arrogance were important drawbacks. Because of an overly-inflated ego, even by Presidential standards, Johnson very seldom allowed his aides to be truly creative or independent in their judgments. As a result, he cut himself off from many of the opinions he later needed when his Presidency entered upon troubled times.

In addition, Johnson fed upon power. He was proud of the fact that he could maneuver and "wheel and deal" with the best politicans. As he once remarked: "I do understand power, whatever else may be said about me. I know where to look for it and how to use it." However, he often squandered this asset by first overstating his political goals and then using questionable means to achieve those goals.

Johnson's style was also irksome. First of all, he was devious and manipulative by nature. These traits may have served him well in Congress, where back-scenes scheming was respected, but in the office of the Presidency these qualities were suspect. As the historian Philip Geyelin has noted:

> Johnson's art of persuasion and influence operates on the theory that almost any argument that isn't demonstrably false is justified in a good cause; if contradictions develop, they can be ironed out and retribution made at a later date.[6]

Again, this approach was plausible when he was Senate Majority Leader, and when he worked with a small group of men and women and held access to the key sources of information. But in dealing with a national audience, this approach backfired. In a national arena, a President must work to seek rapport and to be better understood. Johnson's falsehoods were not appreciated by the general public, and his credibility quickly faded. The best example involved the Vietnam War, where Johnson's repeated assurances were almost always belied by the course of events. Eventually Johnson came to be so distrusted that anything he tried, even when his intentions were good, was suspect.

Further, Johnson's coarseness of manner and speech were often viewed as appalling. For instance, there was his choice of words in expressing gratitude to José A. Mora, Costa Rican Secretary-General of the OAS, for his handling of the Dominican Republic peace-keeping problem: "That José Mora . . . did such a wonderful job, he can have anything I've got. He can have my little daughter Luci. Why, I'd even tongue him myself." This particular incident, though more spectacular than most, conveys the dismay which Johnson could evoke.

Johnson's major weaknesses, however, revealed themselves in the realm of foreign affairs. Besides extreme inexperience, Johnson brought to the conduct of foreign affairs two important liabilities: a self-righteous belief in American moral superiority, and a simplistic approach to the evils of appeasement. Like many other Americans of his generation, Johnson's thinking on foreign affairs was colored by the failure of appeasement at the notorious Munich Conference of 1938. With this event in mind, Johnson interpreted aggression around the world in light of the European experience of the 1930s. At one time or another, Stalin, Mao, and Ho Chi Minh were likened to Adolf Hitler by Johnson, and the paths of their nations likened to the path that Germany took toward National Socialism. Such simplistic reasoning was bound to be disastrous. As the historian Eric Goldman has argued, this type of thought led straight to an escalation of the Vietnam War that was:

> a grave mistake, unnecessary for the national security, inconsistent with a mature foreign policy, disruptive of our world leadership, destructive of urgently needed domestic programs, and dubious in terms both of the American tradition and of Judeo-Christian morality.[7]

But one does not have to hold the view that Vietnam was a grave miscalculation to be critical of Johnson's handling of the war. For instance, Johnson need not have misled the American people with naive historical analogies and patently false statements. He need not have tried to hide the real costs of the war by dodging the funding issue, borrowing money instead of raising taxes to pay for the war. Instead, he might have gone to Congress with forthright statements, declared a state of national emergency, and put the economy on a wartime footing. Instead, he chose a policy which divided the nation against itself and set the basis for a raging inflation in the years to follow. As one Chicago manufacturer commented: "The President may be right in going into Vietnam. I can't make up my mind. What really worries me is the kind of thinking that led to his decision."

Historians are equally critical of Johnson's decision to intervene with military force in the Dominican Republic in 1965. Again, Johnson's handling of the situation revealed characteristic personal shortcomings. First were the extravagant public statements about the problem at hand, statements generally in sharp disagreement with actual events. Then, Johnson put forth an argument with premises which were highly suspect. In this instance, Johnson argued that it was legitimate for the U.S. to intervene with armed force in Latin America and the Caribbean to suppress civil strife that could give the communists a chance to gain a foothold. However, since the U.S. government had a tendency to see in *all* social revolution the hand of communist conspiracy, the implications of such reasoning were frightening. Finally, when the OAS proved to be unenthusiastic about endorsing the Johnson Administration's high-handed actions, Lyndon's disappointed evaluation was typical: "The OAS couldn't pour piss out of a boot if the instructions were written on the heel."

Other aspects of Johnson's foreign policy were in equal disarray. During his tenure in office no real progress was made with the Soviet Union on arms-limitation. There was no workable policy to deal with a smoldering Middle Eastern situation. And China-U.S. relations were conducted as if there were no reality to the ever-growing Sino-Soviet dispute.

There are even harsh critics of Johnson's Great Society programs. Conservatives in particular are critical of Johnson's avid belief that for every problem there was a legislative solution, and that the government could solve most problems by throwing money at them. Even liberals express anguish over the misspent monies, the poorly administered programs, and the burgeoning bureaucracies involved with Johnson's legislative accomplishments. The key failure seems to have been that Johnson pushed his programs ahead too rapidly, so that most were insufficiently studied and prematurely implemented. As a result, despite the high goals and the lofty ideals, no one was really satisfied and in the end Johnson left a legacy of bitterness and disagreement. The historian Jim Heath summarized these frustrating developments:

Blacks and the poor believed that they were still not getting a fair share of the benefits. On the other hand, the middle and working classes increasingly felt that minority groups and those on welfare were receiving too much help compared to themselves. Middle-income earners labored hard and paid sizable taxes but received relatively few federal benefits. In contrast, the rich took advantages of tax loopholes, corporations enjoyed handsome government contracts and subsidies, and government regulatory agencies guarded the special interests they were to police more than they protected the general welfare. Reports of government waste and fraud rankled Middle Americans, as did the huge, costly, and often irritating bureaucracy required to administer federal operations. During the 1960s, the feeling grew that perhaps the "experts" in Washington really did not have answers to the multitude of problems confronting the country.[8]

So ends a catalogue of the major criticisms of the Johnson Presidency. A survey of the current Johnson literature tends to confirm the evaluation that on the whole the Johnson Presidency was a time of failure. Johnson himself seems a tragic figure; a man of so many gifts, a man who excelled so exceptionally in one area of government service, yet so miscast for greatness in the office of Chief Executive. The lesson would seem to be a warning to all Americans that they would do well to re-evaluate how their Vice-Presidents are chosen. For currently the person who is to be second-in-command is most often chosen for the wrong reasons and at the wrong time.

Yet, the failure may not have been solely Lyndon Johnson's. Perhaps Johnson was only coincidentally suffering from years of flawed governmental planning. After all, Johnson was simply operating on the accepted premises of post-World War II America. His domestic program was nothing more than the New and Fair Deals and the New Frontier, brought to their logical culmination. And in foreign policy, Johnson was carrying forth the policy of containment to its ultimate conclusion. Maybe it took a Lyndon Johnson, so out of place in that Washington world of pseudo-sophistication and phony finesse to reveal that America's governing elite were simply not focussing on the right questions.

SELECTED BIBLIOGRAPHY

1. Bornet, Vaughn Davis. *The Presidency of Lyndon B. Johnson.*   Lawrence, Kan.: University of Kansas Press. 1983.
2. Caro, Robert A. *The Years of Lyndon Johnson.* 2 vols. New York: Alfred A. Knopf. 1982 and 1990.
3. Conkin, Paul. *Big Daddy from the Pedernales.* Boston: Twayne. 1986.
4. Divine, Robert A. *Exploring the Johnson Years.* Austin: University of Texas Press. 1981.
5. Dugger, Ronnie. *The Politician: The Life and Times of Lyndon Johnson. The Drive for Power, from the Frontier to Master of the Senate.* New York: W. W. Norton and Co. 1982.
6. Geyelin, Philip. *Lyndon B. Johnson and the World.* New York: F. A. Praeger. 1966.
7. Goldman, Eric F. *The Tragedy of Lyndon Johnson.* New York: Alfred A. Knopf. 1969.
8. Heath, Jim F. *Decade of Disillusionment: The Kennedy-Johnson Years.* Bloomington: Indiana University Press. 1975.
9. Heren, Louis. *No Hail, No Farewell.* New York: Harper and Row. 1970.
10. Johnson, Lyndon. *The Vantage Point: Perspectives of the Presidency 1963–1969.* New York: Holt, Rinehart and Winston. 1971.
11. Kearns, Doris. *Lyndon Johnson and the American Dream.* New York: Harper and Row. 1976.
12. Miller, Merle. *Lyndon.* New York: G.P. Putnam's Sons. 1980.
13. Schandler, Herbert Y. *The Unmaking of a President: Lyndon Johnson and Vietnam.* Princeton, N.J.: Princeton University Press. 1977.

Was the U.S.'s Involvement in Vietnam a Success or a Failure?

Not so very long ago American academicians were fairly unified in their opinion that the Vietnam War was a tragic mistake. The only serious debate among them dealt with the reasons for that error. Essentially there were two broad positions on this matter: for convenience, let us call them the Incrementalist and the Structuralist.

The Incrementalists argued that the Vietnam War and the growing American involvement were the result of a series of seemingly small miscalculations, miscalculations that imperceptibly pulled the U.S. toward an entangling situation. There was no major master plan for intervention, no devious intrigue on the part of the American presidents involved. Rather, they acted incorrectly because of misinformation, or lack of information, and because of their over-reaction, and the U.S. public's over-reaction, to the hysteria of the Joe McCarthy period. Arthur Schlesinger, Jr., summed up the Incrementalist position in 1967 when he argued that:

> Vietnam is a triumph of the politics of inadvertence. We have achieved our present entanglement, not after due and deliberate consideration, but through a series of small decisions.
> . . . Each step in the deepening of the American commitment was reasonably regarded as the last that would be necessary. Yet, in retrospect, each step led only to the next, until we find ourselves entrapped today in that nightmare of American strategists, a land war in Asia—a war which no President, including President Johnson, desired or intended. The Vietnam story is a tragedy without villains.[12]

The Incrementalists concluded with the observation that the U.S. learned valuable lessons from the Vietnam experience, and therefore, another mistake like this was highly unlikely.

The Structuralists disagreed. They saw the cause for American intervention rooted in our aggressive capitalistic system. Structuralists believed that America was truly dominated by a military-industrial complex—an association of imperialistic and counter-revolutionary businessmen in alliance with a warrior caste of high-ranking military officers. Structuralists believed that this highly-placed elite promoted the image of danger abroad so that big corporations' technological and planning needs could be securely, and profitably, decided here at home. Therefore, until this business-military elite was dramatically rooted out of its predominant position, there would be the likelihood of more "Vietnams."

Only the weather, and fashions, change more rapidly than historical interpretations, however. The release of new documents and the opening of new archives have stimulated a major reinterpretation of the Vietnam War, and an attack on both the Incrementalist and the Structuralist positions. Two authors have been particularly important in bringing this turnabout—Leslie Gelb and Guenter Lewy. Both men demonstrate that there was much less governmental blundering, indecisiveness, and self-delusion than was formerly believed.

Gelb, in particular, argues that the irony of the Vietnam experience was that "the system worked."[5] Communism was contained for 25 years, just as the presidents involved aimed to do, and just as the public, the press, and the Congress expected. Gelb adds that American presidents were not taking the nation along with them in a "blind slide down a slippery slope." Nor were American presidents naively expecting an easy military victory in Vietnam. Rather, the presidents involved followed the policy of containment for fear of what would happen domestically and internationally if they did not. Internationally, the presidential fear was that the policy of containment would be badly eroded if Vietnam was lost to the communists. Further, American credibility in the eyes of foreign allies might be lost. Domestically, presidents feared the backlash of voters and politicians on the "right" if they did nothing. Therefore, Gelb maintains, "the costs of raising the ante seemed clearly lower."

Further, Gelb points out that the governmental bureaucracy was not remiss in failing to consider alternatives. Gelb reveals that there was thoughtful and steady questioning of policies regarding Vietnam by the State Department, the Foreign Service, and the military. Particularly surprising is that documentation which shows that CIA analysts began questioning the logic of American intervention in Vietnam as early as 1964. Equally insightful is Gelb's documentation regarding the Gulf of Tonkin resolution. It is now clear that Johnson did not use this resolution as a pretext for escalation of the war. Even after its passage in Congress, Johnson clung to the hope that direct and sustained American intervention might be averted. In sum, Gelb argues that American presidents followed what they considered to be necessary policies, with no illusions as to their success, until the domestic balance of opinion shifted and until Congress finally decided to reduce support to Saigon.

Lewy is even more supportive of American policies in his writings.[9] For him the new documents prove that from the beginning Hanoi instigated, directed, and led the insurgency in the South. The idea that the rebellion in the South was spontaneous or the result of brutal South Vietnamese governmental policies is incorrect, argues Lewy. The U.S., in light of this North Vietnamese attitude, was not remiss in viewing the Vietnam situation as analogous to the aggression in Korea in 1950, and was legally warranted, even in light of the Geneva Accords, in intervening on behalf of the South. In addition, the issue of supposed American war atrocities and war crimes is restudied by Lewy. For Lewy, the new documents support the contention that American atrocities were vastly exaggerated and distorted by the TV and press. Lewy goes so far as to question the inevitability of the final fall of Vietnam in 1975. If President Nixon had not been compromised by the Watergate scandals, and could have provided South Vietnam's government with American air support, the policy of "Vietnamization" might have lasted. Given what has happened since 1975, argues Lewy, this outcome would have been highly beneficial to millions of Vietnamese.

What insights can a historian offer on this controversy and dilemma? I definitely do not pretend to have all the answers, but the following are thoughts that come to mind. We must first recognize that the recently declassified documents are still only a very small part of the story. The U.S. government usually holds the most crucial "classified" documents, ones that it believes might jeopardize current foreign policy, for twenty-five years or more before making them available to scholars and the press.

Secondly, any documents that are released are likely to be slanted in two important ways. First of all, they probably are biased because they are White House and Defense Department papers. These types of archives are generally going to be favorable to the executive and military establishment, and to the governmental bureaucracy in general. For instance, consider the documents that Gelb and Lewy were studying. We must understand that it was no accident that those documents were released. The White House and Defense Department were deeply worried about the credibility of American foreign policy in the face of the SALT II negotiations that were juxtaposed with Soviet aggression. What subtler way to influence public opinion on those matters than by showing competence, capability, and "morality" in the recent past? It was definitely expedient for our government to act in this manner. Significant questions involving the destiny of our nation were at stake, and these decisions were not to be taken without exerting major efforts toward persuasion and influence. A historian attempting to ascertain the truth about the Vietnam War must keep this in mind.

We must be careful, too, of "present-mindedness" in our evaluation of the new works on the Vietnam War. This war was seen as the greatest U.S. policy-failure of the 1960s and early 1970s. Historians and journalists in those years allowed the existence of the war to distort their objectivity regarding many aspects of the American past and present. My warning is that we must not allow current developments to blind us to mistakes that the U.S. truly *did make* in the past, just as the Vietnam War should not cause us to condemn the U.S. for mistakes that the U.S. *did not make.*

Finally, we must recognize that most historians and political scientists still approach the Vietnam War with a characteristic American ignorance. That is, there is the tendency to make very little study of, and pay very little attention to any other country's politics and culture. There was an almost total failure to investigate the feelings and aspirations of the Vietnamese people. Instead, American and alleged Communist actions were seen as the sole motive forces behind these international developments. This is particularly true of the Structuralists, who tend to see nearly all events in the world as almost entirely shaped by the American "counter-revolution."

This last weakness is crucial. The tragic American policy in Vietnam foundered upon one grand imponderable that was beyond our control: the non-Communist Vietnamese were never able to achieve ideological cohesion, organizational discipline, or political legitimacy. They were never able to overcome their differences so as to project one unified policy that would be able to win the support of the peasantry. Given this, America's hopes for success in Vietnam were probably doomed from the beginning.

SELECTED BIBLIOGRAPHY

1. Baritz, Loren. *Backfire: A History of How American Culture Led Us into Vietnam and Made Us Fight the Way We Did.* New York: William Morrow. 1985.
2. Berman, Larry. *Planning a Tragedy: The Americanization of the War in Vietnam.* New York: W. W. Norton. 1983.
3. Brodie, Bernard. *War and Politics.* New York: Macmillan Co. 1973.
4. FitzGerald, Frances. *Fire in the Lake: The Vietnamese and the Americans in Vietnam.* Boston: Little, Brown and Co. 1972.
5. Gelb, Leslie H. and Richard K. Betts. *The Irony of Vietnam: The System Worked.* Washington, D.C.: The Brookings Institution. 1979.

6. Herring, George C. *America's Longest War*. New York: John Wiley and Sons. Second Edition. 1986.
7. Karnouw, Stanley. *Vietnam: A History*. Penguin Books. 1984.
8. Kolko, Gabriel. *Anatomy of a War: Vietnam, the United States, and the Modern Historical Experience*. New York: Pantheon Books. 1985.
9. Lewy, Guenter. *America in Vietnam*. New York: Oxford University Press. 1978.
10. Moss, George Donelson. *Vietnam: An American Ordeal*. Englewood Cliffs, N.J.: Prentice Hall, Inc. 1990.
11. Patti, Archimedes L. A. *Why Viet Nam? Prelude to America's Albatross*. Berkeley and Los Angeles: University of California Press. 1980.
12. Schlesinger, Jr., Arthur M. *The Bitter Heritage: Vietnam and American Democracy, 1941–1966*. Boston: Houghton Mifflin Company. 1967.
13. Sheehan, Neil, et al. *The Pentagon Papers*. New York: The New York Times. 1971.
14. Turner, Kathleen J. *Lyndon Johnson's Dual War: Vietnam and the Press*. Chicago: University of Press. 1985.

Central America and the Vietnam Legacy: What Is the Nature of the U.S. Syndrome?

For the last decade, Republican foreign policy analysts have consistently denied that there is a parallel between the current U.S. involvement in El Salvador and the past U.S. involvement in Vietnam. One remembers President Reagan emphasizing again and again that "there is no comparison with Vietnam" when answering questions about projected U.S. military exercises in and around Central America.

However, notwithstanding President Reagan's comments, there are definite comparisons between El Salvador and Vietnam: the piecemeal escalation of American intervention, the domino analogy, the public-relations battle at home, the protest movement with accompanying demonstrations, search-and-destroy missions against peasant-guerrillas, etc.

Further, despite the repeated assurance of President Bush that this administration will not follow a path that will lead to a major U.S. military intervention in El Salvador, the fact is that the historical interpretation of the Vietnam War which is most in favor with Bush administration officials is an interpretation which argues that continued American presence in Vietnam could have brought eventual victory.

Indeed, a survey of the two major historical interpretations on the mistakes of U.S. policy in Vietnam might shed insight into the reasons why there are such emotional arguments now taking place between Republicans and Democrats on Latin American matters.

First, let us look at the preferred interpretation of many within the Bush administration, the "new nationalist" position, as some have labeled it. A handy summary of the new nationalist position might be the comment made by Peter Duignan, then senior fellow and curator at the Hoover Institution, in an interview with the *Christian Science Monitor* in 1983. "We learned the wrong lessons from Vietnam," argued Duignan. "The great tragedy was that we didn't stay. We lost our nerve and didn't stick to the domino theory. Anyone who just looks at the documents in our archives could never support detente."

For Duignan and other new nationalists, South Vietnam fell as a result of a conventional military attack from the North, not because of the strength of any popular southern rebellion. The press misrepresented the real progress U.S. forces were making, and the war was lost because of pressure from a "misguided minority opposition" at home, as General William Westmoreland once remarked.

"An American commander said of the town of Ben Tre, 'it became necessary to destroy the town in order to save it'. . . . If Communist insurgents or invaders held New York or Washington or San Francisco, we would not leave it to foreigners to take them back, and destroy them and their people in the process. . . . If the government's troops will not or cannot carry the fight for their cities, we cannot ourselves destroy them. . . . For we must ask our government—we must ask ourselves: where does such logic end? If it becomes "necessary" to destroy all of South Vietnam in order to "save" it, will we do that too? And if we care so little about South Vietnam that we are willing to see the land destroyed and its people dead, then why are we there in the first place?" Robert F. Kennedy, Speech Against the War in Vietnam, March 18, 1968.

From the military standpoint, in 1965, if Lyndon Johnson had opted for a rapid escalation in the bombing of the North, rather than a slow, piecemeal approach, or if, as mentioned in the previous chapter, Richard Nixon, in 1975, had not been compromised by the Watergate scandals and could have provided South Vietnam's government with American air support, the independence of South Vietnam might have been secured.

William E. Colby, former director of the Central Intelligence Agency, offers an ingenious analysis of the El Salvador-Vietnam parallels. For Colby, there were a number of "Vietnams." He specifically identifies "four distinct periods of the American wartime experience in Vietnam, each with its own characteristics."[2] The first period was 1960 to 1963, the second from 1964 to 1968, the third appeared between 1968 and 1972 and the fourth between 1973 and 1975.

For Colby, the Vietnam which most obsesses the American public's mind is the one of 1964 to 1968, when growing numbers of Americans became confused and distrustful of President Johnson's handling of the war.

However, the Vietnam of the third period offers an important paradigm of success, argues Colby. "The Vietnam of 1968 to 1972 offers a positive model of a leading role for political, economic and social programs to enlist a nation to develop and defend itself, with American advice and assistance in doing both."[2]

On the other side of the question are those who have learned something very different from America's experience in Vietnam. In this interpretation, the mistakes of American policy were equally monumental, but they were very different mistakes from those cited above, and very different lessons to be learned, too. For convenience, let us call this school of thought the revisionist viewpoint.

For revisionists, one of the key mistakes of Vietnam was the American tendency to view communism as a monolithic force, with the world's Communist nations in certain and conspiratorial agreement. Hence, local realities were incompletely understood.

The fact that the Vietnamese Communists under Ho Chi Minh had largely captured the banner of Vietnamese nationalism during the struggle against the Japanese in World War II was ignored. The fact that the South Vietnamese government was a puppet regime and the war in the South was a civil war was not appreciated by a State Department either picked clean of its best Asian experts by the McCarthyite purges or simply terrorized by them.

Revisionists argue, too, that there was an irrelevance in the U.S. government's anti-Communist approach in Vietnam. For the Vietnamese, the Western industrial paradigm had been an exploitative model during the years of French colonial rule. To argue for Western ideals of political pluralism and liberal capitalism was colossally irrelevant. Ho's brand of communism was more complementary to both the Vietnamese people's historic traditions and their religious aspirations.

Finally, revisionists emphasize that Americans have a persistent tendency to confuse communism as a social doctrine with communism as a valid threat from either China or Russia. As a result, there is the continual danger that our government will be led into clumsy interventions and brutal tragedies just like that in Vietnam.

These, then, are two opposite sets of lessons from America's Vietnam intervention. In a nation yearning for the tranquilities of a golden mean of good sense in foreign policy, these lessons introduce a divisiveness that, as America's military role in Latin America grows, has the power to polarize our citizenry, to dissipate our strengths and encourage our weaknesses and, worst of all, to destroy that composure which befits our stature as a great power.

Is there any basis for national agreement? Are there any common grounds upon which to build? Perhaps the following points might serve as a basis upon which to secure a consensus that is more sympathetic to the plight of the Central American people than the one that the Bush administration is currently working to secure.

First, we might recognize that many Latin Americans view Fidel Castro's Cuba much differently than we Americans do. For Latins, to be sure, Castro's achievements cannot be compared with those of such nations as the U.S., Japan, Great Britain and Sweden, especially in regard to civil liberties, democratic practices and technological breakthroughs.

Rather Castro must be compared with what went on before in Cuba. And on those terms Castro's achievements, while surely imperfect, are impressive. A social revolution was successfully effected which brought to the majority of Cubans progress in their daily lives. This should be compared with many other nations in the Third World which continue to be plagued by major failure and misery.

It is true that many Latins question Castro's continued hard-line communist stance. However, most Latin Americans believe that shortsighted American policies drove Castro into the Soviet embrace, and that more enlightened American actions might have forestalled the worst aspects of the Cuba-Soviet alliance and the lack of Castro's flexibility today.

Secondly, Americans might agree that much of Latin America today is ripe for revolution. With political and economic elites reluctant to share power and wealth with their fellows, with a middle class that is small and inexperienced, with a working class subject to the ills which usually are at their worst in the early stages of industrialization, there are few who will deny the potential of revolutionary turmoil in Latin America.

Finally, Americans, even if they do not like to admit it openly, might agree that "Yankee imperialism" is one of the greatest fears held by Latin Americans. From their point of view, the blessings of U.S. capital investment have been mixed. Often the largest profits have been made either by the few or the absentee.

Even more often there has been an accompanying spiritual poverty about American capital investment as it has transpired in Latin America. And even more sadly, coinciding with a rough-and-ready American economic aggressiveness has been a very condescending belief in American political and intellectual superiority, and a belief in the moral correctness of American interventions.

As Simón Bolívar so poignantly remarked: "The United States appears to be destined by Providence to plague America with misery in the name of liberty."

Perhaps with the recognition of common grounds for agreement we may come to realize that our national weaknesses are not as great as we imagine, nor our enemies as dangerous as they seem, nor our strengths as negligible as they appeared in Vietnam.

We may recognize, too, that despite our military hardware, the key element in any confrontation is the will of our nation. Without the strength of will, without the courage grounded in the conviction that our actions are undertaken after careful consideration and rigorous intellectual thought, and without a concern for moral correctness, any American foreign policy will probably fail in the end.

SELECTED BIBLIOGRAPHY

1. Didion, Joan. *Salvador*. New York: Simon and Schuster. 1983.
2. Gettleman, Marvin E., et. al. *El Salvador: Central America in the New Cold War*. New York: Grove Press. 1981.
3. La Feber, Walter. *Inevitable Revolutions*. New York: W.W. Norton. Expanded edition. 1984.
4. Lowenthal, Abraham F. *Partners in Conflict: The United States and Latin America*. Baltimore: Johns Hopkins University Press. 1987.
5. McMahon, Robert J. ed. *Major Problems in the History of the Vietnam War*. Lexington, Mass. and Toronto: D.C. Heath. 1990.
6. Skidmore, Thomas E. and Peter H. Smith. *Modern Latin America*. New York: Oxford University Press. 1984.
7. Smith, Robert Freeman, ed. *The United States and the Latin American Sphere of Influence*. 2 volumes. Melbourne, Florida: Robert E. Krieger. 1981.
8. Steel, Ronald. *Pax Americana*. New York: Penguin Books. 1977.
9. Tannenbaum, Frank. *Ten Keys to Latin America*. New York: Alfred A. Knopf. 1966.

Uncertain Greatness? Henry Kissinger and American Foreign Policy

For eight dramatic years, 1969–1976, Henry Kissinger was a central figure in our nation's governmental process. Whether as National Security Adviser to the President or as Secretary of State, his presence, at times, overshadowed that of the Presidents whom he served. Yet, whenever I think of Dr. Kissinger's role in the conduct of American foreign policy, Winston Churchill's comment about Lenin and Russia comes to mind: "the worse misfortune was his coming, the next worse—his leaving."

For instance, negative aspects of Kissinger's legacy are readily apparent. He was a cold practitioner of *Realpolitik,* with little interest in the questions of international human rights. Whether in Chile, in Pakistan, or in Biafra, if the requisites of the superpower struggle took precedence in his eyes, he tended, it seemed, to ignore the human costs. On the domestic front, he often ran roughshod over our nation's democratic processes. For example, he was a main influence behind the restructuring of the National Security Council so that it was removed from the checks and balances of the State Department, the Congress, and the force of public opinion. Further, he cultivated a viciously competitive climate in the National Security Council and the State Department bureaucracies so as to disarm and divide his rivals, and to fortify his position with the President. Finally, one remembers the wiretapping incidents, probably initiated by Kissinger, certainly condoned by him, ostensibly to halt the dangerous leaking of important information. But the vast majority of leaked information, as one of Kissinger's former staff members, Roger Morris, has argued:

> only revealed to the American people the actions of their own government that foreign friends and enemies already knew. At stake was not the capacity to keep authentic secrets, but rather the ability of the White House to continue conducting foreign policy even more furtive and closed than its predecessors.[8]

In sum, there were unfortunate questions surrounding Kissinger's conduct of foreign policy. Critical situations were often used as excuses to indulge his power-seeking impulses. At crucial times he appeared to be, in a democratic sense, considerably removed from the essence of American ideals.

On the other hand, Kissinger's "leaving" was to be lamented, too. Kissinger brought to the conduct of diplomacy a rational doctrine and a deliberate design which contrasted favorably with the American government's general tendency to approach foreign affairs somewhat haphazardly on a day-to-day basis. Believing that the U.S. was one of the two dominant powers on the world scene, Kissinger borrowed three lessons from his study of European history which he thought to be particularly relevant to America's contemporary predicament. The first lesson was that a secure peace is not based on the predominance of one nation over the rest, but rather on the basis of a set of negotiated settlements which attains careful equilibria on all sides. Second, to maintain peace, a dominant power should not attempt to overwhelm its opponents, but rather it should attempt to make it worthwhile for them to acquiesce in a general system of order, by offering them tangible benefits. Third, the best guarantee of peace is a balance of power between nations, with one or more nations playing key roles as balancers.

Kissinger applied these principles in the following manner. His first principle was epitomized by the policy of detente with the Soviet Union, and recognition of Soviet parity with the U.S. in strategic weapons. The second principle was implemented in the economic arena, where Kissinger extended extensive credits to the Soviet Union and other nations, in hopes of creating a community of economic interests that would act as a restraint on adventurism. The third principle was illustrated by the rapprochement with China. The stunning reversal of U.S.-China relations created a new triangular relationship among the Soviet Union, the U.S., and China. In this relationship, Kissinger saw the U.S. and China playing the vital role of balancers. To summarize, then, Kissinger brought to the State Department a comprehensive set of principles upon which, he believed, American foreign policy could be solidly based.

But there is yet another reason to lament Kissinger's removal from the summit of foreign policy decision-making; for a decade his absence coincided with a worsening of our relations with the Soviet Union. The Cold War was lessened measurably during Kissinger's tenure in office. He vigorously pursued detente with the Soviet Union, utilizing the concept of "linkage." Linkage simply meant that strategic problems with the Russians were not to be worked out in a vacuum. Rather each vital issue-area between the two nations was to be linked with other key issue-areas, and progress on one would affect progress on all. With this approach, Kissinger developed a close working relationship with Soviet Ambassador Anatoly Dobrynin, orchestrated an important summit conference with the Soviets in 1972, and tried to secure a solid beginning on SALT (Strategic Arms Limitation) negotiations by initialing a first agreement.

Likewise, Kissinger's efforts in beginning a U.S. rapprochement with mainland China were very vigorous. Both Kissinger and President Nixon perceptively measured the extent of the Sino-Soviet rift in 1969 and then swiftly moved to exploit it. Kissinger himself wrote of this achievement:

> To understand the contribution of the China initiative to international stability, we merely need to ask ourselves what the world would have been like if Chinese pressures in Asia had been added to Soviet global adventurism during the Vietnam War and afterward.[5]

In addition, Kissinger argued that the domestic political impact inside the U.S. of this China policy was equally significant:

> After [the U.S. withdrawal from] Vietnam and the despair about the possibility of creative policy . . . the China initiative [was] a breath of fresh air, a reminder of what America could accomplish as a world leader. [It proved] to ourselves and others that the U.S. remained a major factor in world affairs.[5]

Another positive aspect of Kissinger's legacy involved his mediation efforts after the Arab-Israeli "October War" of 1973. He recognized immediately that a stalemated outcome would allow him to utilize diplomacy as a tool to deal extensively with the Arab-Israeli quarrel. His plan was to implement a "step-by-step" approach, at first neglecting the most difficult substantive and ideological issues, in favor of setting a foundation for a pattern of negotiations for a future reconciliation. In short, a principled comprehensive solution was postponed in favor of dealing with minor details until a negotiating process was in place. Added to this was another feature; American bilateral talks were begun with each receptive Arab nation.

Some people believed that Kissinger should have proceeded in exactly the opposite manner; that is, the most difficult substantive issues such as Palestinian representation should have been resolved at the beginning of the peace-making. Nonetheless, Kissinger's achievement has to be regarded as significant. He bought time. He prevented war. He set a process in motion which resulted in the signing of the Sinai Agreement of 1975. And for the first time since World War II, the U.S. appeared to have a viable "Arab policy." In exchange for recognition of Israel's existence, Kissinger offered the Arab nations two key prospects: the eventual return of territories conquered by Israel, and the availability of modern American technology for general economic development throughout the Middle East.

One last example, however, best serves to demonstrate the difficulty of evaluating Kissinger's achievement. Indeed, no issue has been more disputed than Kissinger's Indochina policy. Upon entering office, neither Kissinger nor Nixon had any declared intention of precipitously ending America's involvement in the Vietnam War. For them, American honor, prestige, and credibility were at stake. A "callous" abandonment of South Vietnam, simply to gain a respite from domestic travail, they argued, would weaken the faith that America's allies had in America's alleged ability to "lead the world." Further, it would embolden America's enemies abroad to resort to arms whenever some minor aspect of the *status quo* did not suit them.

For critics, these arguments were not persuasive. They argued that Nixon and Kissinger overestimated the amount of humiliation that the U.S. would suffer if the war were quickly abandoned. On the contrary, critics believed, American credibility would be enhanced by a noble recognition of misjudgment, and a merciful end to the killing and destruction. For these critics, Nixon and Kissinger, with more perceptiveness and persistence, could have gained, as early as 1969, the very terms that were incorporated into the 1973 peace settlement. Further, critics castigated Nixon and Kissinger for not recognizing the strategic weaknesses of their "Vietnamization" policy; that is, their tactic of withdrawing U.S. troops, naively expecting Hanoi to negotiate while U.S. military power was shrinking, and then, more disastrously, in order to salvage their failing strategy, turning to increased bombings in North Vietnam and to a secret widening of the war into Cambodia, in large part creating the tragic situation that later beset that part of Indochina.

Our survey of Henry Kissinger's impact in the making of America's foreign policy during the Nixon and Ford years suggests that foresight and folly seem to be intertwined in almost equal measure. For every grand stroke there seems to be an example of an equally mistaken one. The real significance of Henry Kissinger, however, is that he brought to light a key dilemma that faced all Americans: could violent threats to the *status quo* be condoned in a world bordering always on the possibility of nuclear holocaust? For Kissinger, the pursuit of a stable balance of power between nations was essential. If necessary, dubious means were to be tolerated if extremely dangerous developments in the superpower struggle threatened nuclear disaster. "If history teaches anything," he argued, "it is that there can be no peace without equilibrium and no justice without restraint."[5]

Yet, since most countries in the world social system, as evolved thus far, are essentially unsatisfactory to the poor, and politically undemocratic as well, is not tyranny likely to result from *any* policy "committed to stability as its ultimate standard?" Whatever our final answer to this dilemma, we must grant that Kissinger at least confronted the challenge and presented a comprehensive answer. Many Presidents and Secretaries of State have lacked his comprehension of controlling principles, thereby diminishing their diplomatic effectiveness. Because of Kissinger's "ideological" precision and the depth of his intellect, his most important legacy has been to make clearer the ominous alternatives which confront us.

SELECTED BIBLIOGRAPHY

1. Brown, Seyom. *The Crises of Power.* New York: Columbia University Press. 1979.
2. Gardner, Lloyd C. *The Great Nixon Turnaround: America's New Foreign Policy in the Post-Liberal Era.* New York: New Viewpoints. 1973.
3. Graubard, Stephen R. *Kissinger: Portrait of a Mind.* New York: W. W. Norton. 1974.
4. Hersh, Seymour. *The Price of Power.* New York: Summit Books. 1983.
5. Kissinger, Henry. *White House Years.* Boston: Little, Brown and Co. 1979.
6. _____. *Years of Upheaval.* Boston: Little, Brown and Co. 1982.
7. Mazlish, Bruce. *Kissinger, The European Mind in American Policy.* New York: Basic Books. 1976.
8. Morris, Roger. *Uncertain Greatness.* New York: Harper and Row. 1977.
9. Shawcross, William. *Sideshow: Kissinger, Nixon and the Destruction of Cambodia.* New York: Simon and Schuster. 1979.
10. Stoessinger, John. *Henry Kissinger: The Anguish of Power.* New York: W. W. Norton Co. 1976.

GENERAL ESSAYS ON U.S. HISTORY

Political misjudgments and wrong turns are like tuberculosis, hard to detect and easy to cure in the beginning and easy to diagnose and very hard to cure at the end.

Machiavelli

Are Recent Anti-Draft Protests Simply the Latest in a Long, Long Line?

Recent years have been trying times for "patriotic" Americans. First, was the decade of the 1960s with its anti-war protests and violence. Then came the 1970s, the so-called "Me Decade," when individual hedonism seemed to push national concerns for self-discipline and self-sacrifice to new and dismal lows. Many hoped a different mood would develop in the 1980s. Some people even sought to rationalize the actions of the 1960s and 1970s as normal reactions to an unjust and unpopular war. All we had to do was to look to the early 1920s and early 1950s for confirmation of the psychological and social dislocations which occur during postwar periods.

These hopes for a different mood in the 1980s were dashed, however, by renewed protests. There were zealous criticisms of ill-planned nuclear-energy power facilities, of "inordinate" corporate profits, and of "crafty" oil-industry "manipulations." For many "patriotic" Americans the *coup de grace* was the anger aroused by President Carter's call for the re-implementation of draft registration after the Soviet invasion of Afghanistan.

Before the disillusionment sets in too far, however, it might be beneficial to evaluate the recent draft protests in the light of the past. A historical perspective will immediately awaken one to the fact that vehement draft protests are nothing new for Americans, and can be traced back all the way to our struggle for independence in 1776.

Let us take the Revolutionary War as a first example. One need only peruse George Washington's private papers to recognize what tremendous problems he had with defectors, mutineers, and those of his forces who "lacked public spirit." He complained of the state militias, saying that they "were continually coming and going without rendering the least Earthly Service." He remarked of the Continental Army: "As the army now stands, it is only a receptacle for ragamuffins." Many historians to this day characterize public support of the Revolutionary War as: "one-third in favor, one-third against, and one-third indifferent."

When the U.S.'s alliance with France was signed in 1778, the American letdown in the war effort was so disastrous that it almost cost the U.S. a victory. Now that France had committed troops, most Americans became convinced that "peace and prosperity" were just around the corner, and they rushed off in the pursuit of happiness, i.e., the pursuit of dollars. Again George Washington observed: "Stock jobbing, speculating, engrossing, &c. &c. seems to be the great business of the day, and of the multitude, whilst a virtuous few struggle, lament, and suffer in silence, tho' I hope not in vain."

The War of 1812 was especially notorious for its revelations of national disunity. In fact, it was perhaps the most unpopular war in our history, especially in the Northeast. New England governors refused to allow their militias to fight outside their state boundaries, New England bankers failed to take up wartime loans, and New England farmers and fishermen traded with the enemy. Luckily, the peace treaty with Great Britain was signed before the New England delegates meeting at the Hartford Convention could make good their threat of secession.

The Civil War also provides an intriguing example of what we may already recognize as a typically American approach to patriotism. In 1863, when Northerners passed a National Conscription Law, public protests and draft riots were commonplace. This was despite the fact that this draft law had a provision that a substitute could take a draftee's place, or that a draftee could buy a substitute for $300. Ultimately, only 46,000 of the 255,000 men who were called in the draft actually entered Union military service. The hiring of a substitute was regarded as so respectable that President Lincoln hired one for his own son.

Southern soldiers were equally adept at disregarding their Conscript Act of 1862. After its passage, Southern soldiers expressed their resentment by deserting in droves. Lincoln faced less of a problem, however, than Jefferson Davis, for Union armies could rely on two sources of manpower not readily available to the South: European immigrants and freed slaves. By 1864 one out of every four or five Union soldiers was of European birth. Another 178,895 Union soldiers were blacks, roughly five times the number of men in Lee's army when he surrendered at Appomattox.

World War I is an early twentieth-century example which supports the trends that I have delineated above. Americans were deeply divided over U.S. entry into World War I initially, and an extensive indoctrination and propaganda program had to be launched to ameliorate much of the strongest protest. American soldiers were involved in the heavy fighting for only a few months, however, so national unity was not severely tested in World War I. Nonetheless, there were over 170,000 deserters and draft dodgers during the time that the U.S. was involved (1917-1918).

Even a popular war, like World War II, was not without its negative aspects, though one must recognize that World War II is the exception which proves the rules and conclusions that I will introduce below. To continue my argument, however, one need only remember that as late as 1940 public opinion was so divided as to the real threat of Fascism that the subject of a peacetime conscription measure had to be very adroitly introduced and handled by Franklin Roosevelt.

The main point of this essay is not to denigrate the heroism of American veterans, or to cast aspersions on American character. I am simply attempting to offer a historical perspective into draft protests after the Soviet invasion of Afghanistan.

What key insights emerge from all of this? First of all, Americans do not arouse themselves unless they think the threat from an enemy is imminent and explicit. One can see this reluctance in the reaction after the French Alliance in 1778, in the actions of the New England states in 1812, in the war-weariness of the North during the Civil War, and in the examples of the Korean and Vietnamese conflicts more recently.

Secondly, Americans do not fight well when they suspect there is a question about the justice or legality of a war, or the possibility of injustice or illegality, e.g., when Congress has not been properly consulted or when Congress is deeply divided. Again, one need only look at the War of 1812, the Civil War, the Korean War, and the Vietnam War to substantiate this point.

Finally, Americans do not fight enthusiastically when the burdens of sacrifice are unequally distributed. Today there is concern that U.S. foreign policy is excessively reflective of the wishes of a corporate business elite. This too is not a new anxiety. As early as the American Revolution George Washington commented on that "tribe of black hearted gentry," the monopolizers and profiteers who threatened the nation's ideals: "These murderers of our cause . . . are preying upon our very vitals, and, for the sake of a little dirty pelf, are putting the rights and liberties of the country into the most imminent danger."

In conclusion, it may be true that American national patriotism is ebbing. It may be true that our concern for our national destiny has lost its vigor. It may be true that our materialistic lifestyle has sapped our will power and moral fervor. But one cannot utilize recent draft protests as proof of this argument. Indeed, our nation has always revered resistance and protest when what it believed were vital issues have been involved. We have always sought to stimulate an ability to re-evaluate and criticize our government when it is believed to be necessary. Protestors today are engaging in a typically American characteristic when they march in opposition to a President's call for conscription.

SELECTED BIBLIOGRAPHY

1. Baskir, Lawrence M., and William A. Strauss. *Change and Circumstance: The Draft, the War, and the Vietnam Generation*. New York: Alfred A. Knopf. 1978.
2. Karsten, Peter. "The American Democratic Citizen Soldier: Triumph or Disaster?", *Military Affairs*, Vol. XXX (Spring 1965) pp. 34–40.
3. _____, ed. *The Military in America: From the Colonial Era to the Present*. New York: Macmillan and Co. 1980.
4. Miller, John C. *Triumph of Freedom*. Boston: Little, Brown and Co. 1948.
5. Stouffer, Samuel A., et. al. *The American Soldier: Combat and Its Aftermath*. Princeton, N.J.: Princeton University Press. 1949.
6. Wiley, Bell I. *Life of Billy Yank*. Indianapolis, Ind.: Bobbs-Merrill Co. 1952.
7. _____. *Life of Johnny Reb*. Indianapolis, Ind.: Bobbs-Merrill Co. 1943.

44

Will the World Energy Crisis
Lead to a Less Abundant Future?

Oliver Wendell Holmes, Jr., once observed: "When I want to understand what is happening today or try to decide what will happen tomorrow, I look back." Given the confusion which besets our nation as it faces the challenge of today's energy crisis, a historical perspective might be instructive. Historians have never neglected the place of energy in their portrayal of America's past. But the story, contrary to today, has always mentioned the abundance and wealth of our nation's resources. Beginning with the importance of coal and water in promoting America's initial industrial revolution, through to the birth of America's modern oil industry in 1859, the emphasis has been on easily accessible resources and ingenious technological successes. Even with oil, for instance, by 1909 U.S. production had reached 500,000 barrels a day, more than the rest of the world combined.

True, World War I provided a temporary setback to this record of unsurpassed growth. The strains of war led to a scarcity panic among top governmental and oil-industry executives, and for a few years after the war the U.S. became a net importer of oil. This fact is not surprising when one remembers that 80 percent of all Allied oil supplies came from the U.S.

Nonetheless, two developments returned the U.S. to its position of predominance. The first was the discovery of major new oilfields in Texas. The second was the success of government and oil-industry cooperation in securing domination over foreign sources of oil. By World War II the U.S. was the major force in controlling the world's oil network. Five U.S. companies were especially prominent in this endeavor: Exxon, Gulf, Mobil, SoCal, and Texaco. These five companies, when joined by British Petroleum, and Royal Dutch/Shell, were known as the "Seven Sisters."

Once again, however, the requisites of war cast an ominous shadow. This time it was World War II, a historical turning point in the American energy story. Seven billion barrels of oil were used to achieve victory in World War II, with almost 6 billion provided by U.S. wells. In 1948, as a result, the U.S. became for the first time a permanent net importer of oil.

This foreboding development was overlooked by contemporaries because of several factors. First, the U.S. continued to produce half of the world's oil. Second, the 1950s were the heyday of the "Seven Sisters." Lastly, there was a glut of oil throughout the 1950s as new sources of oil from around the world became available, especially from the Middle East.

229

The zenith of American power over the international oil network might be dated precisely at 1954. It was in that year that the U.S. government forced a favorable settlement upon troublesome forces in Iran, demonstrating to the world America's potent influence. Problems in Iran dated back to 1951, when Iran's Prime Minister Mohammad Mosaddegh nationalized British Petroleum's Iranian properties. The U.S. government reacted quickly to this unique precedent. American officials feared that Mosaddegh's example might persuade other oil-producing nations to do the same, causing a loss of effective control by the West. In addition, State Department officials were concerned that the Soviet Union's influence might be allowed to increase in Iran if Mosaddegh succeeded.

Such was the rationale behind a tragic series of decisions that has left its embittered legacy on our own times. With a push from the CIA, Mosaddegh was ousted and the Shah Pahlavi was reinstalled. The U.S. government then forced through the aforementioned Iranian Settlement of 1954, two aspects of which unexpectedly had important ramifications for the future. First, Iran was designated as the unquestioned proprietor of its own oil fields; previously the ownership and production of Iranian oil was exclusively in the hands of British Petroleum. This change in itself was a novel development. Very soon it was to become the norm. Second, the U.S. government persuaded the "Seven Sisters" to allow "independent" oil companies to own a small share of a reorganized Iranian consortium. This second precedent eventually was to create a situation where the oil-exporting nations could develop bargaining leverage by playing the independents against the "Seven Sisters." This was especially to be the case later in Libya.

For the short term, however, stability was the rule in the Middle East oil situation—until 1959. With the price of oil under one dollar a barrel, Exxon in that year made one of the most short-sighted decisions that an American oil company has ever made—it lowered the price even more. Although there was a glut in the oil market at the time, and the Russians were purposely adding to that surplus, apparently in hopes of creating economic problems in the West, the critical point about Exxon's decision was that it was made unilaterally, with no attempt at consultation with other oil producers.

The immediate response was outrage on the part of the governments of five key oil-producing nations—Iraq, Iran, Saudi Arabia, Venezuela, and Kuwait. They convened a meeting at Baghdad in September 1960 where a cooperative organization, OPEC, was founded. The power of OPEC remained minimal throughout the 1960s. Nonetheless, the potential power of the West was weakened further throughout that decade as the gap between oil supplies and industrial demands began to narrow. This was the result of two factors: 1) increased production on the parts of the established industrial powers and 2) the entry of new nations into the mechanized fold.

A dramatic shift in oil-producing power away from the West began in 1970. As U.S. production hit its peak that year at 11.3 million barrels a day, a series of crucial events commenced in the Middle East. The first was triggered by an accidental break of a key oil pipeline from the Persian Gulf to a Mediterranean seaport by a bulldozer in May 1970. As the 1967 Arab-Israeli war had closed the tanker route through the Suez, this main pipeline put Libya in a key bargaining position, which her new dictator Colonel Moammar Khadafy exploited to the full. His example was quickly followed by the rest of OPEC. By February, 1971, what was then considered to be a hugh price increase was squeezed from the West: 50 cents a barrel.

The stage was now set for the year 1973. With the outbreak of another war between Egypt and Israel in October, and the ensuing Arab oil-boycott, OPEC muscle was flexed as never before. Within two years the price of oil was pushed upward from $2.60 a barrel to over $10. A pattern began to emerge which has now become all too familiar: oil price hikes, followed by inflation and recession in the industrial nations.*

Luckily for the West this situation stabilized somewhat between 1974 and 1978. The price of oil rose steadily, but not very steeply. In fact, the price of oil did not keep pace with contemporary rates of inflation. Nonetheless, danger signals were ever present. Any crisis could throw the whole network of oil supply into chaos.

In late 1978, the international oil network was jolted by news of the Iranian Revolution. Before long, most Iranian oil shipments were stopped, resulting in another round of price hikes. The price of oil jumped in a short time from $13 a barrel to $26. Again, the price hike was ominously followed in industrial countries by surging inflation and deepening recession.

With this brief summary of key events and trends, it is easy to see why historians have found the energy-crisis to be a useful and unifying theme for presenting the disparate events of the 1970s. A focus on energy is important not only because of its own significance, but also because it allows the historian to elaborate upon the two other key developments of that decade: the rise of the Middle East to much greater international influence, and the growing problem of inflation, spreading from industrial countries to all the rest of the world.

By following the energy story from its inception to today, it becomes obvious how and why the U.S. became dependent on an oil-based technology and economy. It also becomes obvious just how revolutionary the Middle Eastern events of the 1970s were, and why the U.S. was so unprepared for the ensuing energy crisis. Contrary to much popular opinion, then, historical trends seem to indicate that the U.S. is beset with a long-term problem, the ramifications of which require decisive action and may require a transition to a future of far less abundance and even some scarcity.

SELECTED BIBLIOGRAPHY

1. Blair, John. *The Control of Oil*. New York: Pantheon Books. 1976.
2. Chester, Edward W. *United States Oil Policy and Diplomacy: A Twentieth-Century Overview*. Westport, Conn.: Greenwood. 1983.
3. Engler, Robert. *The Brotherhood of Oil: Energy Policy and the Public Interest*. Chicago: University of Chicago Press. 1977.
4. Jacoby, Neil H. *Multinational Oil*. New York: Macmillan Co. 1974.
5. Mitchell, Edward J., ed. *Dialogue on World Oil*. Washington, D.C.: American Enterprise Institute. 1974.
6. Randall, Stephen J. *United States Foreign Oil Policy, 1919–1948.: For Profits and Security*. Kingston, Ont.: McGill-Queens University Press. 1985.
7. Rocks, Lawrence, and Richard P. Runyon. *The Energy Crisis*. New York: Crown Publishing Co. 1972.
8. Sampson, Anthony. *The Seven Sisters*. London: Hodder and Stoughton. 1975.
9. Stobaugh, Robert and Daniel Yergin, ed. *Energy Future: Report of the Energy Project at the Harvard Business School*. New York: Random House. 1979.

*I do not mean to imply that the rising price of oil alone was responsible for U.S. inflation. The inflation of the 1970's was stimulated by a heavy demand for almost all commodities. I simply emphasize the energy aspect of the story because the U.S., with only 6 percent of the earth's population, was consuming 33 percent of all energy produced. Of this total, oil accounted for nearly 46 percent, and natural gas another 32 percent.

10. Szulc, Tad. *The Energy Crisis*. New York: Franklin Watts Inc. 1974.
11. Tanzer, Michael. *The Energy Crisis: World Struggle for Power and Wealth*. New York: Monthly Review Press. 1974.

In the Shadow of the Past: The Impact of History on U.S. Foreign Policy

In a number of instances in this book, the reader has been acquainted with great debates regarding the correctness of U.S. decision-making involving war: War of 1812, World War I, World War II, Korea and Vietnam. Perhaps now it is appropriate to confront the larger issue—what exactly has been the U.S. record and the American tradition in world affairs? Beneath the continuous and rapid change that has characterized the American past, what has been the nature of our heritage in foreign relations? As might be expected, the controversy is heated and antipodal. The following is a sampling of the diverse positions that historians hold.

One of the most popular approaches is that put forward by Dexter Perkins.[7] In a book first published in 1951, and then reprinted extensively and translated into eight languages, Perkins argues that our traditions are conciliatory and peaceful, that "Americans are not a warlike people in the proper sense of the word. [We] have not, in general, glorified war." Why is this?

For one thing, according to Perkins, the U.S. has been powerfully influenced by a history characterized by extraordinary security. The Atlantic and Pacific oceans were great barriers to Old World intervention, plus the U.S. was lucky to have peaceable neighbors to the north and south, and plenty of room for expansion.

Secondly, Perkins draws attention to the great impact that the Enlightenment made upon the U.S. national development. According to Perkins, America was the child of the Enlightenment's rationalistic and optimistic view of human nature. Because of this influence, warlike attitudes ran counter to our national ideals, ideals which were formulated during that great Age of Reason.

Thirdly, our nation's unity was forged during the nineteenth century, a period of almost unparalleled peace in the history of Western Europe, a fact which also went far to condition American attitudes and expectations in the realm of international relations.

Further, the economic circumstances of American life, the coexistence of abundant natural resources and great economic progress, predisposed the average American toward "getting ahead materially," and toward a predominant focus on domestic matters. "The dream of the 'good society', of a world in which there is plenty for all, caught the American imagination and seemed incompatible with perpetual strife."

Fifthly, our democratic system of government, by placing the issue of war before a national forum, was generally a restraint upon any headlong rush into conflict. "For, though democracies are capable of great excitement, though popular pressure may sometimes force a reluctant administration along the path of war, the very fact that this issue must be debated, and cannot be decided by fiat, tends to reduce the opportunities for conflict."

Finally, our Judeo-Christian traditions encouraged a search for peaceful solutions, an exploration of viable methods of international arbitration, and a careful weighing of the moral correctness of any position before a resort to force.

To prove these generalizations, Perkins brings forward some intriguing examples. There is the even-handed, non-militaristic manner in which history is taught in the U.S.; there is the prolific use that the U.S. has made of "the processes of peaceable adjustment of international disputes"—Jay's Treaty, Jefferson's Embargoes, Wilson's League, Roosevelt's United Nations; there is the fact that we have never instigated a war in the manner of a Stalin or a Hitler; and there is the fact that the American people have usually been very slow to anger and very reluctant to impose compulsory military service on its young men and women. In summary, argues Perkins, "the American people have not surrendered their long–practiced democratic customs and ideals in the arena of foreign policy."

Other historians adamantly disagree with Perkins. For instance, Wayne S. Cole argues that the story of our nation's past has been one of "expansion, conquest, and aggrandizement without parallel in modern history."[2] Beginning with the Indian wars, followed by the Purchase of Louisiana, the ousting of the Spaniards from the Floridas, the annexation of Texas and over half a million square miles of Mexican Territory, the maneuvering of the Russians and then the British out of the Pacific Northwest, the purchase of Alaska, the establishment of hegemony in the Caribbean, and the acquisition of the Panama Canal territory—expansion has been the dominant pattern in America's history.

To be sure, Cole adds, expansion was not always characterized by territorial and colonial gains. Expansion of trade investments, expansion through religious organizations and missionary activities, and intellectual, cultural and ideological expansion have all been part of our past. But whatever the expansionistic approach, one of the most consistent patterns in the history of U.S. foreign affairs has been the steady growth of American power, influence, and control in other parts of the world.

Richard Van Alstyne concurs with Cole and argues that we can see these expansionistic dreams as early as 1776, in the Continental Congress's draft of a proposed treaty with France.[10] The king of France was to agree never to:

invade, nor under any pretense attempt to possess himself of Labrador, New Britain, Nova Scotia, Acadia, Canada, Florida, nor of the Islands of Newfoundland, Cape Breton, St. John's, Anticosti, nor of any other Island lying near to the said Continent, in the Seas, or in any Gulph, Bay, or River, it being the true Intent and meaning of this Treaty, that the said United States, shall have the sole, exclusive, undivided and perpetual Possession of the Countries, Cities, and Towns, on the said Continent, and of all Islands near to it, which now are, or lately were under the Jurisdiction of or Subject to the King or Crown of Great Britain, whenever they shall be united or confederated with the said United States.

Expansionism is even more blatant in Jedediah Morse's *American Geography* of 1789:

It is well known that empire has been travelling from east to west. Probably her last and broadest seat will be America . . . the largest empire that ever existed. . . . We cannot but anticipate the period, as not far distant, when the AMERICAN EMPIRE will comprehend millions of souls, west of the Mississippi.

For William Appleman Williams, more tragic than the expansionism in our history itself, is the way that Americans have lied to themselves about it.[11] "A process of reification has occurred—a transformation of the realities of expansionism, conquest, and intervention into pious rhetoric about virtue, wealth, and democracy." And, continues Williams, "the cost of empire is not properly tabulated in the dead and the maimed, or in the wasted resources, but rather in the loss of our vitality as citizens. We have increasingly ceased to participate in the process of self-government. We have become ever more frustrated and fatalistic, and hence concerned with individual gratification. Indeed, we cannot say no to our desires. And we witness immediate national disillusionment when it appears that our desires must be limited."

Still other historians, such as Armin Rappaport[8] and Henry Steele Commager,[4] contend that nothing is more enduring in the American heritage than a sense of mission. This sense of mission was present right from the beginning, when the Puritan religious leader John Winthrop, in 1630, warned his congregation:

> We shall be as a City upon a Hill; the eyes of all people are upon us; so that if we shall deal falsely with our God in this work we have undertaken and so cause him to withdraw his present help from us, we shall be made a story and a by-word through the world.

Though this sense of mission was mostly implicit in our early colonial years, it grew stronger with independence and national expansion. Our great success in terms of national progress went to our heads, laments Rappaport. We believed that anything was possible, and we began to become boastful, presumptuous, and vain. Soon American messianic attitudes were reinforced and justified by the arguments of Manifest Destiny and Social Darwinism. Strength, power and wealth were transmogrified into signs of God's grace. Indiana Senator Albert Beveridge's speech in favor of annexing the Philippines in the debate of 1900 gives some small indication of how strong this sense of mission really was:

> Mr. President, the times call for candor. The Philippines are ours forever, territory belonging to the United States as the Constitution calls them. And just beyond the Philippines are China's illimitable markets. We will not retreat from either. We will not repudiate our duty in the archipelago. We will not abandon our opportunity in the Orient. We will not renounce our part in the mission of our race, trustee under God, of the civilization of the world. And we will move forward to our work, not howling our regrets like slaves whipped to their burdens, but with gratitude for a task worthy of our strength, and thanksgiving to Almighty God that He marked us as His chosen people, henceforth to lead in the regeneration of the world.

President McKinley's rationalization of U.S. actions in the Philippines is still another example of how easily American leaders could amalgamate aggressive business practices, *Realpolitik*, and brotherly love.

> We could not turn the islands over to France or Germany, our commercial rivals—that would be bad business and discreditable. We could not give them back to Spain—that would be cowardly and dishonorable. We could not leave them to themselves—they were unfit for self-government. . . . There was nothing left for us to do but to take them all, and to educate the Filipinos, uplift them and Christianize them.

As America moved into and through the twentieth century, the crusades of two world wars, and the post-World War II challenge of communism strengthened our sense of mission even more. We went into World War I with a great crusader, Woodrow Wilson, at our helm, aiming "to make the world safe for democracy," and aiming "to fight the war to end all wars." We ended World War I with feelings of disillusionment, but we never doubted our mission. We were a world power and we believed in the superiority of our political institutions and our economic system.

Given the clear-cut brutalities of the Fascist powers on the eve of World War II, we entered that war with our sense of destiny still intact. And we emerged from World War II with few feelings of disillusionment about ourselves. We had the atomic bomb; we were technologically superior; and we were in so many ways unchallenged. We kept our sense of mission then, and even strengthened it; it seemed more important than ever, for now we had to save the world from communism and for democracy. Hence, it became easy for us to support odious dictators, to wage pitiless wars abroad, and, according to Commager, "to feel justified in pursuing policies of intervention, subversion and aggression which we have always judged to be reprehensible in others." Such is the strength of our messianic dream today, adds Commager, that we are willing to "go it alone," if necessary, so sure are we in the overall rightness of our cause.

Though this sampling of divergent views does not exhaust the many approaches to this issue, nonetheless it lends insight into the perplexities of the arguments. Is there some common ground in this disparate situation? How might one reconcile such an array of seeming opposites?

First of all, it might be said that none of these positions is mutually exclusive. There is in each a kernel of truth about our complex and paradoxical national character. We have at different times acted in completely different ways. And we have reacted differently with different peoples. Toward Europeans our relations have been diplomatic and correct for the most part. Toward Latin Americans, our attitudes of superiority, and rationalizations of national security have led us to be more self-righteous and high-handed. So, ironically, we have played each of the above roles at various times and under various circumstances. We were surely the missionaries vis-à-vis the Indians and the Mexicans, and the expansionists, too. Yet, regarding the balance of power in Europe, our policies seem to have been more inclined toward peacefulness and international consultations.

Secondly, we might recognize how ethnocentric all these attitudes are. There is a tendency to believe that the rights essential to our own existence and healthful development are equal to the rights of all humankind. There is a tendency in each of these positions to judge the behavior of other peoples, including their revolutionary behavior, by its correspondence with "the American way."

Finally, we must toss to the winds the shibboleth that the great concern Americans currently have for foreign policy is something new, stimulated by the unique circumstances of the Cold War. There have been periods of intense preoccupation with international matters beginning with the origins of our republic.

The very existence of the nation for a time depended upon events in Europe, and questions of foreign policy were debated with a sense of extreme urgency. Our early statesmen were nurtured with the understanding that European rivalries could determine the fate of the American people. It was this realization that caused American leaders to comprehend the possibility and importance of a French alliance if victory were to be achieved in the Revolution. After the Revolution, the American nation did not cease to be involved in the rivalries, the politics, and the wars of the Old World. The British, French, and Spanish empires embroiled the U.S. in one dramatic issue after another: Jay's Treaty, the XYZ Affair, the Louisiana Purchase, Pinckney's Treaty, the Embargo Acts, and the War of 1812.

There was no self–perception on the part of our early founders that youth and inexperience made Americans more gullible than the worldly Europeans. Rather, the complexities of international issues were approached with confidence. Our leaders believed that difficult problems could be made intelligible to the public, that the American citizenry could then be trusted to yield an eventual consensus, and that a democratic republic could more than hold its own against the Great Powers of Europe. There was a recognition that hard work, patience, and subtlety were requisites for diplomatic success. Perhaps that is why the foreign policy achievements of that first generation of American leaders remain unparalleled in our history.

To conclude, we might recognize the import of understanding our very own heritage. For true peace in our time, we must not only understand the nature of the challenge of our adversaries, but we must also understand the nature of the traditions that have shaped our view of today's reality.

SELECTED BIBLIOGRAPHY

1. Bailey, Thomas A. *The Man in the Street: The Impact of American Public Opinion on Foreign Policy.* New York: Macmillan. 1948.
2. Cole, Wayne S. *An Interpretive History of American Foreign Relations.* Homewood, Ill.: Dorsey Press. 1968.
3. Combs, Jerald A. *American Diplomatic History: Two Centuries of Changing Interpretations.* Berkeley and Los Angeles: University of California Press. 1983.
4. Commager, Henry Steele. *The Defeat of America.* New York: Simon and Schuster. 1974.
5. Gilbert, Felix. *To the Farewell Address: Ideas of Early American Foreign Policy.* Princeton, N.J.: Princeton University Press. 1961.
6. Hoffman, Stanley. *Gulliver's Troubles.* New York: McGraw–Hill. 1968.
7. Perkins, Dexter. *The American Approach to Foreign Policy.* Cambridge, Mass.: Harvard University Press. Rev. ed. 1962.
8. Rappaport, Armin. "The American Mission: A 200–Year Perspective." A Lecture delivered at De Anza Community College in honor of the Bi–Centennial of the American Revolution. 1976. See also his book, *A History of American Diplomacy.* New York: Macmillan. 1975.
9. Stoessinger, John G. *Crusaders and Pragmatists.* New York: W.W. Norton. 1979.
10. Van Alstyne, Richard W. *The Rising American Empire.* New York: Oxford University Press. 1960.
11. Williams, William Appleman. *Empire As A Way of Life.* New York: Oxford University Press. 1980.

Has Excessive Violence Characterized America's Domestic History?

There used to be a time, particularly in the 1950s, when we Americans convinced ourselves that we were among the most well-behaved and law-abiding people in the world. In those days of general self-satisfaction and somnolence, we revelled in our ability to solve difficult political and social problems by resorting to artful compromise and ridiculed those nations which were characterized by revolution and rioting. American scholars often reflected the popular attitudes by displaying a "historical amnesia" when it came to violence in our past.

Today, the popular and scholarly self-satisfaction has passed. Not only are we quite aware of the violence in our midst, but we are positively frightened by it. Yet, we should not lose our perspective when calculating the amount of civil strife which characterizes our society. There is nothing in the American experience to compare with the killing and slaughter of some totalitarian regimes, particularly Stalin's Russia and Hitler's Germany. Nor has the U.S. been plagued with the domestic turmoil that has been a feature of the history of Algeria, Nigeria, Indonesia, Iran and Venezuela.

Nevertheless, the magnitude of U.S. civil strife is alarming, especially when we compare ourselves with the advanced industrial nations of the world. The murder rate in the U.S. exceeds that of any advanced industrial nation. In a typical year there are more homicides in Houston or on Manhattan Island than in all of England and Wales. A historical study of the years 1960–1968 showed that the gun-homicide rate in the U.S. was 40 times that of the British Isles, the Netherlands and Japan. More recently, researchers from the National Center for Health Statistics released a study, for the year 1990, showing that the murder rate among young men in the United States was almost 22 per 100,000; that contrasted to 0.5 per 100,000 in Japan, 1.2 in England, and 1 in East Germany.

America's consumer society and popular culture seem to thrive on the merchandising of violence. Children are schooled in violence from their first shoot-out with toy guns to their first encounter with popular comics. In the six weeks following Martin Luther King, Jr.'s assassination, a survey of the prime times when children watched TV discovered 372 threats or acts of violence, including 84 killings, in the span of 85 1/2 hours. Just recently it was estimated that violence occurs on TV at the rate of five incidents per hour in prime time. No wonder Alfred Hitchcock remarked: "Television has brought back murder into the home where it belongs."

What are the sources for this violence? Psychologists might talk of "frustration-aggression syndromes" and biologists might emphasize the "territoriality instincts" of all humans and animals. But one assumption that underlies almost all historical studies is that nature has provided humans only with the capacity for violence; what determines whether or how that capacity is exercised depends on social circumstances.

To gain a perspective on the roots, or seeds, of today's civil violence, a brief historical survey of the types of civil strife in the American past is in order. This historical perspective quickly reveals that Americans have never been a very law-abiding people, and that we have consistently rewarded illegal violence. We have consistently lacked a full respect for the law and have tended to obey only those laws with which we were in agreement.

America's frontier experience has had an important influence on contemporary patterns of violence. The fact of white-Indian conflict alone, a unique American frontier experience, must have had a brutalizing impact on the development of American attitudes toward violence. For Indian wars were the longest and most merciless of all wars in American history. It is significant to note that the most emotionally compelling myth-hero of the early American Republic was not an enlightenment rationalist modeled after Benjamin Franklin or Thomas Jefferson, rather it was the solitary hunter and Indian-fighter of the deep woods, Daniel Boone. Americans today like to think of our Founders as those reasoned men of Philadelphia who amicably met, and in the light of natural law, produced the Constitution which forged the bonds of our nation. But we must also remember that our Founders (to paraphrase the historian Richard Slotkin) included the rogues, adventurers, land-boomers, Indian fighters, traders, missionaries, explorers, hunters, and settlers who killed and were killed in their aim of mastering the American wilderness. These latter Founders defined their national aspirations not in terms of "checks and balances" or "separation of powers," but in terms of bears destroyed, land pre-empted, trees hacked down, and Indians and Mexicans dead in the dust.

Americans have also had a notorious historical experience with vigilantism. All in all, there have been 326 documented vigilante movements in American history. It might be argued that, in the short run, vigilantism played a positive role in the development of American society. For it was at first directed mainly at horsethieves, counterfeiters, and outlaws, and was introduced in those frontier areas where lawlessness was rife. After the Civil War, however, vigilantism was resorted to as a desperate response to emerging urban, industrial, racial and ethnic problems. Its chief victims became Catholics, Jews, immigrants, blacks, laboring men, political radicals, and proponents of civil liberties. In these changed circumstances, its results were wholly negative and pernicious.

Another thread of violence in American history has been labor unrest. Though there were workingmen's protests and riots going back to Colonial times, the modern labor movement was associated with America's Industrial Revolution of the late nineteenth and early twentieth centuries. It was in these years that America's workingmen literally fought for their rights to organize, strike and improve their living conditions. The height of American industrial violence was the period from 1877 to World War I. A great burst of union activity also occurred in the 1930s. Despite the fact that labor violence has ebbed considerably, one should not underestimate the amount of industrial unrest in the past. As two prominent labor historians have observed: "The United States has had the bloodiest and most violent labor history of any industrial nation in the world."[4]

Another key type of American violence has been the violence associated with prejudice. Early examples include the anti-Catholic riots before the Civil War and the anti-Chinese agitation that characterized the West in the late nineteenth and early twentieth centuries. However, there are other examples too numerous to fully discuss in the space available which involve Irishmen, Jews, Slavs, Italians and other nationalities from Southern and Eastern Europe.

The most persistent factor in racial violence, of course, has been the friction which has been prominent in relations between Caucasians and Negroes. The history of black-white violence might be dated from the first slave uprising which occurred in New York City in 1712. With the end of slavery, racial violence between blacks and whites continued, gaining momentum during the period of Reconstruction and leading eventually to the rise of the Ku Klux Klan. Klan activity surged again during the 1920s as white Americans were swept up into a psychological frenzy and into a backlash of racial hatred in what historians have called the "Red Scare." Today, the black uprisings which have stirred America since the 1960s also have at their heart the issue of race.

As the above examples indicate, the cities in America have been the arena for most of the violence. Beginning with the Stamp Act protest of the Revolutionary period down to recent black riots, the "city" has been no stranger to violence. Indeed, America's urban experience has exacerbated the racial, ethnic, religious and labor tensions already discussed. The reasons for this are numerous. First of all, the spectacular growth of American cities was a disruptive influence. Further, America's cities were characterized by youth, weak traditions, weak external controls, large-scale migrations, rapid social change and diverse social structures. Thirdly, the anonymity of city life enhanced the tendency toward crime and violence. In the city, people were often strangers to each other, and the shame of arrest and the fear of detection were no longer strong inhibiting factors. For these and other reasons, the 1830s, 1840s and 1850s were decades of sustained urban rioting. Such was the violence of those years that public officials were prompted to develop America's first professional city police system. Similarly, it was the great urban violence of the 1880s and 1890s which made apparent the inadequacy of the state militias and led to the creation of the National Guard.

Another factor that might be noted, in this partial survey of historical forces behind today's civil violence, has been the American tendency to glorify violence when it has been associated with a "good" cause. Whether we talk of the American Revolution, the Civil War, the wars against the Indians, police violence or simply the shoot-out at high noon between the town marshal and a notorious bad man, there has been a tendency among Americans to condone violence when the majority considered the cause just. Again and again in American history, the fact of violence has been overlooked as a means when the ends have been widely accepted and applauded.

There is also a great paradox in the story of American civil violence. At the same time that there has been a substantial amount of civil strife in America, there has also been a high degree of political and institutional stability. Indeed, political stability and domestic strife have coexisted quite comfortably. Why has this been so? The following are a sampling of the answers given by American historians.

First of all, politically, America's system of diffused power and authority has never made Washington, D.C., the central target for all protest and, economically, private institutions have been much more important in American history than public institutions. Hence, in political and economic confrontations, groups have been pitted against groups rather than groups against the state. For instance, labor has confronted industrialists, farmers have confronted railroad magnates, farmworkers have confronted farmers, and so forth. In essence, America's federalistic and capitalistic structure has served to deflect attacks on the state.

A second answer which is offered for this paradox focuses on the fact that most American violence has had a "conservative" bias. Generally, it has not been initiated by the underdogs in American society, but rather by the topdogs and the "middle-dogs." There has been a proclivity toward maintaining the *status quo*. American violence has been repressive rather than insurrectionary. Hence, governmental stability has been promoted by such an orientation. In fact, this is why the violence of the 1960s so worried the majority of Americans. It was more politically oriented and more determinedly directed toward changing basic social, economic and political structures than most violent protests of the past.

A third answer emphasizes American affluence. Despite noted pockets of inequality in its economic experience, prosperity has been the rule in American life. To some historians this fact has, to a large extent, served to legitimize the U.S. form of government in the eyes of the great majority of Americans.

To conclude, what might one say in summary about the violence in American domestic history? First of all, there has been a huge amount of it. It has formed an important part of both America's most demeaning and most noble historical episodes. Secondly, Americans have often resorted to violence without thought to the consequences of their actions, or without regard for the fact that violence rarely leads in the direction intended, or brings about the results expected. Finally, there remains the paradoxical thought that perhaps high levels of civil strife are accepted because Americans are confident that it will not disturb the essential political stability and security of our country.

SELECTED BIBLIOGRAPHY

1. Brown, Richard Maxwell. *Strain of Violence*. New York: Oxford University Press. 1975.
2. Friedman, Leon, ed. *Episodes of Violence in U.S. History.* 3 vols. New York: Chelsea Publishing Co. 1970.
3. Graham, Hugh Davis and Ted Robert Gurr, ed. *Violence in America*. Beverly Hills: Sage Publications. 1979.
4. Hofstadter, Richard and Michael Wallace, ed. *American Violence*. New York: Alfred A. Knopf. 1970.
5. Hollon, W. Eugene. *Frontier Violence: Another Look*. New York: Oxford University Press. 1976.
6. Limerick, Patricia Nelson. *The Legacy of Conquest: The Unbroken Past of the American West*. New York and London: W. W. Norton. 1987.
7. Rose, Thomas, ed. *Violence in America*. New York: Random House. 1970.
8. Slotkin, Richard. *Regeneration Through Violence: The Mythology of the American Frontier, 1600–1860*. Middletown, Conn.: Wesleyan University Press. 1973.

America's Great Presidents:
Historical Insights for the 1990s

Greatness, like beauty, is in the eye of the beholder. John Kennedy realized this when he remarked in 1963: "A nation reveals itself not only by the men it produces but also by the men it honors, the men it remembers."

As the events of Election '92 begin to rouse the emotions of America's political partisans, perhaps a retrospective look at our great presidents will offer insights into which of today's candidates is best suited for what is generally called "the toughest job on Earth."

The selection of America's premier presidents is, of course, not one that is devoid of argument. Nonetheless, the names of eight men repeatedly appear at the top of almost all of the rating surveys. (See Presidential Performance Chart.) In the category of the "great" are Washington, Jefferson, Lincoln and Franklin Roosevelt. In the category of the "near-great" are Jackson, Theodore Roosevelt, Wilson and Truman.

What insights do these men's careers offer us as American citizens today? Specifically, what personal characteristics led to their success? What was the nature of their legacies? What general lessons might be learned from a survey of their presidencies?

In the area of personal attributes, honesty, integrity and strength of character are at the top of the list in the qualities that Americans desire of their presidents. The Father of Our Country was a man "who did not tell a lie." Our next greatest president was known as "Honest Abe." In the twentieth century, a soft spot in our hearts is reserved for Harry Truman, the man of forthright opinions and the man guaranteed "to shoot straight from the hip." Americans look to the chief executive to inspire trust in government, and to preserve confidence in our democratic system. Without a sterling character, and without honesty and integrity, our presidents, in the long run, do not hold the respect of either professional historians or the general public.

Secondly, Americans prefer their presidents to be intelligent, though not necessarily intellectual. Indeed, an intellectual might prove to be a liability as president. But a president has to be smart enough to gain the respect, cooperation and loyalty of his peers. He has to be smart enough to be able to "pick brains," to choose good advisers and to attract people of intelligence to his side. A president has to be smart enough to develop a keen sense of timing, and sense of discrimination about which crucial issues need to be tackled immediately and which can be left for later. The perfect example is George Washington. Though overshadowed in pure intellect by

"I have learnt to expect that it will rarely fall to the lot of imperfect man to retire from this station with the reputation and the favor which bring him into it. . . . I shall often go wrong through defect of judgment. When right, I shall often be thought wrong by those whose positions will not command a view of the whole ground. I ask your indulgence for my own errors, which will never be intentional, and your support against the errors of others, who may condemn what they would not if seen in all its parts." Thomas Jefferson, First Inaugural Address, March 4, 1801.

PRESIDENTIAL PERFORMANCE RATINGS[7]

Schlesinger Poll 1948(1)

Great
1. Lincoln
2. Washington
3. F. Roosevelt
4. Wilson
5. Jefferson
6. Jackson

Near Great
7. T. Roosevelt
8. Cleveland
9. J. Adams
10. Polk

Schlesinger Poll 1962(2)

Great
1. Lincoln
2. Washington
3. F. Roosevelt
4. Wilson
5. Jefferson

Near Great
6. Jackson
7. T. Roosevelt
8. Polk
9. Truman
10. J. Adams
11. Cleveland

Maranell Accomplishment Poll 1970(3)

Accomplishments of Administrations
1. Lincoln
2. F. Roosevelt
3. Washington
4. Jefferson
5. T. Roosevelt
6. Truman
7. Wilson
8. Jackson
9. L. Johnson
10. Polk

U.S. Historical Society Poll 1977(4)

Ten Greatest Presidents
1. Lincoln
2. Washington
3. F. Roosevelt
4. Jefferson
5. T. Roosevelt
6. Wilson
7. Jackson
8. Truman
9. Polk
10. J. Adams

Chicago Tribune Poll 1982(5)

Ten Best Presidents
1. Lincoln
2. Washingotn
3. F. Roosevelt
4. T. Roosevelt
5. Jefferson
6. Wilson
7. Jackson
8. Truman
9. Eisenhower
10. Polk

Murray Poll 1982(6)

Presidential Rank
1. Lincoln
2. F. Roosevelt
3. Washington
4. Jefferson
5. T. Roosevelt
6. Wilson
7. Jackson
8. Truman
9. J. Adams
10. L. Johnson

1. Arthur Schlesinger Sr.: 55 Scholars polled.
2. Arthur Schlesinger Sr.: 75 Scholars polled.
3. Gary Maranell and Richard Dodder: 571 Historians polled.
4. Robert E. DiClerico: 93 Historians polled.
5. Chicago Tribune: 49 Scholars polled.
6. Robert K. Murray: 953 Historians completed a 17-page questionnaire containing 155 questions.

his secretary of state and his secretary of the treasury, Jefferson and Hamilton respectively, he eclipsed both in balance of judgment and in common sense.

Thirdly, America's great presidents also have been flexible and openminded. Though all had definite goals in sight, they were "compromising battlers" on the way toward achieving those goals. They were men with the ability to weigh both sides of an issue, to have compassion for those of different beliefs, and to convey an idealism that sought to bring out the best in the American people. One is reminded of Washington's pardoning of the leaders of the Whiskey Rebellion, of Jefferson's generosity toward the defeated Federalists, of Lincoln's sympathy with the defeated South and of Franklin Roosevelt's empathy with the downtrodden and unemployed. Americans have not respected presidents who have demonstrated rigidity, defensiveness or vindictiveness—presidents who have consistently blamed their problems on "enemies."

Fourthly, Americans have tended to revere those presidents with the capacity to clarify, communicate and mobilize. Clement Attlee once said in reference to Winston Churchill: "Words at great moments of history are deeds." And so it has been in American history. Eloquence of either the tongue or the pen, or both, has been an attribute of greatness. Except for Washington, this has been true of all of our great presidents. (And even Washington is noted for his justly famous Farewell Address.) Jefferson's and Lincoln's written eloquence are legendary. FDR's ability to clarify complex ideas through the use of simple metaphors brilliantly aided him, and the nation, through the Depression and the Second World War. In the near-great category, Theodore Roosevelt and Woodrow Wilson were eloquent leaders in their time. So was the unscholarly and ungrammatical Andrew Jackson, who, despite errors of syntax and spelling was a man of moving and dramatic rhetoric. Americans, then, have revered those commanders-in-chief who have also been teachers-in-chief.

We need, however, to distinguish eloquence from glittering oratorical gifts. Americans have generally passed by their great orators for the office of the presidency: Patrick Henry, Alexander Hamilton, Henry Clay, Daniel Webster, John C. Calhoun, Charles Sumner, Stephen Douglas, James G. Blaine, Robert Ingersoll, Roscoe Conkling and William Jennings Bryan.

In the area of executive leadership, our great presidents have left durable legacies—either great programs, great victories in war or great "revolutions" furthering political democracy. Perhaps Franklin Roosevelt said it best: "All of our great presidents were leaders of thought at times when certain historic ideas in the life of the nation had to be clarified." All our great or near-great presidents have led the nation during periods of dramatic activity. These men have had a sense of destiny and a sense of history, and they have placed the stamp of their personality and the impact of their vision upon their day and age. They have all been idealists, and men of steadfast purpose.

Washington set the tone for all future presidents during the unpredictable and dangerous transition from the Articles of Confederation to the new Constitution. Jefferson healed the wounds of the nation after the unexpected emergence and virulence of political parties. Lincoln kept the faith of union when the young nation was threatened with its very life. Franklin Roosevelt shored up capitalism with the introduction of the welfare state during our greatest depression.

In the category of the near-greats, Jackson symbolized the new wave of equality and democracy touted as the "rise of the common man." Teddy Roosevelt and Woodrow Wilson brought cohesiveness and direction to the great reform watershed known as the Progressive movement. Harry Truman ended a world war, inaugurated the age of atomic energy, faced the new and perplexing challenges of the Cold War, kept his head during the Chinese Revolution

246

and the Korean War, eased the American economy's transition from a wartime footing to a peacetime basis and laid the foundation for the prosperity of the 1950s.

In sum, all of our great and near-great presidents have been decisive men of action. They have been strong, vigorous leaders. To varying degrees, they all have offered moral leadership of an elevated nature that has transformed the politics of their time and of ours. Americans will overlook personal shortcomings in their presidents, but they will rarely forgive a president's failure to provide leadership when urgent action is believed to be needed.

There are other, more general insights that become apparent from a look at America's great presidents.

First, there is an interesting mathematical calculation that emerges from the latest presidential ranking (Murray's). No other fifty-year period in American history, except the period of our Founders, ranks as high as the fifty-year period since the Great Depression. This might prove a surprise to those who have been highly critical of our presidential leadership in the recent past. (See U.S. Dynasties Chart.)

Second, it is an ominous thought that three of four great presidents and three of four near-great presidents probably would be bypassed in today's era of television promotion. Only FDR and Wilson possessed the requisite style and charisma that would project well across the TV screens of the 1990s. Washington's stiffness and coldness, and his positively terrible public-speaking abilities would not make him first in the hearts and minds of his present countrymen. Jefferson's soft-voiced diffidence and Lincoln's country-bumpkin manner would not make them great media personalities. Further, their careful, calculated manner of deep thinking would be out of place in a media age which fosters the glib answer and the genius for the noncommittal comment. Jackson's gaunt, almost emaciated physique, Teddy Roosevelt's high, near-falsetto voice, Truman's clumsiness when reading a speech—all would be miscast with our over-emphasis on personal looks and personal magnetism.

A third general factor that emerges from a study of America's great presidents is that none was without his mistakes and/or his periods of intense unpopularity. Washington's unpopularity was during the signing of Jay's Treaty. Jefferson's was during the Embargo Acts before the War of 1812. Lincoln's was during much of the Civil War, until the final victories of late 1864 and 1865. Franklin Roosevelt's occurred during the deepening of the Depression in 1937 and during the turmoil surrounding the Yalta Conference after 1945.

U.S. DYNASTIES RATED[7]

Presidential Era	Average Murray Rank	Rank Order
The Virginia Dynasty (Washington–J.Q. Adams)	10.1	1
The Super Power Era (F. Roosevelt–Carter)	15.8	2
The USA is a New World Power (T. Roosevelt–Hoover)	19.5	3
The Gilded Age (Lincoln–McKinley)	21.7	4
The Jacksonians (Jackson–Buchanan)	23.3	5

The fourth general point involves the unveiling of a myth. Many Americans have been taught to believe that great crises in a democracy necessarily bring forth great leadership. The events leading to the War of 1812, however, brought out little of the best in either the nation or in James Madison; the secession crisis did not ennoble the efforts of James Buchanan; and financial crisis did not crown the efforts of Martin Van Buren, Grover Cleveland or Herbert Hoover. More correctly, it would be closer to the truth to say that all of our great presidents have lived during great crises, or during "revolutionary" times.

However, it was the animated energies of the American people rather than presidential leadership that made these revolutions possible. The character and abilities of our presidents counted for much. But their statesmanship was brought to fruition because more was expected of them. They produced great legacies because public expectations were higher.

In sum, with each presidential election, we must remember that WHO we vote for is important. There are significant issues facing our nation, issues upon which the various political candidates differ markedly, and issues which will be decided by the men and women who are elected.

But we must also remember that each election is a renewal of each of our personal responsibilities toward politics. Great breakthroughs in political history usually have occurred because of pressure from the bottom of society, or at least from the middle.

As historians look back to our own time, they more than likely will see our major turning points as having been precipitated by the activism of civil rights workers, consumer organizations, women's rights activists, environmental protectionists, tax-revolt champions and anti-war protestors.

SELECTED BIBLIOGRAPHY

1. Bailey, Thomas A. *Presidential Greatness: The Image and the Man from George Washington to the Present*. New York: Appleton, Century, Crofts. 1966.
2. Barber, James David. *The Presidential Character*. Englewood Cliffs, N.J.: Prentice–Hall. Second edition. 1977.
3. Cronin, Thomas E. *The State of the Presidency*. Boston: Little, Brown and Co. Second edition. 1980.
4. _____. "Thinking and Learning about Leadership." *Presidential Studies Quarterly*. Vol. 14, No. 1 (Winter 1984).
5. Ketcham, Ralph. *Presidents above Party: The First American Presidency, 1789–1829*. Chapel Hill: University of North Carolina Press. 1984.
6. McCormick, Richard P. *The Presidential Game: The Origins of American Presidential Politics*. New York: Oxford University Press. 1982.
7. Murphy, Arthur B. "Evaluating the Presidents of the United States." *Presidential Studies Quarterly*. Vol. 14, No. 1 (Winter 1984).
8. Schlesinger, Jr., Arthur M. *The Imperial Presidency*. New York: Houghton Mifflin. 1973.

48

The Supreme Court: Insights from History

"'Tis funny about th' constitution,' remarked Mr. Dooley, the philosophic Irish bartender created by Finley Peter Dunne, "it reads plain, but no wan can understant it without an interpreter."

For the most part that interpreter has been the Supreme Court, and this year marks 201 years of decidedly controversial interpreting. Even omitting the recent decisions on abortion, school prayer, criminal rights, etc., that have so divided Americans, the earlier history of the Court has been equally contentious. Time and again the Court has seemed to put its approval upon some of the grossest social inequities in our history, and has had to finally reverse itself after long years of sanctioning terrible abuses.

In *Hammer v. Dagenhart*, it declared a child-labor law unconstitutional; in *Adair v. United States*, it voided a law that banned yellow-dog contracts; in *Matter of Heff*, it ruled that the illegal sale of liquor to Indians could not be punished. Perhaps Louis Brandeis was right when he argued: "A lawyer who has not studied economics and sociology is very apt to become a public enemy." All these decisions have been reversed.

The income tax law of 1894 was struck down in *Pollock v. Farmers' Loan and Trust Co.* The effect of this decision was to delay for two decades, until the passage of the Sixteenth Amendment, the effective imposition of a federal income tax, and a fair basis of taxation for most Americans of that time. The notorious *Dred Scott* decision denied the right of blacks to be citizens of the United States and denied the right of Congress to interfere with the holding of slaves in the territories.

If many of the decisions of the Court have caused dismay, still more Americans remain chagrined about the Court's independence to review and overturn laws passed by Congress. Because the Justices are neither directly elected by nor directly responsible to the people, many believe that the Court anachronistically perpetuates a deep distrust of democracy. In a democratic state, one in which the ideal is majority rule and minority rights, many argue that it is the legislative branch which is better suited to protect the fundamental laws of our land. The history of Great Britain, where parliamentary government is supreme, offers incontrovertible proof to many scholars of the superiority of having the legislative branch predominant.

The record of the Court is not all negative, of course, and there have been times when the Court has moved on social abuses and inequities when the other branches of our government have lacked either the courage or the inclination. But the key point remains, are we justified in placing such significant powers in the hands of appointed, life-tenured Justices? Is there particular merit in having our government balanced so carefully between three separate branches? Don't people learn to admire the forms of government they become used to, and then argue that those forms are infinitely wise since they fit the national character? Given its record, is there truly a compelling reason for us to be celebrating 201 years of the Supreme Court's decision-making?

It is hoped that a historical perspective might offer insights into these questions and also into the possible trends that might shape the future. For it was Justice Oliver Wendell Holmes, Jr., who said: "a page of history is worth a volume of logic."

First, the issue of proper representation in a democracy should be discussed. A democracy need not directly elect all the officers who hold crucial authority under its power; nor is government by referendum nor government by town meeting necessarily the best form of democracy. Rather, whatever the system of representative government, the key is to place one's leaders under some ultimate form of effective control and responsibility, and our Constitution, with its central principles of popular sovereignty, separation of powers, limited government, and "checks and balances," does exactly that.

Further, great institutions of government generally emerge in response to deeply-felt human needs and aspirations. The growth of judicial review is simply the result of 200+ years of American concern with protecting the individual against the encroachments of unjust government. It is true that parliamentary supremacy, rather than judicial review, has become the norm in Great Britain. But the situation here in America was different. Because of our colonial beginnings, it was the British Parliament that was looked upon by American colonials as the threat to the individual's sacred rights. Repeatedly, colonial Americans turned to the courts for protection and intercession on behalf of their fundamental rights, and eventually it was that need that came to be institutionalized. Finally, ours is a "written" Constitution, with its majestic ideals stated in the broadest of terms: "freedom of speech," "freedom of religion," "due process of law," "equal protection of the laws," etc. Hence, there are ambiguities within it and within the Bill of Rights which form such an integral part of it. The genius of our Constitution is that it has provided only the general framework of government, while the exact details are left for each generation's reworking. However, interpreting these broad ideals and working out those details requires careful study and argument, and hence another reason for the existence of a strong appellate judicial tradition in our nation.

In sum, our history demonstrates that there is an important rationale for having crucial constitutional issues decided by men and women utilizing a judicial perspective. Such a perspective can be a steadying influence and a source of accumulated wisdom. It can be a protection to unpopular individuals and minorities who are shut out of, or inadequately represented in, the political process.

What, then, of the Court's aforementioned record of notorious decision-making? The fact of the matter is that, though we might quarrel with particular decisions, over the long term the record of the Court has complemented the perceptions and beliefs of the majority of our nation. For proof, let us turn first to a brief survey of U.S. political and judicial history.

The real beginnings of the Supreme Court's authority coincided with the appointment of John Marshall as Chief Justice in 1801. Before Marshall, the Court's impact was minimal, its main characteristics being that of disorganization and disunity. Between 1790 and 1801, the Court decided only fifty-five cases; the most notable, *Chisholm v. Georgia*, was overruled by the Eleventh Amendment. Worst of all, the Court became embroiled in partisan politics in 1798 when Congress passed the Alien and Sedition Acts. By failing to declare these acts unconstitu-

250

tional, the way was open for James Madison's and Thomas Jefferson's Virginia and Kentucky Resolutions, Resolutions which reserved ultimate review of Congressional legislation to the States. These Resolutions were the very negation of the concept of judicial review.

Marshall's transformation of the Supreme Court was to be the most significant in its history. He instituted the practice of having a single Justice—often himself—issue an opinion for the entire Court, rather than each Justice giving his opinion individually as was the previous practice. Now the Court spoke as a single voice, thus adding to its prestige and power vis-a-vis the executive and legislative branches. In the thirty-five years that Marshall was on the Bench, 1106 opinions were issued, with Marshall writing 519. Of the sixty-two decisions involving major constitutional questions, Marshall wrote thirty-six. A Court which could easily have remained insignificant was invigorated by Marshall's three predominating goals: strengthen the Union, strengthen the Constitution, and strengthen the federal judiciary.

In the context of the attitudes of the majority of Americans, Marshall's actions fulfilled a great need felt by the young nation for the establishment of a stable national power, and the establishment of a security for property rights. Both these needs had not been met under the Articles of Confederation, as the excesses of state power made both national unity and property rights precarious. Further, the famous cases of *Marbury v. Madison, Fletcher v. Peck, Martin v. Hunter's Lessee, Cohens v. Virginia, McCullough v. Maryland,* and *Gibbons v. Ogden* offered a clear, strong answer to the question of which institution was to interpret the fine technicalities of the Constitution. The Supreme Court, because of Marshall, came forward as the authoritative voice without which the whole new plan of government might have faltered. This was a generation that had already witnessed the failure of two systems of government—the British imperial alternative and the Articles of Confederation. Marshall fulfilled the aspirations of a generation that yearned for solidity and strength in a national government.

By the time of Marshall's retirement and the Chief Justiceship of Roger Taney, the U.S. was in the wake of a tremendous economic, industrial, and urban transformation. The first major moves of the U.S. away from a traditional, pre-industrial society were made; on the horizon were major battles between the contradictory impulses of economic life in a modern age—security v. progress, stability v. expansionism, and order v. efficiency. That generation had to tackle the uneasy coexistence of these dilemmas for the first time. Great pressure was put upon some of the major doctrines of the Marshall Court—i.e., the primacy given vested rights in the *Dartmouth* case, the interpretation of the Commerce Clause in *Gibbons*—as a result of the tremendous economic expansion of the early-nineteenth century. New forms of private and semi-private enterprise had emerged, such as internal improvement franchises, public utilities, and powerful corporations. Dynamic theories of property-holding threatened static theories; the emergence of a rhetoric of mass democracy challenged the legacies of a stratified, restrictive polity; humanitarianism confronted slavery. The Taney Court is best remembered for its terrible failure in the *Dred Scott* decision. However, as far as keeping pace with the shifting needs of the young nation, the Taney Court was to be a significant success. Its decisions were flexible and non-doctrinaire, a course of decision-making which furthered the growth of corporate enterprise and prevented its restriction by the deadening hand of established monopoly, on the one hand, while also representing the "common man" motif of Jacksonian America, on the other. For instance, it was in 1844, under Taney, that the Court overruled Marshall's decision in *Bank of the United States v. Deveaux* and accorded to corporations the status of "citizens" with the right to sue in federal courts. Yet Taney also broadened the concept of a state's police power as a means of promoting the welfare of the community; as a means of justifying judicial recognition of a state's efforts to promote social welfare legislation.

The Civil War and Reconstruction era brought yet another period of revolutionary change upon the nation. In these crises, the federal government had to assume powers that took it into new constitutional arenas and tested to the limits that generation's accepted social and economic attitudes. During the war, at least in the eyes of the North, the federal government was a beneficent force fighting the twin, repugnant evils of slavery and secession. Therefore, it was worthy of all sorts of newly-expanded powers in order to secure victory for the Union cause. During Reconstruction, federal powers increased further as three Amendments were added to the Constitution and the fate of the newly-freed slaves eventually came to be placed under Congress's authority. The Court again kept pace with the rest of the government and the northern mood—in the *Slaughter-House* cases, in *Mississippi v. Johnson,* in *Georgia v. Stanton,* and in the second *Ex parte McCardle* case, all of which strengthened the prerogatives of the Reconstruction governments.

Another great age of economic transformation was the next crucial development in U.S. history. Between 1890 and 1937, the U.S. became the greatest of the world's industrial powers. Because of revolutions in transportation, communication, and production, markets became truly national and highly complex. The final conquest of the American continent was completed. In this age of opportunity and expansionism, *laissez-faire* economics and Social Darwinism were held up as two religions, and the Supreme Court kept in step with the suppositions of that time. The theories of Substantive Due Process and Liberty of Contract appeared and were used by the Court to strike down 228 state statutes that were deemed restrictive of the rights of private property. From our perspective, the Court decisions of this period remain among the most questionable, and the excesses of *laissez-faire* capitalism the most lamentable. For that generation, Herbert Spencer's opinions reflected much of the callousness of the age:

> The whole effect of nature is to get rid of [the poor], to clear the world of them, and make room for the better. If they are sufficiently complete to live, they *do* live. If they are not, they die, and it is best they should die.

This was a time when the predominant belief in our nation was that equality of opportunity and economic success could best be achieved by the absence of governmental interference with the economy. The Supreme Court's use of the Due Process Clause of the Fourteenth Amendment in favor of business was part of the exaltation of property rights so characteristic of the thinking of that time. To this day, there are historians who argue that if the U.S. was to be successful in its expansionism in that era, certain functional requirements were a necessary accompaniment—among them dynamic and unfettered entrepreneurialship, and friendly, helpful government toward business. It would have been non-functional to have been anti-capitalist at that time of tremendous industrial potential. Whether or not this latter argument is correct, a search for unifying principles did mark American life in this period, and after years of division and war, the sweeping doctrine of *laissez-faire* seemed especially suited to the contemporary situation in the economic realm.

Disturbingly, the same inclination that moved the nation to safeguard the property rights of entrepreneurs was matched by a disinclination to protect the civil rights of blacks. A great retreat began in the 1880s and 1890s when it came to matters of civil rights. The lynching of blacks reached new peaks; a backlash against the Populist Party began; in 1894 Congress removed from federal statutes a number of Reconstruction laws aimed toward the protection of equal rights; and Booker T. Washington's "Atlanta Compromise" speech of 1895 was widely interpreted as an acceptance of a subordinate status for blacks by the foremost leader of that race. Again, the Court reflected the shift in national perceptions. The *Civil Rights* cases of 1883—whereby the Court condoned private, personal acts of discrimination—destroyed that delicate balance of federal guarantees, black protest, and private enlightenment that might have created a foundation for a future improvement in the plight of the nation's blacks. Then, the Court sealed the fate of black inequality before the law with the subsequent decisions in *Plessy v. Ferguson* (1896) and in the *Berea College* case (1906).

For most Americans, the Great Depression reversed the previous era's shibboleths and signaled the need for more government control of a *laissez-faire*, buccaneering economy too long without adequate restraints. As the Depression deepened, Americans warily discussed alternative economic philosophies. Many came to question the free enterprise model as a sure prescription for success; government involvement in economic affairs was now seen as mandatory for security and progress. The acclamation for Franklin Roosevelt's New Deal and his landslide victory in 1936 reflected the dramatic shift in national attitudes. Moreover, the American businessman, who had been glorified for over a generation, became a figure of greed, manipulation and pathos.

However, the Charles Evans Hughes Court proved to be a reluctant convert to the new thinking. Between 1934 and 1936, twelve New Deal measures were invalidated. Among the most adamant Justices against change were the so-called "Four Horsemen"—Willis Van Devanter, George Sutherland, Pierce Butler and James McReynolds. Then dramatically, beginning in April 1937, the Court changed course and went on to uphold every New Deal measure presented to it thereafter. Part of the shift might have been due to political pressures—the long-term impact of FDR's personal popularity and the immediate threat of his "Court-packing" plan. More significant, in all probability, was the shift in ideology that came to pervade the entire legal profession. Important here were the earlier arguments of Justices Oliver Wendell Holmes and Louis Brandeis. Holmes argued that human values rightly adjust to changing social conditions and that such changes should not provoke alarm. One must guard, warned Holmes, against the imposition of rigid, outworn absolutes. Brandeis argued that empirical indices of change could be observed and analyzed, and, in the process, public policies could be matched to the dictates of contemporary life. Modern liberalism, with its belief that governmental institutions could intervene to make the world more livable, was now at hand and finally triumphed with the Court's 1937 decision in *National Labor Relations Board v. Jones and Laughlin Steel Corporation*. In this judgment, and in subsequent ones, the interpretations of both the Due Process Clause and the Commerce Clause were reversed, and a vast Congressional expansion of power over the economy was allowed. By 1955, the Court would resoundingly declare:

> The day is gone when this Court uses the Due Process Clause of the Fourteenth Amendment to strike down state laws, regulatory of business and industrial conditions because they may be unwise, improvident, or out of harmony with a particular school of thought.

The high tide of modern judicial liberalism is generally associated with the tenure of Chief Justice Earl Warren (1953–1968). During this wave of liberalism, the emphasis shifted to protection of the individual and a focus upon personal rights (Important examples in the area of criminal cases included *Mapp v. Ohio, Gideon v. Wainwright, Escobedo v. Illinois,* and *Miranda v. Arizona.*) In the process, it was inevitable that the rights of blacks and of women would be re-evaluated. The new political power of both blacks and women, their enhanced economic positions, and the vast shift ideologically in the moral attitudes of the nation naturally spilled over into the federal courts. Corresponding to the changed ideological climate was a new belief in judicial activism. The argument arose that the ultimate protection for minorities, for religious liberty, for freedom of speech, etc., rightfully came from the Judiciary. The political process, it was believed, with its arbitrary compromises and its susceptibility to short-run pressures, was inadequate to be the caretaker of long-range and enduring values. The egalitarian impulse of the Warren years reigned triumphant in *Brown v. Board of Education*, and in the *Reapportionment Cases*. With its new activism, the Court made law on an extensive scale, substituted national rules in the place of local determinations, and mandated such changes in American society that might generally be associated with revolutions or wars. The Warren Court did indeed seem to embrace Lord Acton's maxim: "The most certain test by which we judge whether a country is really free is the amount of security enjoyed by minorities."

In the America of the 1990s it seems as if the policies identified with welfare liberalism have become a political liability, and that the egalitarian assumptions of the Warren years have lost their force. The current issues on the conservative agenda include reversing the Court decisions involving abortion, school prayer, constitutional protection for persons accused of crimes, school busing, affirmative action, and the regulatory power of government agencies. There is also a move to return some of the power to the States that has gravitated to the federal government.

Whatever the future trends or the strength of the present shift, we must emphasize the insights from this brief historical overview. As the conditions change which face a people and a nation, the major institutions undergo a shift also, especially in the area of social and economic affairs. The arc of the pendulum of Supreme-Court change is less drastic than in the political process, as the Judiciary is meant to be the "sober second thought" on constitutional matters. Further, the Court has to constantly weigh the short-term conditions of a particular time against the enduring truths of a written constitution. Nonetheless, despite acknowledged "judicial-lags" (gaps between the changing needs of the times and the doctrines followed by the Justices), by and large the Court through history has appreciated that the Constitution is a "living" instrument that must be constantly fine-tuned to the necessities of contemporary government.

Another insight which emerges from a study of the Supreme Court comes from Alexis de Tocqueville's *Democracy in America*, published in 1835: "Scarcely any political question arises in the United States that is not resolved sooner or later into a judicial question." In this perception, Tocqueville was characteristically unerring. The Supreme Court makes decisions that are political as much as legal. What in other nations is settled solely at the political level, is often decided at the judicial level in the U.S. However, there are key limits to the Court's success in the political arena. When Americans themselves are deeply divided on important social values, or first principles, then the Court has not proved to be suited to a final resolution of the problem. The persuasiveness of judicial decision-making is that it appeals to core values within the nation or affirms the underlying shared beliefs which unify our people. When no set of first principles emerges from the analysis of a case, however, the Court itself cannot effectively function and the results have brought great failures in the past. The *Dred Scott* decision is a perfect example of the moral and political limits of the Court when our nation was deeply divided over first principles—in this case between freedom and slavery. Timing is important when it comes to the writing of great formulas into the Constitution. In 1857, in *Dred Scott*, the timing was not right and Taney overstepped the limits of judicial power. Instead of taking a more prudent tack, he aimed to affirm what for him were overriding truths. But undeniable truths in this instance were impossible; instead there were two opposing sides holding deeply entrenched values. No amount of judicial decision-making can paper over the rifts of a deeply-divided nation. (Other examples where the Court overstepped its limits were: the first *Legal Tender* case which resulted in the enlargement of the Salmon P. Chase Court in order to secure a reversal; the *Income Tax* decision which stimulated the passage of the Sixteenth Amendment; and the Four Horsemen's intransigence which led to FDR's "Court-packing" attempt.)

Finally, one cannot come away from a study of the Supreme Court without recognizing the institutional restraints which weigh upon each Justice. Supreme Court Justices are expected to be collegial, detached, self-restrained, and deferential to important institutional principles. The text of the Constitution, the "intention" of its Framers, prior judicial precedent, and the relevant contemporary context are all expected to be considered in the final judicial decision. Justices who are too ideological, and too involved in the political realm betray the judicial tradition. In contrast to politicians, Supreme Court Justices have an *intellectual* obligation to give adequate reasons for their decisions in written form; an *institutional* obligation to defer to the power of the other branches of government in enumerated instances; a *political* obligation to be restrained on hotly partisan issues; and a *psychological* obligation to recognize the role of their bias in decision-making. The success or failure of the Court in the past has depended to a great degree on whether or not the public has perceived the Justices to have fulfilled their institutional obligations.

In conclusion, perhaps the most enduring truth which emerges from this study is that in the end it is the health and character of the American people as a whole which determines the success or failure of the Supreme Court, just as it is with America's other institutions. The strengths and weaknesses of the American people, along with their prejudices, determination, and intelligence inevitably mold the final decisions of the Court. Our democratic life is fraught with contradictory principles where free speech may clash with privacy, egalitarianism with racial justice, liberty with patriotism, freedom to hold property with freedom to acquire it, etc. Each generation has had to grapple with the hard, temporary choices which best fit its era. In the struggle, the actions of the Court may come under fire and attack. But the ultimate responsibility rests with the average American citizen.

One could make a strong argument that our dilemma today is not an absence of leadership—Supreme Court or otherwise. Rather it is an absence of "followship"—an absence of national virtue, or a paucity of national values, with which to sustain our leadership.

There is a truism about governing which emerges from the study of history: no institution, not even one as powerful as the Supreme Court, can save a people from themselves.

SELECTED BIBLIOGRAPHY

1. Abraham, Henry J. *Justice and Presidents: A Political History of Appointments to the Supreme Court.* New York and Oxford: Oxford University Press. 1985.
2. Cox, Archibald. *The Court and the Constitution.* Boston: Houghton Mifflin Co. 1987.
3. Fribourg, Marjorie G. *The Supreme Court in American History: Ten Great Decisions.* Philadelphia: Macrae Smith Co. 1965.
4. Friendly, Fred W. and Martha J. H. Elliott. *The Constitution: That Delicate Balance.* New York: Random House. 1984.
5. Garraty, John S., ed. *Quarrels That Have Shaped the Constitution.* New York, Evanston and London: Harper and Row. 1964.

6. Levy, Leonard W., ed. *Judicial Review and the Supreme Court*. New York, Evanston and London: Harper and Row. 1967.

7. Mason, Alpheus Thomas. *The Supreme Court: From Taft to Burger*. Baton Rouge and London: Louisiana State University Press. Third Edition. 1979.

8. McCloskey, Robert G. *The American Supreme Court*. Chicago and London: University of Chicago Press. 1960.

9. Pfeffer, Leo. *This Honorable Court*. Boston: Beacon Press. 1965.

10. Schwartz, Bernard. *A Basic History of the U.S. Supreme Court*. Princeton, New Jersey: D. Van Nostrand Co. 1968.

11. White, G. Edward. *The American Judicial Tradition*. Expanded Edition. New York: Oxford University Press. 1988.

EPILOGUE

America! America!
God mend thine every flaw,
Confirm thy soul in self-control,
Thy liberty in law!

Katharine Lee Bates
From the second verse of:
''America the Beautiful'' (1893)

The "Back-to-Basics" Movement in American History

Styles in the writing of history ever change, but hopefully the writing of history will never go out of style. Currently, in the mode of what is happening nationally, there is a back-to-basics movement in the narration of our national past. Just as E.D. Hirsch, Jr., has argued in *Cultural Literacy: What Every American Needs to Know*[7] and Allan Bloom in *The Closing of the American Mind*,[3] there are historians who are emphasizing the need for reviving past precepts and creeds for the purification of the present. On the whole, these recent trends have been positive, but there have been some weaknesses in this reassertion of past traditions and this renewed national historical pride that have been overlooked.

For example, John Garraty, professor of history at Columbia University, has just published his *1001 Things Everyone Should Know About American History*.[6] On one level, this book is useful. It is always interesting, and generally beneficial, to expand one's knowledge and understanding of both the trivial and the major events of the past (especially if one happens to be a history professor). But, on another level, is there really a pool of historical facts, or trivia, that an educated person simply must know?

What are these supposed things called "facts" anyway? Very often the only points that can be claimed as undeniably accurate and beyond question are matters of little significance. When it comes to an issue of real import, dispute and interpretation inevitably enter in. The "fact" that Jimmy Carter followed Gerald Ford, and that Ronald Reagan followed Jimmy Carter in American presidential succession is a matter beyond dispute. (And we surely would prefer our future historians to get this sequence straight.) But the truly significant point in the years ahead will be the impact that each man had on the course of our political history; and that issue will be contested as long as there are interested people taking the time to study the 1970s and the 1980s. Besides, the facts about Carter and Reagan will read very differently to Democrats and Republicans, as does the story of the creation of Israel to Arabs and Jews and the progress of political freedom in early America to blacks and whites.

Facts are problematic in other ways, too. For instance, there can be both "too many" and "too few." We in the West still have too little information on important turning points in the history of Africa and Asia—even too little on our own pre-Columbian era. Paradoxically, we also have "too many"—too many about the recent past, about the lives of the rich and powerful, etc., so this overwhelming information increases the difficulty of writing with objectivity about remote eras or about the great majority of humanity. My pet peeve in this regard involves the monarchs of Western Europe. Here the facts, in contrast to the information about the lives of the great majority, are too obtrusive. How often have we historians manufactured a heroic king or queen of England (or France or Germany) simply because they occupied a prominent position and we have had intimate details about their period of rule? Few today would dispute that heredity is a poor method of choosing leaders. And yet we historians follow, as a profession, the trials and tribulations of one hereditary monarch after another—often with an excess of concern and with an excess of devotion. Frankly, only a handful of these monarchs rank as high as Calvin Coolidge as a leader of men; perhaps none ranks higher.

These difficulties do not preclude the writing of objective history. There are truths about the past which we can most assuredly ascertain. What is being argued is that the real issue for the historian is not the memorization of a host of specific facts. Rather, the student of history should recognize that there are many factual patterns, an infinite number of them, which can be superimposed upon past events. The historian's task is to find the pattern which is the most relevant to his or her problem. To emphasize, the key is to ask an open-ended question about the past. And then answer it with an explanatory paradigm that best fits the original question.

Moving on, another pitfall in recent historical scholarship that is frequently being overlooked is the rule that one should not allow nationalistic feelings to prejudice the merits or demerits of great issues. One of the worst sins of the historian is to confuse national history with universal history, to find a cornucopia of absolute values and absolute virtues in the course of one's national past. A perfect example of overweening nationalistic attitudes justifying and sanctifying questionable means is our annual glorification of Commodore John Sloat's victory here in California in 1846, and James K. Polk's determined diplomacy that afforded Sloat his opportunity. What red-blooded American doesn't believe that Mexico's loss of California (and the American Southwest) was civilization's gain? Yet leading up to this American victory was a diplomatic record and a national expansionistic policy vis-a-vis Mexico and the Mexican people that was punctuated with much aggression and brutality. Polk's responsibility for the origins of the Mexican-American War was paramount. Polk both instigated the war and lied to Congress and the American people. Nonetheless, most students blink at Polk's notorious means to emphasize the gains of the war. Typical is the synopsis of historian Samuel Flagg Bemis: "Notwithstanding all this, it would be well-nigh impossible today to find a citizen of the United States who would desire to undo President Polk's diplomacy, President Polk's war and the Treaty of Guadeloupe Hidalgo."[2] Few Americans today draw the conclusion that should be drawn from Polk's great drain upon our nation's moral capital: That a quality attributed to a result is not transferable to the cause; that an argument cannot be made valid simply because we approve of its consequences.

However, our greatest shortcoming as students of American history is our failure, still, to truly come to terms with the painful experience of black people in our nation's past. Despite all the literature about the black experience in America, as a nation we still fail to adequately assess the dramatically different effects that our national history has had upon blacks as compared with whites. Because of their past, black-Americans think different things and think about them differently than do whites. Nonetheless, Americans as a whole underestimate the significant and lingering impact of the African inheritance on black Americans. We imperfectly understand the complications of the black acculturation process. We have not even built a consensus opinion about the nature of the impact of slavery upon them. As a result, our nation today has neither the proper empathy for nor the solutions to the challenging social problems of our black citizenry.

To conclude, historical insights can be elusive. Just as we feel secure in one set of truths, there are dangers that we overlook, pitfalls that we fail to avoid. We must remember that supposedly indisputable points can turn out to be like the Cheshire cat in "Alice in Wonderland"— as we ponder them they elusively fade from view; all, that is, but the grin.

SELECTED BIBLIOGRAPHY

1. *The American Historical Review.* Volume 94, No. 3, (June 1989). Much of this volume of the AHR was devoted to a "Forum" discussing "The Old History and the New."
2. Bemis, Samuel Flagg. *A Diplomatic History of the United States.* 4th ed. New York: Alfred A. Knopf, 1955.
3. Bloom, Allan. *The Closing of the American Mind.* New York: Simon and Schuster. 1987.
4. Commager, Henry Steele. *The Nature and Study of History.* Columbus, Ohio: Charles E. Merrill, Inc. 1965.
5. Fischer, David Hackett. *Historians' Fallacies: Toward a Logic of Historical Thought.* New York: Harper and Row.
6. Garraty, John A. *1,001 Things Everyone Should Know About American History.* New York: Doubleday. 1989.
7. Hirsch, E. D. *Cultural Literacy: What Every American Needs to Know.* Boston: Houghton Mifflin. 1987.

American Character in the Nuclear Age

One of the invaluable rewards of a study of history is its demonstration of how much character counts. There are a host of examples where individual character was crucial to the success or failure of a great project or great event. In our own country one wonders how the Revolutionary-era patriots would have managed without the monumental good character of George Washington. In our own time, one expects that the horizons of American women would have been immeasurably lowered without the striking example of Eleanor Roosevelt.

Indeed, the study of history demonstrates that the character of a nation counts for so very much, too. One marvels at the courage of the Athenians who faced the Persian Empire in ancient times; the Florentines who, with their brilliant civic humanism, launched the Age of the Renaissance; the British who pioneered the creation of political democracy; and those hearty Virginians of Colonial America who helped to found one of the noteworthy success stories in the history of our modern age.

Such a perspective naturally brings to the fore certain questions. What can one say about the current American national character? Do we measure up to the great examples of the past? Or are we possibly in a period of decline? The critical literature is significant and substantial. Many social scientists and political commentators find America's culture, economy, and politics to be deeply flawed.

Some critics point to the compulsive egoism, the lack of self-discipline, the obsessive preoccupation with self-esteem and instant gratification that hallmark American culture. Where in the capitalist economy of today, they ask, is the sense of fiduciary obligation to posterity that animated the generation of Founders? Where in the capitalist economy of today are the ideals of compassion, frugality, generosity, gentleness, humility, and simplicity consistently presented? A "more is more" philosophy and a "flaunt-it-if-you-have-it" style are far more revered. How long, the critics ask, before the mass of Americans come to realize that most of the trappings of our everyday life are merely status symbols devoid of intrinsic worth?

In the area of our domestic economy, many political commentators are angered by a national government that refuses to pay its bills, and that refuses to recognize that it cannot spend astronomical amounts for defense and live extravagantly at the same time. What, they ask, can be said of a government that seems unable and unwilling to reform or trim its excesses? The stoic self-sacrifice of our George Washington, Thomas Jefferson, Abraham Lincoln, and even Harry Truman, glaringly contrasts with the wealth that is made in political service today.

In the arena of foreign policy, critics point out that our nation, born of revolution and the midwife of republicanism, has evolved into the policeman of the world in the latter twentieth century; we have become obsessed with curbing incipient revolution, callously impatient with emergent governments and their struggle to make a new life for themselves, and smugly self-satisfied with an inequitable status-quo in international affairs. A careful review of U.S. foreign policy by critics finds an excessive, knee-jerk anti-communism ruinous of both our best morals and our best national interests. Some writers have persuasively argued that the anti-communists in America have done as much harm to our rich democratic legacy as any communists ever have, or realistically, will probably ever do.

Finally, critics ask, what use is it for the U.S. President to covertly authorize and perpetrate terrorism through the CIA and then to publicly deplore it in other nations. People believe what they see, not what they hear. What they have seen since World War II are U.S. leaders who have incessantly intoned the ideal of law and order while resorting to insensate covert violence, violations of international law, and violations of the U.N. Charter.

In sum, for critics, these national characteristics surely do not represent qualities of greatness. Both within our culture, our economy, and our politics are problems that are on the verge of uncontrollability and that are possibly indicative of a nation in decline—a nation, at the very least, with a flawed sense of morality and a skewed outlook upon the world.

In the face of the seriousness of such charges, what might a historian bring forth as a counterbalancing argument? Rather than trying to refute the above points one by one, possibly the best tack is to enjoin the concerned citizen to consider a broader perspective, and a comparative approach.

First, regarding our national culture, a historian might note that there has always been, from Colonial times, a tension between "accumulating goods and cultivating goodness" here in America.[6] Both mundane and visionary motives first drove English colonists to the New World. Even among those whose concerns were pious, the work ethic and the rigorous diligence that they also practiced often led to prosperity in the environment of the New World. Already by the second generation, we can find American ministers condemning their parishioners for impieties and intemperances, and highlighting what they considered to be the purity and material austerity of the original colonists! The truth of the matter, as David Shi has argued, is that "there is no way of knowing the true extent of saintly and selfish behavior in society at a given time. Generalized assessments of cultural behavior and values . . . are notoriously intuitive, and therefore inexact. . . . Too often the past seems far more virtuous, simpler, and happier than it actually was."[6] Earlier generations are never as saintly as we believe them to be, nor are later generations as debauched. There is the common mistake, when evaluating ourselves, of taking the vices of our society as its norms.

In the political arena, the historian, reflecting upon the resurgent, self-righteous patriotism and the self-consciously vigorous presidential leadership of today, might emphasize an important reality in political history: it has often been necessary to be strong in order to bring forth sweetness. There has frequently been an intriguing symbiotic relationship between national self-assertion and political, economic, and cultural creativity.

One can take the Ancient Greeks as a first example. Their military victories over the Persian Empire inspired Greek artists and political leaders onward into what came to be their "Golden Age." The victory of the Greeks, especially against the odds, stimulated their pride and lifted up their spirits. Is it an accident that the battles of Marathon and Salamis were so soon followed by the works of Aeschylus and Sophocles?

The Florentines of the Renaissance provide yet another example. In this case, too, it is important to note that the achievements of the Florentines closely followed military success against the Visconti dynasty of Milan. As with the Greeks, civic pride and military prowess were to combine to arouse superb human endeavors and achievements.

A final example might be that of Elizabethan England. Whatever else might be said of the Tudors, through successive political challenges they provided the ballast for a divided English society. The Tudor form of government provided the bone and sinew for social progress. Genius needs looking after, and in their haphazard way the Tudors were able to provide the structural support which allowed the English genius to develop and flourish. Again, is it an accident that the Tudor victory over the famous Spanish Armada would be so soon followed by the works of Shakespeare, and the creative explosion associated with the English Renaissance?

To conclude, whatever our perspective, few would doubt that we live in a uniquely difficult age. On the one hand, critics should be wary of the fact that bitter criticism continuously applied can enervate and sterilize the human spirit. On the other hand, there are enough ominous problems to stimulate the most complacent citizen into an anxious concern for reform and change. Further, the reassuring lessons of the past often have limited applicability in our nuclear age. For, even in periods of anarchy, Ancient Greece, Renaissance Italy, and Elizabethan England were not truly "revolutionary" worlds. Even in times of peace, our modern world is confronted with sweeping political, economic, and social change.

Perhaps, then, we have come upon a partial answer for our age: the need to be wary of conceptualizing the puzzles of a nuclear world in prenuclear terms; the need to be particularly aware of applying yesterday's programs to today's challenges; and the need to guard against pursuing the ideological objectives of the nineteenth century in the latter part of the twentieth.

A postnuclear world, a tomorrow pregnant with new possibilities, and a twenty-first century are what hang in the balance.

SELECTED BIBLIOGRAPHY

1. Baron, Hans. *The Crisis of the Early Italian Renaissance*. Princeton, N.J.: Princeton University Press. 1966.
2. Commager, Henry Steele. *The Nature and the Study of History*. Columbus, Ohio: Charles E. Merrill, Inc. 1965.
3. Fine, John V.A. *The Ancient Greeks*. Cambridge, Mass.: Harvard University Press. 1983.
4. Lasch, Christopher. *The Culture of Narcissism*. New York: Warner Books. 1979.
5. Morris, Christopher. *The Tudors*. Glasgow: William Collins Sons and Co. 1966.
6. Shi, David E. *The Simple Life*. New York and Oxford: Oxford University Press. 1985.